The New Institutions
of Federalism

Recent American History

Kenneth E. Hendrickson, Jr.
General Editor

Vol. 1

PETER LANG
New York • Bern • Frankfurt am Main • Paris

William K. Hall

The New Institutions
of Federalism

The Politics of Intergovernmental
Relations 1960-1985

PETER LANG
New York • Bern • Frankfurt am Main • Paris

Library of Congress Cataloging-in-Publication Data

Hall, William K. (William Keeny), The new
institutions of federalism.

    (Recent American history ; vol. 1)
    Bibliography: p.
    Includes index.
    1. Federal government — United States.
I. Title.   II. Series.
JK325.H26   1989   321.02'0973   88-12854
ISBN 0-8204-0782-8
ISSN 0899-2371

CIP-Titelaufnahme der Deutschen Bibliothek

Hall, William K.:
The new institutions of federalism : the politics
of intergovernmental relations 1960–1985 /
William K. Hall. – New York; Bern; Frankfurt
am Main; Paris: Lang, 1989.
  (Recent American History; Vol. 1)
  ISBN 0-8204-0782-8

NE: GT

© Peter Lang Publishing, Inc., New York 1989

Printed by Weihert-Druck GmbH, Darmstadt, West Germany

DEDICATION -

To Carla and to Justin and Kirsten

TABLE OF CONTENTS

ACKNOWLEDGMENTS

The writing of a book is never easy, and it is a task never undertaken solo. All authors have a long string of chits outstanding. This author is certainly no exception.

There are so many who are owed a "thank you" and much more. This is especially true when a book has had as long a gestation period as this one! Bradley University provided me with a sabbatical leave, a time I used to do the original research and interviewing. A special word of thanks along that line to the several dozen governors who gave of their time and agreed to be interviewed. The anonymity promised is still intact.

Some of the many who have helped in this effort deserve special attention. Governor William Guy, the father of the Midwestern Governors' Conference, who gave generously of his time. Brevard Crihfield, longtime executive director of the Council of State Governments, who shared his many insights. The staff of the Council of State Governments headquarters in Lexington, who were always helpful. The two directors--James Bowhay and Virginia Thrall--who headed the CSG/Chicago office during the period of the writing of this book were most generous with their time and willingly made available to the author their office archives. The CSG/Chicago staff was super! A University colleague, Dr. Gregory Guzman, was helpful in locating a publisher. Colleague and friend, Professor Larry Aspin did a thousand things I could not do--from Tokyo--in finishing up the final details.

There were two who provided invaluable secretarial assistance. The first was the late Ruth O'Brien, longtime departmental secretary. The second is Kathie Strum.

CREDITS

The author wishes to express his gratitude to the following writers and publishers who have given permission to quote from their works:

Robert H. Salisbury, "An Exchange Theory of Interest Groups," reprinted from the Midwest Journal of Political Science, vol. 13, no. 1, February 1969, by permission of the author and the University of Texas Press. Megatrends, copyright 1982 by John Naisbitt, reprinted by permission of Warner Books, New York. Scott M. Matheson with James Edwin Lee, Out of Balance, Gibbs M. Smith, Inc., Salt Lake City, Utah, 1986. Robert Lorch, State and Local Politics, 2nd edition, copyright 1986, Prentice-Hall, Englewood Cliffs, NJ. Robert Gruenberg, Peoria Journal Star, September 25, 1977, Chicago Daily News Wire Service. Ivor Peterson, New York Times, May 24, 1984, copyright 1984 by the New York Times Company, reprinted by permission. Ira Sharkansky, The Maligned States, copyright 1972, McGraw-Hill Book Co. Dick Herman, Lincoln Journal, August 30, 1967, reprinted by permission of Lincoln Journal, Lincoln, Nebraska by Dick Herman. Randall W. Myers, Kansas City Times, August 9, 1977, all rights reserved. T. Wayne Mitchell, Kansas City Times, July 29, 1976, reprinted by permission, The Kansas City Times, copyright 1976, all rights reserved. Ray Morgan, Kansas City Times, July 22, 1971, reprinted by permission, The Kansas City Times, copyright 1971, all rights reserved. From "Interview with Michael S. Dukakis: in American Government: People, Institutions and Policies by John H. Aldrich, Gary J. Miller, Charles W. Ostrom, Jr., and David W. Rohde, copyright 1986 by Houghton Mifflin Company, used with permission. John Herbers, Governing, vol. 1, October, 1987, reprinted with permission, copyright 1988, Governing Magazine. Martha Derthick, Between State and Nation, 1974, The Brookings Institution. Robert Howard, Chicago Tribune, September 12, 1964, reprinted by permission, Chicago Tribune, copyright 1964. Editorial, Columbus Dispatch, August 27, 1985, reprinted by permission, The Columbus (Ohio) Dispatch, copyright 1985. Kathryn Waters Gest, Congressional Quarterly Weekly Report, May 14, 1977, reprinted by permission, CQ Inc., copyright 1977. Alan Ehrenhalt, Congressional Quarterly Weekly Report, August 20, 1977, reprinted by permission, CQ Inc., copyright 1977. Mercer Cross, Congressional Quarterly Weekly Report, April 9, 1977, reprinted by permission, CQ Inc., copyright 1977. Larry Sabato, Goodbye to Good-Time Charlie, 2nd edition, 1983, reprinted by permission, CQ Press, Inc., copyright 1983. Laurence J. O'Toole (ed.), American Intergovernmental Relations, 1985, reprinted by permission, CQ Press, Inc., copyright 1985. Congress and the Nation, 1965-1968, 1969, reprinted by permission, CQ Press, Inc., copyright 1969. John M. McCabe, Book of the States, 1976-1977, Council of State Governments, reprinted by permission of the Council, copyright 1976.

CHAPTER ONE

INTRODUCTION

The form and shape of the system of American intergovernmental relations have not been the result of any great democratic master plan. The form and shape are more accidental than planned, more serendipitous than anticipated. The present set of arrangements exists not because the Founding Fathers tried to foresee what would be needed in terms of an intergovernmental system, but because they were wise and trusting enough to know better than to lock the system into any preconceived eighteenth-century mold. Today's federalism is the evolutionary result of 200 years of fluctuating forms of federalism.

Federalism is said to be the "central characteristic of the American political system."[1]   Without undue exaggeration, it is possible to state that one of the most basic questions confronting the delegates to the constitutional convention in Philadelphia was how to apportion authority between a national government and the state governments.

The Articles of Confederation had provided evidence of serious problems which had resulted from the creation of a weak central government based on a confederacy of states. Even so, there remained remnants of real fear of a too strong national government in the minds of many citizens and a sizable portion of the constitutional convention delegates.

The convention delegates discussed their expectations as to what a national (federal) government should and should not do. They agreed that efforts necessary to ensure a common defense, and provide for liberty and the general welfare had not been possible under the Articles. Indeed, there was broad agreement that without "national government"[2] these objectives would be very difficult if not impossible to achieve.

Not every delegate in attendance at the convention opposed a strong central government. There was also a sizable bloc of delegates committed to the idea of a strong, centralized national government. These two different and distant positions created a most difficult political dilemma. These two contradictory forces in American politics clashed head-on at the convention that steamy summer in Philadelphia.

Like many other political dilemmas confronted at the convention that summer, this one was settled by a complex series of political compromises. In the body of writings urging ratification of the proposed Constitution, leading Framers tried to explain these compromises this way: "The proposed Constitution, therefore, is, in strictness, neither a national nor a federal Constitution, but a composition of both."[3] James Madison carried the explanation further when he observed that the proposed government was national with regard to the "operation of its powers," but there was evidence of a federal influence on the extent of that government's powers.[4] In fact, wrote Madison, "...the proposed government cannot be deemed a national one, since its jurisdiction extends to certain enumerated objects only, and leaves to the several states a residuary and inviolable sovereignty over all other objects."[5]

Madison's argument was not absolutely correct. The national government was not, in fact, strictly limited only to "certain enumerated" powers. The framers of that marvelous political document had taken care not to tie the political hands of future generations.

The new nation's constitution provided for both a strong national level of government and a presumably parallel level of state governments. Some powers were granted expressly to the national government. Other powers were given by implication to the national government. Some powers were considered the nearly exclusive domain of state governments. Yet other more vaguely-worded powers were left to the states as noted in the

Tenth Amendment, which had been ratified within three years of the ratification of the Constitution itself. Furthermore, the national government and the state governments were to share concurrent powers in certain areas.

Federalism, therefore, was thought to be "...a system of authority constitutionally apportioned between central [federal] and regional [state] governments."[6] Thus, the mechanistic view of federalism was that it was "a legal concept, emphasizing a constitutional division of authority and functions between a national government and state governments, with both levels having received their powers independently of each other from a third source--the people."[7]

In an effort to gain ratification of the proposed Constitution, the Founding Fathers sought to dismiss concerns about a too-powerful national government. Speaking to the issue of national dominance, they noted: "The powers delegated by the proposed Constitution to the federal government are few and defined. Those which are to remain in the State governments are numerous and indefinite."[8] Alexander Hamilton continued the effort to allay fears: "It will always be far more easy for the State governments to encroach upon the national authorities than for the national government to encroach upon the State authorities."[9]

Two hundred years after these words were penned, Americans would find a far different America than the one promised and prophesied in The Federalist. The state governments do not resemble the state governments envisioned by either Madison or Hamilton. The federal government is hardly the meek and mild-mannered federal presence envisioned 200 years ago.

How did this turn of events happen? What forces led to a system of intergovernmental relations which has evolved into quite a different system than the one envisioned by those who drafted the Constitution?

The forces which have contributed to the present state of affairs can be grouped under four general headings. First, there are a number of historical precedents which have contributed to this evolution. These precedents would include the impact of the failings of the Articles of Confederation and the apparent need for a stronger federal government. In addition, precedents have resulted from the "winning" by one set of forces over another set. For example, there has always existed a strong feeling of national unity, a strong sense of national pride, or nationhood. Simultaneously, there has been a counter force of local pride which resulted from the dividing up of the nation into geographical divisions for the purposes of governing. The principal divisions are state governments and to an even greater extent, local governmental units. Thus, even though the Founding Fathers argued that "...the people of each State would be apt to feel a stronger bias towards their local governments than towards the government of the Union;..."[10] such has not in reality been the case. The anticipation that citizens would display a greater loyalty to the local (state and local) governments than to the distant federal government[11] has never been realized.

A second set of forces which is "winning" involves the principle of national supremacy versus maximum local control. Americans are more interested in and more likely to participate in national political contests than either state or local political contests. Citizens express a greater interest in what the federal government is doing than in the activities of either of the levels of government closer to home.

A second set of explanations of this evolution of federalism include important political events. These events include the ratification of the Sixteenth Amendment in 1913, which gave Congress the power to impose a federal personal income tax. The ratification of the Seventeenth Amendment later in the same year changed the method of electing members of the United States Senate from selection by state legislatures to direct election by the citizenry. This would come to have a major impact on the role the states would directly play in congressional deliberations.

The devastation of the Great Depression was also an important event in this evolution. The magnitude of the suffering caused by the Depression was so great that the federal government began to directly involve itself in providing for the welfare of its citizens. Numerous federal social welfare programs of varying types were the result of Franklin D. Roosevelt's New Deal proposals.

Of even greater importance than a sharp reversal of the direction of the federal government occasioned by the Depression, was the dramatic change in the thinking of many Americans. Prior to the New Deal, most Americans had expected little of their federal government in terms of domestic involvement. They were seldom disappointed. But, when the Depression hit, solutions of the past paled alongside the hugeness of the problem. The people turned--in desperation--to the federal government because there was nowhere else to turn. Even so, the startling change of mind by millions was not nearly as easy as it might be made to sound.

The New Deal also gave a giant boost to federal grant-in-aid programs. These programs--which involved the carrot of federal dollars and the stick of restrictions on the use of those dollars--were additional reasons for the increases in size and power of the federal government.

The growth in size and influence of the national government has been furthered by the decisions and actions to make America a world power, a leader of the free nations of the world. Those decisions which moved America in this direction, the need for defending the nation and America's national interest, and American participation in several of the twentieth-century wars have all contributed to the strengthening of the power and influence of the national government. This is especially true in the area of influence resulting from federal involvement in the nation's economy.

Finally, the federal government has grown in power more rapidly than either the state or local governments because of the "nationalness" of certain problems such as poverty and civil rights. Events such as the civil rights revolution of the late 1960s hastened this growth, this expansion of power.

The third set of forces which has shaped the evolution of the system of federalism are the "formal" or legal reasons--the

U.S. Constitution and the interpretation of that document's meaning by the United States Supreme Court. Beginning in the late 1930s, the Court expanded the powers of the federal government, while--in the opinion of some--it has "eviscerated the states' political authority...."[12]

The Supreme Court has often acted to expand the power of the federal government at the expense of state and local governments essentially by interpreting the commerce clause and the supremacy clause favorably for the federal government. In a decision handed down late in 1985--Garcia v. San Antonio Metropolitan Transit Authority (469 U.S. 528)--the Court ruled that the Tenth Amendment no longer protected state and local governments from the Fair Labor Standards Act.[13]

Ten years before in the case of National League of Cities v. Usery (426 U.S. 833, 1976), the Court had ruled the Act did not apply to the states in areas of "traditional governmental functions." In Garcia, however, the Court took the position that any restraint on the power of Congress to control state and local governments "is most appropriately obtained through the national political process rather than through judicial review."[14] To many, the decision seemed to make more real the possibility Associate Justice Sandra Day O'Connor warned about in 1982 when she noted further expansion of the powers of the federal government "could turn state legislatures and administrative agencies into 'field offices of the national bureaucracy.'"[15] It was this continued lessening of the role and authority of state and local powers which led Governor Richard A. Snelling (R-Vt., 1977-1985) to lament: "State and local governments have lost much of their identity, becoming more like 'sub-national units' than independent members of the federal system."[16]

Are these conclusions about the evolution of federalism correct or are there other conclusions which can properly be drawn? Without denying the continued growth of the central government, there would seem to be ample evidence to indicate that state and local governments are not now nor have they ever teetered on the brink of extinction. Rather, the long course of federalism, especially the course of federalism over the past 25 years has been one in which federalism could be defined as "...a political and pragmatic concept, stressing the actual interdependence and sharing of functions between Washington and the states, and focusing on the mutual leverage that each level is able to exert on the other."[17] In this kind of system of federalism, relations [between governments] are "flexible, fluid, and pragmatic, ever changing and adjusting with shifts in power loci and public attitudes."[18]

In the chapters which follow we will examine the system of federalism which prevailed during the period 1960-1985, and how it changed. We will also examine the efforts of state governments to adapt to those changes. Especial emphasis will be placed on those cooperative efforts aimed at improving interstate relations. An additional focus will be the phenomenon of the new regionalism, so much a part of the story of this quarter-century.

One of the most prodigious writers on federalism, Daniel Elazar, has underscored the critical importance of the adaptability of the American system when he observed that "...federalism is more than an arrangement of governmental structures; it is a mode of political activity that requires the extension of certain kinds of cooperative relationships throughout any political system it animates."[19] The adaptability, the political activity, and the cooperative relationships are the foci of this examination of the new institutions of American federalism.

NOTES
==

[1]Daniel J. Elazar, American Federalism: A View From the States (3rd ed.; New York: Harper & Row, Publishers, 1984), p. 2.

[2]The Federalist No. 39.

[3]Ibid.

[4]Ibid.

8

[5] Ibid.

[6] Laurence J. O'Toole, Jr., ed., American Intergovernmental Relations (Washington: Congressional Quarterly Press, 1985), p. 2.

[7] Michael D. Reagan, The New Federalism (New York: Oxford University Press, 1972), p. 3.

[8] James Madison in The Federalist No. 45.

[9] Alexander Hamilton in The Federalist No. 17.

[10] Ibid.

[11] William H. Riker, Federalism: Origin, Operation, Significance (Boston: Little, Brown & Co., 1964), p. 111.

[12] W. John Moore, "Just a Principle," National Journal, XIX (January 17, 1987), p. 161.

[13] Advisory Commission on Intergovernmental Relations, Reflections on Garcia and Its Implication for Federalism (Washington: Government Printing Office, 1986).

[14] Ibid., p. 1.

[15] Quoted in Moore, "Just a Principle," p. 161.

[16] Richard A. Snelling, "American Federalism in the Eighties," State Government LIII (Autumn, 1980), p. 168.

[17] Reagan, The New Federalism, p. 3.

[18] Parris N. Glendening and Mavis Mann Reeves, Pragmatic Federalism: An Intergovernmental View of American Government (Pacific Palisades: Palisades Publishers, 1977), p. 8.

[19] Elazar, American Federalism, p. 2.

CHAPTER TWO

TWO HUNDRED YEARS OF FEDERALISM: THE AMERICAN EXPERIMENT

As the architects of the yet-to-be-written-constitution gathered
in Philadelphia that summer of 1787 to construct a new
government and write a new constitution, they knew they had to
find remedies for the republican diseases which had plagued the
new nation under the ill-fated Articles of Confederation. The
challenge before them--to combine the states into a political
system which would create a federal system, rather than a
confederacy. The term federal had then and has now two
meanings. The term is frequently used in reference
(synonymously) to mean the national government. It is also used
to indicate a division of authority and power between the
central (national) government and regional (state) governments.
That is essentially what a contemporary scholar of federalism,
Daniel Elazar, said when he defined the American system of
federalism as:

> ...the mode of political organization that
> unites separate polities within an overarching
> political system by distributing power among
> general and constituent governments in a
> manner designed to protect the existence and
> authority of both.[1]

That the founding fathers would design a _federal_ system is
so typical of the pragmatic compromises which shaped their
design of the system. The Framers had had firsthand--and very
unpleasant--experience with a unitary form of government as
British colonial subjects. When the colonies achieved
independence following the Revolution, Americans vowed never
again to establish a governmental system which would vest all

power in a single individual, a single branch of government or a single level of government. At the same time, the Framers viewed with dismay the failures of the confederation established under the Articles of Confederation which gave too little power to the national government.

What was needed, it seemed, was a political system with appropriate constraints built into it. Constraints which would prevent a strong central government from riding roughshod over the "regional" governments it created. Constraints which would prevent the states from interfering with each other and with the central government as had often been the case under the Articles of Confederation. To solve these two serious problems, the constitution writers proposed a governmental framework which would create a nation and a national government able to act "in a unified and central fashion for certain purposes."[2] Simultaneously, the framers proposed that the states remain as independent sovereign governments with independent jurisdictions. Indeed, the principle of federalism is one of the three principles upon which the American democratic system is built. Coupled with the doctrine of the separation of powers and the concern over the protection of individual rights, federalism was to be the third line of defense against an overpowerful national government. It was, as has been said, an additional expression of the Framers' effort to fragment power by using the self-interest (power) of one institution to check the self-interest of another.[3]

Indeed, one of the intriguing constitutional questions is whether the states preceded and created the nation or whether the national government created the states. If the states did give birth to the nation as some scholars believe,[4] then it was not a matter of the states being thrown a few leftover crumbs from a national jurisdiction; rather, it was a matter of the states offering up powers to the national government for national purposes, while at the same time retaining control over their own internal affairs.

Even though some of the Founding Fathers such as Alexander Hamilton might have preferred a strong and highly centralized national government, it was politically impossible. The Founding Fathers were far too practical as politicians to move in that direction. As these men looked about for examples of federalism in operation, however, they found precious few examples. Madison candidly admitted as much when he urged citizens to:

> Hearken not to the voice which petulantly tells you that the form of government recommended for your adoption is a novelty in the political world; that it has never yet had a place in the theories of the wildest projectors; that it rashly attempts what it is impossible to accomplish.[5]

The nation had had no experience with this type of political system. It was obvious that this new, novel approach to intergovernmental relations would have to slowly develop out of the American experience over time.

The decision to propose a federal system was not intended to quash all controversy about the appropriate roles of the national and state governments. There is evidence to indicate that clarification of those roles was deliberately left ambiguous and unsettled. That ambiguity made it possible to design a system which--in developing over time--created "a mode of political activity that requires the extension of certain kinds of cooperative relationships throughout...."[6] One of the key principles of this new political order was partnership. A form of partnership which implied the existence of several centers of power, each of which would have to negotiate with and bargain with one another in order to achieve the common goals spoken of by James Madison and the other federalists.

In the new nation's earliest decades under the new Constitution, the system was known as "dual federalism." In that system of dual federalism, each level of government operated within its own bailiwick without much interference from the other. As long as the national government operated on a small budget, had few employees, and exercised generally only those powers specifically delegated to it (including the power to lay and collect taxes; to borrow money; to regulate foreign and interstate commerce; to coin money; to declare war; and to raise and support armies), there was little reason to doubt the value of such a system. Conflict between the two levels of government was mostly minimal and there were numerous opportunities for cooperative interaction between the levels including land grant programs, technical assistance, and exchanges of expert personnel. Instances of conflict and cooperation served to reinforce one of the underlying principles of the system of American federalism--the interdependence of the levels of government. It was a system--as envisioned by Madison and others--which featured a delicately-balanced series of intergovernmental relationships designed to protect the existence and dual authority of each of the various governments.

Commencing at about the time the twentieth century was beginning, the seemingly clear distinction between federal and state interests and powers has been blurred and distorted. The delicate balance was often upset. Although the progression has been neither uniform nor constant, there has been a gradual, long-term shift toward emphasizing the federal government and "federal interests." This shift has usually come at the expense of state government and "state" or "local interests," and has usually been accompanied by a measurable expansion of the national government's powers. In simplest terms, the federal government has acquired more duties and powers, over the years, than have the states.[7]

Many factors have contributed to this shift. The national government's responsibilities for maintaining a strong national defense and the conscious political decision of the nation's leaders to make America a world leader have been factors. American involvement in World War I and World War II as well as in the Korean War and the Vietnam War plus the arrival of the Cold War have all contributed to an expansion of the size and role of the national government.

Certain provisions of the Constitution have often been interpreted by the federal judiciary in such a way as to contribute to this shift, among them: the national supremacy clause, the necessary and proper clause, the commerce clause, the provision giving Congress the power to provide for the general welfare, as well as the due process and equal protection clauses of the Fourteenth Amendment. All have been used as justification for the expansion of the responsibilities and powers of the national government.

As noted, the roots of this expansion can be traced to the dawning of the twentieth century. At that juncture, problems with laissez faire economics, the concentration of corporate power and wealth and the concern over conserving precious and scarce natural resources encouraged the carving out of a bigger role for the national government. National regulatory agencies began to be created. With the ratification of the Sixteenth Amendment (okaying imposing a federal income tax) in 1913, the federal government at last had the means to fund an expansion of its activities and involvements. It would not be long before the federal government would begin giving cash grants to state and local governments and not long after that, that cash grants to those governments would overshadow all other forms of intergovernmental assistance. Even so, the roles of state and local governments had changed but little.

> While the states' regulatory, intrastate commerce and, in a few cases, taxing authorities were constrained by some of the federal government's regulations, none of these state powers was denied or in any real sense undermined. Most important, state and local governments enacted, performed and funded nearly all of the growing number of public services provided directly to the citizenry.[8]

The 140-year period from 1789 to 1932, can be described as one in which the national government and the states quarreled on more than one occasion, but essentially it was a period in which both levels grew--not equally, but steadily--in power. It is best described by the label dual federalism. Those clashes which did occur, however, led one leading scholar of intergovernmental relations to describe that phase as the "conflict" phase.[9]

The period was also one marked by few relationships between

local governments and the national government. Tightly
controlled by the states for most of these years, local
governments had few contacts--fiscal or otherwise--with the
national government. The few programs of aid for local
governments which existed were usually funneled through the
states.

The states and the national government were presumed to
have separate, identifiable and protected spheres of influence,
powers, and responsibilities. The efforts of the states--at
least in terms of dealing with the two foremost challenges of
the period (the settlement and economic development of the
nation and the process of industrialization) generally exceeded
the efforts of the national government in these areas.

The beginning of the decade of the 1930s marked a watershed
in recent American federalism and a dramatic change in the
direction of the system. The period of 1932-1960 is often
characterized as the period of "cooperative," "concentrated,"
and "creative" federalism.[10] The political, social and
especially the economic devastation wrought by the Great
Depression, the subsequent election of Franklin D. Roosevelt in
1932 to the first of four terms, and the passage of many New
Deal programs signaled a basic change in the character and
nature of American intergovernmental relations, and indeed, a
basic change in the entire American political system.

Because of the Great Depression, the need for public
welfare services was so great that the states could not meet the
need. The nation's federal structure was transformed as New
Deal programs fostered all kinds of new intergovernmental
relationships. The extent of the transformation can be seen in
the changes in public expenditures. In 1929, federal
expenditures totaled $2.6 billion while state and local
governments spent $7.6 billion. A decade later, the state and
local governments were spending $8.5 billion while federal
government spending had increased to $8.9 billion.

Even though the concept of dual federalism seemed alive and
well, the acceptance of the New Deal and its programs meant
significant changes in the conduct of federalism. In the early

months of the New Deal, congressional acceptance of New Deal ideas and proposals came easily. Acceptance of those same New Deal ideas and programs was much slower in coming in the judicial arena. It was not until President Roosevelt unveiled his "court-packing" plan in early 1937 that the United States Supreme Court stopped invalidating important New Deal legislative programs.

Because of the high unemployment rate and other equally serious economic woes, state and local governments suffered terrible losses in revenue. That was especially true of local governments which were tied to the property tax as their major source of revenue. Many state legislatures, controlled by conservative, rural interests worried about fiscal insolvency and acted--protectively--to limit local governments' ability to borrow money or find new tax revenue sources. Cities were particularly hard hit.

The federal government had to step in. Roosevelt and his New Deal created massive public works programs designed to ease the problem of unemployment. These programs were administered cooperatively by federal, state and local officials. Roosevelt also changed the character of the system by working to bring local governments into a more active role in the intergovernmental partnership. This constituted a major break in the tradition of very limited federal-local relations, a break so significant that Roscoe Martin called 1933 the "geologic fault line" in the development of direct federal-local relations.[11]

Many of the changes which were begun as part of the New Deal would outlast it. Foremost among these changes was the growth of the federal government and its assumption of the role of senior partner in the nation's domestic affairs. World War II and the subsequent Cold War contributed to the increase in the size of the federal presence in the system.

Dwight D. Eisenhower took the oath of office for the first time in 1953, and he was dismayed by the imbalance he saw in the federal system. Over his two terms in office, he sought to

upgrade the role of the states, to shift some governmental tasks
and responsibilities to state and local governments, to shift
other responsibilities from them to the federal government, and
to expand the number of federal-state cooperative programs.
Among his first official acts was a call for legislation to
create the Commission on Intergovernmental Relations (see
Chapter Three). In his message to Congress on the establishment
of the Commission, the President noted:

> The present division of activities
> between Federal and state governments,
> including their local subdivisions, is the
> product of more than a century and a half of
> piecemeal and often haphazard growth. This
> growth in recent decades has proceeded at a
> speed defying order and efficiency. One
> program after another has been launched to
> meet emergencies and expanding public needs.
> Time has rarely been taken for thoughtful
> attention to the effects of these actions on
> the basic structure of our Federal-state
> system of Government.
>
> Now there is need to review and assess,
> with prudence and foresight, the proper roles
> of the Federal, state and local governments.
> In many cases, especially within the past
> twenty years, the Federal government has
> entered fields which, under our constitution,
> are the primary responsibilities of state and
> local governments.[12]

That Commission (established in 1955) would undertake the first
fundamental review of the system of federalism since the
adoption of the Constitution. In its final report, the
Commission noted: "The national government and the states should
be regarded not as competitors for authority but as two levels
of government cooperating with or complementing each other in
meeting the growing demands on both."[13]

Eisenhower would implement a number of the Commission's
recommendations including the appointment of a Deputy Assistant
to the President for Intergovernmental Relations and the
establishment of a Joint Federal-State Action Committee. These
actions accurately reflected Ike's view of the basic role and
purposes of not only the federal level of government but of the
state governments. President Eisenhower also proposed that

there be a rearrangement of some programs and that some federal programs be turned over to the state and local governments and that the federal government assume the total burden for the nation's welfare programs and costs. The Joint Federal-State Action Committee was to designate those functions which the states were willing to assume and finance, and to recommend the revenue adjustments (federal and state) necessary for the states to assume those functions. The proposed realignment fell apart when it got down to answering nitty-gritty questions about the specific shifts of money and political power.

A MOST IMPORTANT QUARTER-CENTURY OF FEDERALISM: 1960-1985

Ike and his Joint Federal-State Action Committee worked diligently to reduce the federal budget and turn over some responsibilities to the states. But, beginning with John Kennedy's New Frontier (1961-1963), and reaching its zenith in Lyndon B. Johnson's Great Society (1963-1969), the federal government again changed its basic approach and outlook. The nation entered into a period of "competitive" intergovernmental relations,[14] a period which saw a major expansion in the role of the federal government, not only in programs, but in regulations and requirements.

This third period or era of federalism has been called by some the period of "cooptive" federalism.[15] In this case the term "cooptive" refers to the cooptation or usurpation by the national government of powers previously exercised by the state governments.

The keynote of this new phase of federalism was the development of national purposes and national goals as seen in various federal assistance programs. Previously, federal dollars had largely been aimed at state and local governments to help them accomplish their objectives.[16] The federal government established the objectives, spelled out the details of the programs, came up with some of the funding and "induced"--by carrot and stick methods--widespread subnational participation. If that were not enough, the federal government also began to involve itself in policy areas previously left to the state governments. Included as examples are social welfare policies, civil rights policies, environmental and pollution control policies, and intergovernmental regulation.

Lyndon Johnson's brand of federalism was labeled "Creative Federalism," and like so many of the thrusts of his Great Society, "Creative Federalism" had something for everyone. The federal government, under the Great Society, channeled massive amounts of money to state, county and municipal governments, essentially through federally-supervised, conditional categorical grant-in-aid programs. By 1970, there were nearly 450 categorical grant programs totaling some $24 billion in federal government expenditures, amounting to nearly 20 percent of state-local revenues.

Lyndon Johnson spent a great deal of time publicizing his ideas and programs leading to increased intergovernmental cooperation. He was fond of pointing out to audiences that the expansion of federal power need not mean a weakened position for state and local governments. Indeed, he argued the expansion of federal power was good because it also meant an expansion of the powers of state and local governments. His arguments seldom dealt with the fact that during his Administration--which witnessed a substantial increase in federal power--a number of established state prerogatives were squashed.

In 1980, Governor Richard A. Snelling (R-Vt., 1977-1985) looked back at the legacy of Lyndon Johnson's Creative Federalism:

> What we call American federalism today is far from the delicately-balanced intergovern- mental relationship dreamed of in Madison's day. Today, the federal system is not really federal--it isn't even systematic. The text- book distinctions between state and federal interests have been blurred by the evolution of the federal grant-in-aid system,... States and local governments have lost much of their identity, becoming more like "sub-national units" than independent members in a federal system.[17]

Although the programs of the Great Society were not, by

themselves, responsible for these changes, Johnson's dreams, efforts and successes accelerated the earlier trends by means of massive infusions of federal aid to state and local governments. These infusions were invariably accompanied by more stringent federal guidelines and controls. As long as there seemed to be an ample supply of federal dollars, there was little grumbling. But, the huge costs of the war in Vietnam, the civil unrest resulting from protests opposing American involvement in the war, the social upheaval resulting from the civil rights revolution, plus the difficult political and budgetary choice of guns or butter ultimately drove Lyndon Johnson from office. His successor was Richard M. Nixon.

Lyndon Johnson had justified his expansion of the federal government's role largely on the claim that the states had not responded to the problems of their cities. His claim had considerable merit and could be substantiated by reams of statistics. Johnson saw this urban neglect as reason enough for the federal government to tackle those urban (as well as non-urban) ills ignored by the states.

Richard Nixon came into office with a much different outlook. The new president summed up his basic philosophy of federalism by calling federalism:

> A cooperative venture among government at all levels...in which power, funds, and authority are channeled increasingly to those govern- ments which are closest to the people.[18]

This philosophy evidenced Nixon's deep commitment to bringing government closer to the people. In so doing, he hoped to restore Americans' loss of faith and trust in government at all levels and strengthen state and local governments so they would be able to provide the leadership believed to be lacking in recent years. His Administration was to be much more supportive of the state and local governments.

Partly as a reaction to the growth of the federal government in the 1960s, Nixon proposed a major departure from recent trends. His proposals, called the "New Federalism," sought to channel the flow of power, funds and responsibilities away from the federal government and toward state and local governments. Nixon sought to trim the power of the federal government by reducing the size of the federal bureaucracy.

Nixon also tried to pry power out of the hands of the federal government in another way. He urged Congress to enact a series of six consolidated block grants. These grants--which included some new federal programs as well as the combining of some 129 old categorical grant-in-aid programs--were designed to provide federal dollars for broad purposes, while at the same time increasing the discretion of state and local officials in the specific use of the funds.[19]

The proposals for creating the six block grant programs quickly ran into trouble in Congress as the vested interests rallied against them. After a difficult struggle, Nixon would finally get congressional approval for a Comprehensive Employment and Training Assistance (CETA) block grant program (combining 17 old categoricals); a Community Development Block Grant (CDBG) program and a Social Services block grant. Unlike the two block grant programs approved during the Johnson Administration (the Partnership for Health Act and the Safe Streets Act), these block grant programs provided for funding local governments directly. This was one of the reasons Nixon's proposals created such a furor in Congress.

This bypassing of states was also part of another element in Nixon's legislative package. Nixon formally proposed as part of his legislative package the adoption of general revenue sharing, a program which would distribute federal funds to state as well as local governments with few strings attached. The funds could be used for almost any legitimate government purpose and were calculated on a formula based on population and tax burden.

Nixon saw in general revenue sharing a way to restore power to state and local officials by not only providing them with massive amounts of federal aid, but by reducing the federal requirements and guidelines. General revenue sharing was an integral part of the initiatives of the New Federalism. In sending his legislative proposal to Congress, Nixon noted:

> Our ultimate purposes are many: To
> restore to the States their proper rights and
> roles in the Federal system with a new
> emphasis on and help for local responsiveness;
> to provide both the encouragement and the
> necessary resources for local and State
> officials to exercise leadership in solving
> their own problems; to narrow the distance
> between people and the government agencies
> dealing with their problems; to restore
> strength and vigor to local and State
> governments; to shift the balance of political
> power away from Washington and back to the
> country and the people.[20]

He tried--throughout his nearly six years in office--to
seek an intergovernmental restructuring. His efforts were
reminiscent of the proposals made by the man he had served as
vice president, Dwight D. Eisenhower. Like Eisenhower, Nixon
tried to sort out and rearrange governmental responsibilities.
His New Federalism not only proposed the idea of devolving power
and authority through general revenue sharing, but he also
proposed to consolidate more than 100 federal aid programs into
just six broad functional grant programs. His $11 billion
special revenue sharing proposal never made it through
Congress. Both Nixon and Gerald Ford who followed him into
office, believed that the consolidation which would result from
these block grants would curb the rapid increase in the number
of the categorical grant programs. Both believed state
governments should be the basic delivery mechanisms. Both,
however, lost the war of grant reform to the legislative branch
of government.[21]

Gerald Ford sought to continue Nixon's brand of federalism
and proposed three additional block grant programs in child
nutrition, health, and education. Congress turned down all
three reform proposals. Instead, Congress created a number of
new conditional categorical grant programs. These programs were
even more complex than their predecessors and sub-national
governments found themselves forced to seek professional help in
the important and complex game of grantsmanship.

In trying to be elected president in his own right in 1976,

Gerald Ford was defeated by Jimmy Carter. A former governor of Georgia, Carter chose to call his program of federalism a "New Partnership." It was an oddly eclectic blend of the programs and approaches of Lyndon Johnson and Richard Nixon, but with a mixture of budget restraints and budget cuts. These had been forced on the President by the state of the nation's economy.

Reflecting his service as a state chief executive, President Carter's New Partnership sought to involve state and local government officials much earlier in the planning stages of policy and budget decisions. Only a month after he took office, he sent this memo to executive departments and agencies:

> Throughout the campaign and transition period, I made a firm commitment to state and local officials that they would be involved in the development of my Administration's policy and budget priorities and programs. I pledged that such consultation would occur at the earliest possible stages in order to make it significant and fruitful....
>
> In order to assure that these objectives are met, please include in any major policy, budget or reorganization proposal which has significant state and local impact, a brief description of how you fulfilled this commitment on my behalf.....[22]

As a former governor, Carter had felt the anger and frustration which comes from having programs and regulations imposed from above. It was his belief, therefore, that consultation such as the type he proposed would not only increase the "practicality and effectiveness" of the programs, but would also be likely to insure broad-based support for Administration proposals.[23]

In 1980, Jimmy Carter became the second consecutive president to be defeated in a bid for re-election. The election of 1980 signaled the dawn of a new age of federalism. Republican nominee Ronald W. Reagan was elected president and the Republicans erased twenty-five years of electoral frustration by capturing control of the United States Senate. It surprised them almost as much as it did the Democrats. Most observers credited the take-over to a national reaction to the intergovernmental developments of the preceding twenty years, especially a reaction to the growth of the federal government.

The era of cooptive federalism had led to some significant systemic changes. There have been changes in the federal-state balance, changes in the institutional capabilities of these two levels of government, as well as changes in the policies the two levels of government pursue jointly. While many arguments can be made supporting the positive or negative results of these changes, our task is not to judge these changes, but only to note them.

Reagan took the oath of office January 20, 1981 and in his Inaugural Address, the new President--a former chief executive of the nation's most populous state--clearly declared his intentions:

> It is time to check and reverse the growth of government, which shows signs of having grown beyond the consent of the governed. It is my intention to curb the size and influence of the Federal establishment and to demand recognition of the distinction between the powers granted to the Federal Government and those reserved to the States or to the people. All of us need to be reminded that the Federal Government did not create the States; the States created the Federal Government.[24]

Ronald Reagan made it clear from the start that he intended to raise fundamental questions about the role of the national government in the federal system. In a brief statement of his goals, he noted: "Steps will be taken aimed at restoring the balance between the various levels of government."[25] There could be little doubt that he sided with those who held the opinion that the federal government had become too large, too powerful and too demanding of the states and the local governmental units. Reagan announced--perhaps prematurely--the death of cooptive federalism.

Reagan soon introduced the elements of his own version of federalism; a federalism which he--like Nixon--labeled the "New Federalism." It was there, however, the similarities between the two stopped. Reagan's New Federalism was to be much different. He set down four goals for Phase One of his New Federalism: (1)

to repair the economy and to develop a strong monetary system; (2) to shift (devolve) a number of federal programs as well as funding sources to state and local governments (this was partially designed to help reduce the size of and the problems created by a huge federal deficit); (3) to begin the process of deregulation; and (4) to "deinstitutionalize most federally encouraged regional bodies."[26]

Because of the state of the nation's economy, the key battleground for these goals would be the 1981 economic recovery package which included proposals to reduce government spending, lower taxes for individuals and businesses, deregulate industries, and stabilize monetary growth. Ostensibly the budget and tax cut proposals were aimed at strengthening the economy, but it is clear that cuts in the budget were designed, in part, to cut or eliminate a large number of categorical grant programs. Concomitant with these cuts were his proposals for the creation of seven new block grant programs.

Congress--even with a Republican Senate--received the President's proposals with lukewarm enthusiasm. The Congress then proceeded to make a sizable number of important changes in them. Reagan quickly learned about the role of the legislative branch in decisions regarding the system of federalism.[27] His original proposals sought to combine 90 categorical grant programs into more comprehensive, less-conditional block grant proposals. Nine block grants ultimately emerged from the congressional give-and-take. Even though a number of the nine block grant programs were not among the President's initial proposals, Congress--though disagreeing as to the role of the national government--did give the President a good deal of what he had requested. Fifty-seven (as opposed to 90 in the President's original proposals) categorical grant programs were approved for consolidation into new block grant programs. The President had every right to be pleased with his success.

On February 17, 1981, the President moved on another front. He issued Executive Order 12291 authorizing the Office of Management and Budget to review all regulations proposed by executive agencies with an eye toward eliminating unnecessary federal mandates and regulations.

The President's federalism initiatives also affected various regional bodies. Since the early 1960s, the federal government had been encouraging and providing financial support for the formation of these organizations. By the time of Reagan's inauguration, the number of these governmental regional bodies had grown to twenty: twelve regional economic development planning commissions, two interstate compact river basin commissions and six Title II river basin commissions. Every state in the union was a member of at least one of these regional bodies. In addition to these multistate regional organizations, there were more than 600 sub-state regional councils of government and nearly 1,500 planning units of various types operating at the sub-state level.

In the first few months of his first term, Reagan proposed cutting off most of the federal monies going to these regional organizations. Unsuccessful at that, Reagan tried a different approach when in July of 1982, he weakened the regional planning units by ordering the old A-95 grant review process scrapped and replaced it with a new and much more decentralized consultation process, one which allowed state and local governments to establish their own consultation processes.

In his 1982 State of the Union address, Reagan sounded the clarion call for Phase Two of the New Federalism--a swap of governmental programs and responsibilities between the federal government and the states. At the heart of his proposal was the swapping of some 40 programs and $47 billion in revenues between Washington and the state capitals. The struggle soon turned into a struggle over which programs would be swapped. The specific programs under consideration included the federal food stamp program (to the states), Medicaid (to the federal government), and Aid to Families with Dependent Children (to the states).

The states seemed to be in the most difficult position in terms of the proposals of Phase Two. Not surprisingly, the "big swap" proposed by Reagan galvanized the governors into action and they came within an eyelash at their 1982 annual meeting of presenting their own list of "swappable" programs to Congress. Only lengthy negotiations (see Chapter Three) prevented that from happening.[28]

The various initiatives Reagan proposed constituted a distinct break with the past. He spoke out in favor of fewer federal strings and regulations; he favored the creation of more block grants and the elimination of numerous categorical grants; and he sought reductions in federal domestic spending. He viewed the states as "middlemen" for federal funds. At the same time, he proposed reducing the funds flowing to state and local governments. This led at least one governor to label Reagan's federalism as "pick and choose federalism," "retrenchment federalism," or "austerity federalism."[29] Although it is not yet possible to assess the final outcome, it seems certain that Reagan envisions an America which would operate under an updated system of dual federalism with the federal government and the states having distinctly separate spheres of authority and responsibility. He has tried to remold the system of intergovernmental relations in that image.

Because of Reagan's New Federalism, state and local governments have gained a new sense of independence from the federal government and have taken on new responsibilities.[30] As the federal presence has been cut back, there has been "an explosion of innovations and initiatives by state and local governments...."[31]

State and local governments have been reinvigorated. Subnational governments are increasing taxes and raising large amounts of money to replace (or often exceed) funds eliminated at the federal level. State and local officials have put aside their ideological and partisan differences and have begun to unify, to work together. Public institutions such as schools have been helped by these "waves of reform." Even state governments have caught the spirit by loosening the financial reins on local governments, especially in terms of taxation.[32]

CHANGES IN THE AMERICAN SYSTEM OF FEDERALISM 1960-1985
This quarter-century has witnessed almost revolutionary

changes in America federalism. From Eisenhower's efforts to identify the fundamental principles of federalism to the changes in the basic roles of the national government and the states, these last 25 years have seen dramatic changes and the dawning of some serious rethinking about the very fundamental principles of federalism. The most important of these changes include:

(1) The degree of interdependence in the federal system. The states and the federal government--and the local governments as well--participate in a wide sharing of functions. This theory of shared governance has moved American federalism out of the age of "layer cake federalism" and into the age of "marble cake federalism."[33] The various governments share--at least partially--in the decisions regarding governmental actions as well as cooperating in the implementation of public policies. One analysis of the new federalism has gone so far as to state: "Federalism--old style--is dead."[34] That old style federalism emphasizing a constitutional division of authority and functions has given way to a new, more fluid style of federalism known as intergovernmental relations.

(2) Even with this interdependence, the federal government has assumed the primary role in the system. This can be measured in terms of a twelve-fold increase in total federal grant outlays, from $7 billion in 1960 to nearly $106 billion in 1985. It can also be measured in terms of a sizable jump in the number of federal grant-in-aid programs, from 132 in 1960 to over 530 a quarter of a century later.

(3) Even with the federal budget reductions there have been additions of new federal grant-in-aid programs (e.g., medical assistance for the needy and regional economic development) and the expansion of some old ones (e.g., AFDC and public health programs). These programs and hundreds of others have demonstrated the federal government's "continued reliance on grants as a means of furthering national purposes...[and] a new reliance on the same device for advancing what formerly were purely local functions."[35]

(4) Changes in federal-local relations. Aided by the passage of general revenue sharing and various block grant

programs, the amount of federal money which bypassed the states on the way to local governments rose from 8 percent in the early 1960s to a high of 28 percent in the late 1970s before leveling off at 24 percent in 1980.

(5) Unprecedented changes in fiscal federalism. From the development of block grants in the late 1960s, to the passage of general revenue sharing, these changes contribute to changes in all three levels of government. It is also important to document the reliance of state and local governments on federal dollars. That reliance has become a habit-forming dependency. In 1960, federal aid funds accounted for less than 15 percent of state and local expenditures. By 1980, the figure had hit 26 percent. State and local governments would find, however, that the government that giveth can also taketh away. By FY 1986, the federal share of state and local receipts was expected to drop less than 21 percent.

Fiscal federalism has meant even more than that and the dominance of the federal government has put the sub-national governments in "a distinctly subordinate role--that of middle-management supplicants."[36] If their supplications are granted then they must continually look up to a federal bureaucrat to see if they are performing in accordance with the rules in administering the grant.

(6) The strangling effect of intergovernmental regulation, including cross-cutting conditions applied to grants; threats by the federal government to cut off funds to state governments for refusal to comply with related federal requirements, such as those involving the 55-mile-per-hour speed limit; direct federal mandates; and full and partial federal preemption. The number of regulators has grown rapidly, with fourteen new federal regulatory agencies created during this quarter-century. They have been busy. By the early years of the decade of the 1980s, the requirements they had written and published in the "Code of Federal Regulations" exceeded 85,000 pages.[37]

(7) The establishment of literally hundreds of multi-state and sub-state regional units--resulting from various grant programs. These single-purpose planning and grant review bodies

are often nothing more than intergovernmental paper tigers.

(8) Changes in the role of the states in the system and in their relationship with the federal government. While he was still president of Princeton University and just two years before he became governor of New Jersey, Woodrow Wilson noted how important and enduring the question of the states' rule would be:

> The question of the relation of the States to the federal government is the cardinal question of our constitutional system.... It cannot...be settled by the opinion of any one generation, because it is a question of growth, and every successive stage of our political and economic development gives it a new aspect, makes it a new question.[38]

The states retain their constitutional role as "keystones" of the American governmental arch. They retain a major role in authorizing and carrying out federal programs. The states also retain their political role--as polities--in the American political system. They were designed to govern within their jurisdictions, not to be merely the middle level of management in the federal scheme of things.[39] The states continue to maintain a firm grip on the sentiment of loyalty of their citizens.

(9) The galloping intergovernmentalization of fiscal, administrative and political arrangements of American federalism.[40] The rapid expansion of the role of the federal government in this quarter-century has "exacerbated the difficulties of governance."[41] This process of intergovernmentalization, or marbleization as some call it, has allowed the federal government to accomplish its goals and policies by an explosion of conditional categorical grant-in-aid programs coupled with regulations and guidelines, programs administered by state and local governments, and often paid for by state and local taxes. All of this accomplished without the politically dangerous task of expanding the federal bureaucracy. In fact, while state and local employment figures have skyrocketed, the size of the federal bureaucracy has actually declined since the late 1960s.[42] This process of

intergovernmentalization has involved not only state and local governments but "a host of public, quasi-public, and private actors--institutions, groups, interests, and individuals"[43] as well.

(10) Comprehension of the fact that during this quarter-century, Congress has become the principal architect of intergovernmental relations. Beginning with Nixon, each of the next four presidents pushed for a decentralization of the system of federalism and a reduced role for the national government. Congress generally refused to go along. One description of the theory of the congressional view of federalism maintains it is "incremental, confrontational, strongly categorical, heavily conditional [as in federal regulations], and politically co-optive."[44] Another view is equally as blunt in its assessment:

> There is a Washington establishment. In fact, it is a hydra with each head only marginally concerned with the others' existence.... Contrary to what is popularly believed, the bureaucrats are not the problem. Congressmen are. The Congress is the key to the Washington establishment. The Congress created the establishment, sustains it, and most likely will continue to sustain and even expand it....
>
> Congress is the linchpin of the Washington establishment.... Congress does not just react to big government--it creates it.[45]

Congress has tended to favor the use of conditional categorical grant programs as opposed to the less restrictive block grant approach. The use of these "narrow intergovernmental devices" allows members of Congress to further their personal political ambitions by program sponsorship. These devices have become the preferred way of doing business because of the proliferation of congressional subcommittees with narrow jurisdictions. This explosion of subcommittees resulted from the efforts at congressional reform in the 1970s. That same pattern of congressional decentralization increased the pressures interest groups can bring to bear on committees and committee members.[46]

In federal programs designed to involve several levels of government, "the congressional act does not result in a joint venture between equal, participating partners. Rather...the national government assumes the role of landlord or provider while the state government is relegated to the status of a tenant."[47]

These views of federalism have contributed—among other things—to the birth (or revitalization) of a number of new institutions of federalism, especially those involved as participants in the intergovernmental lobby in Washington. This is because Washington is not only where national policy is determined, but it is also the place where many policies affecting state andlocal governments are decided.

(11) The increasing influence of the professional bureaucratic complex which has resulted from functional specialization.[48] This complex is made up of individuals with scientific or other professional training. These "technocrats," as Beer calls them, wield enormous decision-making powers.[49] But, they do not wield these powers by themselves. They must share them with interested legislators, usually members of relevant congressional subcommittees and with spokespersons for the groups, the "topocrats" that benefit from such programs.[50] These three comprise what is commonly known as the "triple alliance,"[51] or the "iron triangle."[52]

(12) The emergence of new (or revitalized) intergovernmental and regional organizations and institutions. These new organizations and institutions have sprung up because of many of the changes noted above. Some of these institutions have been the result of federal legislation; others resulted from changes in the role of political officials, such as governors and mayors. Yet others were the children of new problems, new divisions in the system. This is especially true of many of the regional organizations born during the phase of intergovernmental relations (in the 1960s and 1970s) which Deil Wright has identified as the "competitive" phase of federalism.[53]

One of the most important effects of the emergence of these

institutions and organizations has been the arrival on the Washington scene of representatives of many of these institutions and organizations coupled with the arrival of representatives of other governmental units, such as states and cities and counties.

By the end of this quarter-century, no fewer than two-thirds of the states maintained offices in Washington. These state offices are on the lookout for federal grant programs, they keep an eye on federal regulatory developments, they often attempt to influence the shaping of public policy, they work with other states on issues of mutual concern and they serve as information clearinghouses. This control of information is one way governors have tried to maintain control of state agencies which have grown increasingly dependent upon the federal government.[54]

In addition to these state offices, the intergovernmental lobby includes the so-called "corporate interests" of the different levels of government and various groups of public officials. These corporate interests are represented by such groups as the National Governors' Association, the National Conference of State Legislatures, the U.S. Conference of Mayors and the National Association of Counties, to name only a few of the more prominent ones. The members of these organizations maintain a "capacity for independent political involvement,"[55] a capacity to participate in Washington politics on their own.

This "intergovernmental lobby" is an important new development in this quarter-century, resulting from the federal government's decisions and actions to continue to increase its role in the federal system. This surge of lobbying activity dates only from the mid-1960s and came as a response to the increase in federal programs spawned by technocratic professionals.[56]

There are many who contend that the last twenty-five years have witnessed changes in the intergovernmental patterns never before seen in such scale. These changes, this loss of innocence of a simpler, less complex pattern of federalism have had profound implications for the functioning of the system over the past quarter-century. Many of the manifestations of these changes, of the growing complexity, interdependence and interrelatedness of the system can be seen in the new institutions and organizations of federalism examined in the next chapter.

NOTES

===

[1]Daniel J. Elazar, American Federalism: A View from the States (3rd ed.; New York: Harper & Row, Publishers, 1984), p. 2.

[2]Laurence J. O'Toole, Jr., ed., American Intergovernmental Relations (Washington: Congressional Quarterly Press, 1985), p. 3.

[3]Jerome J. Hanus, ed., The Nationalization of State Government (Lexington, Mass.: Lexington Books, 1981), p. 31.

[4]Raoul Berger, Federalism: The Founders' Design (Norman: University of Oklahoma Press, 1987), pp. 24-61.

[5]The Federalist, Number 14.

[6]Elazar, American Federalism, p. 2.

[7]William H. Riker, Federalism: Origin, Operation, Significance (Boston: Little, Brown & Co., 1964), p. 81.

[8]David B. Walker, "American Federalism—Then and Now," in The Book of the States, 1982-83 (Lexington, Ken.: The Council of State Governments, 1982), p. 23.

[9]Deil S. Wright, Understanding Intergovernmental Relations (2nd ed.; Monterey, Calif.: Brooks/Cole Publishing Co., 1982), pp. 31-66.

[10]Deil S. Wright, "Intergovernmental Relations in the 1980s, A New Phase of IGR," in Intergovernmental Relations in the 1980s, ed. by Richard H. Leach (New York: Marcel Dekker, Inc., 1983), pp. 15-19.

[11]Roscoe C. Martin, The Cities and the Federal System (New York: Atherton Press, 1965), p. 111.

[12]"Special Message to the Congress Recommending the Establishment of a Commission to Study Federal, State, and Local Relations," March 30, 1953, Public Papers of the Presidents of

34

the United States, Dwight D. Eisenhower, 1953 (Washington: Government Printing Office, 1960), p. 140.

[13]Commission on Intergovernmental Relations, Report to the President for Transmittal to the Congress (Washington: Government Printing Office, 1955), p. 2.

[14]Wright, Understanding Intergovernmental Relations, pp. 31-66.

[15]David B. Walker, "American Federalism--Then and Now," in The Book of the States, 1982-83 (Lexington: The Council of State Governments, 1982), pp. 23-29.

[16]James L. Sundquist, Making Federalism Work (Washington: Brookings Institution, 1969), p. 3.

[17]Richard A. Snelling, "American Federalism in the Eighties," State Government LIII (Autumn, 1980), p. 168.

[18]"Address at the National Governors' Conference," September 1, 1969, Public Papers of the Presidents of the United States, Richard M. Nixon, 1969 (Washington: Government Printing Office, 1971), p. 696.

[19]Richard S. Williamson, "Block Grants--A Federalist Tool," State Government LIV, #4 (1981), pp. 114-117.

[20]"Special Message to the Congress on Sharing Federal Revenues with the States," August 13, 1969, Public Papers of the Presidents of the United States, Richard M. Nixon, 1969 (Washington: Government Printing Office, 1971), p. 668.

[21]Donald H. Haider, "Intergovernmental Redirection," Annals CDLXVI (March, 1983), pp. 170-171.

[22]Mercer Cross, "Carter's Federalism: How Real in Practice," Congressional Quarterly Weekly Report, XXXV(April 9, 1977), p. 679.

[23]Ibid.

[24]"Inaugural Address," January 20, 1981, Public Papers of the Presidents of the United States, Ronald W. Reagan, 1981 (Washington: Government Printing Office, 1982), p. 2.

[25]Ibid., p. 3.

[26]David B. Walker, "The Federal Role in the Federal System? A Troublesome Topic," National Civic Review LXXII (January, 1983), p. 13.

[27]David B. Walker, "Dysfunctional Federalism--The Congress and Intergovernmental Relations," State Government LIV, #2 (1981), pp. 53-57.

[28]"State, Local Groups Still Asking for Details of the New Federalism," National Journal, XIV (July 17, 982), pp. 1243, 1269; "Two Baby Steps," National Journal, XV (De ember 3, 1983), p. 2536; "Is this the End for Reagan's New Feder lism?" National Journal, XIV (August 14, 1982) pp. 1407, 14 2; "Revised New Federalism Plan Would do Little to Change Power, Authority," National Journal, XV (March 5, 1983), pp. 487, 518-519; Haider, "Intergovernmental Redirection," pp. 170-171.

[29]Scott M. Matheson, "Sovereign States--Sovereign Nation," National Civic Review, LXXI (November/December, 1982), p. 506.

[30]John Herbers, "The New Federalism: Unplanned, Innovative and Here to Stay," Governing, I (October, 1987), p. 28.

[31]Ibid., pp. 28-37.

[32]Ibid.

[33]Morton Grodzins, "The Federal System," in President's Commission on National Goals, Goals for Americans (Englewood Cliffs: Prentice-Hall, Inc., 1960), pp. 265-282.

[34]Michael D. Reagan and John G. Sanzone, The New Federalism (2nd ed.; New York: Oxford University Press, 1981), p. 3.

[35]Walker, "American Federalism--Then and Now," p. 25.

[36]Robert S. Lorch, State and Local Politics: The Great Entanglement (2nd ed.; Englewood Cliffs: Prentice-Hall, Inc., 1986), p. 35.

[37]Richard D. Bingham, State and Local Government in an Urban Society (New York: Random House, Inc., 1986), pp. 74-75.

[38]Woodrow Wilson, Constitutional Government in the United States (New York: Columbia University Press, 1908), p. 173.

[39]Lorch, State and Local Politics, pp. 34-36.

[40]Mavis Mann Reeves, "Galloping Intergovernmentalization as a Factor in State Management," State Government, LIV, #3 (1981), 102-108; see also Thomas J. Anton, "The New Federalism in Illinois," Illinois Issues, VIII (March, 1982), pp. 6-14.

[41]Reeves, "Galloping Intergovernmentalization," p. 105.

[42]Alan V. Stevens, "State Government Employment," in The Book of the States, 1984-85 (Lexington, Ken.: The Council of State Governments, 1984), p. 271.

[43]Haider, "Intergovernmental Redirection," p. 166.

[44]Walker, "Dysfunctional Federalism," p. 54; see also Reeves, "Galloping Intergovernmentalization," pp. 102-107; Haider, "Intergovernmental Redirection," pp. 165-178.

[45]Morris P. Fiorina, Congress: Keystone of the Washington Establishment (New Haven: Yale University Press, 1977), pp. 3, 49.

[46]Ibid., pp. 62-67.

[47]Jerome J. Hanus and Gary C. Marfin, "State Dependency and Cooperative Federalism," State Government, LIII (Autumn, 1980), p. 176.

[48]Samuel H. Beer, "Federalism, Nationalism, and Democracy in America," American Political Science Review, LXXII (March, 1978), pp. 9-22.

[49]Ibid.

[50]Ibid., p. 18.

[51]Anita S. Harbert, Federal Grants-in-Aid, Maximizing Benefits to the States (New York: Praeger Publishers, 1976), p. 8; Charles R. Warren, "State Governments' Capacity: Continuing to Improve," National Civic Review, LXXI (May, 1982), pp. 234-239.

[52]Harold Seidman, Politics, Positions and Power (New York: Oxford University Press, 1970), p. 32; "Two Baby Steps," National Journal, XV (December 3, 1983), p. 2536.

[53]Wright, Understanding Intergovernmental Relations, pp. 60-68.

[54]David L. Cingranelli, "State Government Lobbies in the National Political Process," State Government, LVI, #4 (1983), pp. 122-124.

[55]Kay Lehman Schlozman and John T. Tierney, Organized Interests and American Democracy (New York: Harper & Row, Publishers, 1986), pp. 55-56.

[56]Beer, "Federalism, Nationalism and Democracy in America," p. 18; Hanus, The Nationalization of State Government, pp. 139-142.

CHAPTER THREE

THE POLITICS OF INTERGOVERNMENTAL RELATIONS
AND THE NEW INSTITUTIONS OF FEDERALISM

As noted in Chapter Two, today's system of intergovernmental
relations and intergovernmental relationships is quite different
than it was a short twenty-five years ago. All of the
players--the federal government, the state governments and local
governments--are still in the game, but the power positions and
hence the political relationships have changed dramatically.
The federal government is still king of the hill, the single
most dominant force in the federalism of the 1980s. The states
(and local governments), however, have refused to leave the
field of battle.

The nationhood-long struggle between the federal government
and the states continues unabated. As important a restraint as
the U.S. Constitution is in restraining centralized federal
power, the power base of the states rests on more than this
constitutional status. Politically, the states are crucial.
States--although a part of the national political fabric--are
separate political entities. There is a variance in the nature
as well as the content of many of their programs and policies.
The states, not the federal government, have most often been the
program innovators. The states are also important because they
are regarded as "communities." They have political, economic,
historical and social commonalities--and differences. They are
symbols and sources of identification to their citizens. State
governments are still the keystones in the governmental arch.

In this volume, the terms "federalism" and "intergovernmental relations" are used interchangeably. In analyzing these intergovernmental relationships, once called the "hidden dimension" of government, Professor Deil Wright has argued that the most accurate and useful model of intergovernmental relations is the "overlapping-authority" model, a model with three essential characteristics:

1. Substantial areas of governmental operations involve national, state and local units (of officials) simultaneously.

2. The areas of autonomy or single-jurisdiction independence and discretion are comparatively small.

3. The power and influence available to any one jurisdiction (or official) is substantially limited. The limits produce an authority pattern best described as bargaining.[1]

One of the most important implications of this intergovernmental relations model is that the overlapping, interdependent nature of the American system of federalism makes it necessary to "alter the authority relationships among participants (officials)."[2] These alterations have had a significant impact on the roles, functions, and power relationships of the system's governmental officials.

INTERSTATE RELATIONS--REGIONALISM

American federalism is a very complex, overlapping and duplicative system of government. It involves both intergovernmental cooperation as well as intergovernmental competition. To date, most of the studies which have been done have examined intergovernmental relationships from the interlevel standpoint--federal-state, federal-local, state-local, or federal-state-local. This study joins those few studies which have concentrated on intra-level relationships, and focuses primarily on the interactions and relationships among states:

Interactions among states are increasing.... An interesting aspect of this

>expanding intergovernmental intercourse is the growing acceptance of regional organizations on a multistate...basis. Such regional interaction progresses unevenly, with starts and stops; nevertheless it is now a major aspect of the American governmental system....
>
>Another important development is the increase in cooperation among the states as they move positively to solve the problems confronting them.[3]

The result has been a "new regionalism."[4] As the Advisory Commission on Intergovernmental Relations (ACIR) has correctly noted: "Regionalism has been a persistent if not always persuasive part of the American political tradition."[5] The institutions and organizations examined in this chapter are indications that "national and subnational governments find it both necessary and desirable to accommodate regional tendencies in the body politic and to satisfy multi-jurisdictional needs within the system."[6]

As has been observed, regions are a phenomenon unto themselves.[7] Regions do not have formal places in the political system. Such status comes only from interstate, federal or federal-interstate action.

Establishing regional political mechanisms is never easy. Creation of such institutions is a delicate, sensitive, highly political task with few precedents to serve as signposts. It is a task of fitting regional organizations into a political system which is not organized along clearly differentiated and agreed-on regional lines.[8]

Acceptance of regionalism as a political and governmental concept and of regional organizations has gained increasing prominence over the past quarter-century. So much so, in fact, that regionalism is seen by some observers as "...a major new development in modern American federalism."[9]

This new regionalism has historical roots reaching back as far as the constitutional convention. Regionalism--like federalism--has been through different phases. The new regionalism, spawned during the period 1960-1985, is fed by three trends of the period. First, the expansion of the role of the federal government and subsequent withdrawal of the national government from many programs and areas of concern. Second, new, revitalized, higher-quality and more capable state and local governments. Third, a series of events and activities including a decline in real federal aid, the rise of stronger regional organizations, lengthy periods of national economic stagnation, and a realignment of the relative standing of the regions.

Because of the prominent position of the states in the system, any analysis of regionalism must be based on the understanding that the states have to be a part of the operational definition. Such regionalism must be at least bi-state, if not multistate, in character. Although there are sub-state regional organizations, this analysis will confine itself to regional arrangements built around the states as the basic political units.

There are a variety of new political institutions which have resulted from changes in intergovernmental relations and relationships. Some of these institutions are governmental, others are extra-governmental. The latter may have been caused by t..e formation and actions of the former. Extra-governmental institutions are the subjects of the second half of this chapter. The first half of this chapter focuses ₒn the changes caused by and the effects of the new governmental institutions and organizations (and programs), some of them representing rather radical departures from previous types of governmental activities. Rather than an exhaustive analysis of these institutions and organizations, the idea of this chapter is to explore the nature, range, and scope of some of these new governmental and extra-governmental institutions and organizations (and programs) of federalism.

NEW GOVERNMENTAL INSTITUTIONS OF FEDERALISM

Interstate Compacts: The interstate compact is a device, a legal instrument for formal cooperation between states, used since 1783. The first interstate compacts were proposed before the ratification of the Constitution. The early compacts were used by the colonies to settle boundary disputes. Up until 1920, the settling of boundary disputes was about the only purpose of interstate compacts.

The adoption of the Constitution gave constitutional recognition to interstate compacts in Article I, Section 10: "No State shall, without the consent of Congress....enter into any Agreement or Compact with another state...." Legally, interstate compacts are unique in the American governmental system. They are contracts which bind compact states. The United States Supreme Court has expressed a willingness to enforce such agreements. Interstate compacts are superior to and take precedence over states' statutes.[10]

Although the language of the Constitution would seem to require congressional consent to all interstate compacts, this has not been true in practice. In the critical Virginia v. Tennessee (148 U.S. 503 [1893]) decision and in later decisions, the Supreme Court interpreted the compact clause to mean consent by implication as well as by express congressional action. The Court determined that consent was necessary only when the agreements between states "tend to increase and build up the political influence of the contracting states, so as to encroach upon or impair the supremacy of the United States or interfere with their rightful management of particular subjects placed under their entire control."[11]

The first multi-state interstate compact was the Colorado River Compact, designed to allocate water resources on a regional basis among the seven member states. More new ground was broken with the interstate compact which created the Port of New York Authority (between New York and New Jersey) in 1921. The Authority was empowered to develop transportation, terminal and other facilities in the port area. This was the first compact in which the powers to finance, build and operate public works were given over to a bistate agency.

Many of the other six interstate compacts proposed during the 1920s attacked regional problems. In the 1930s, the emphasis shifted. Functional compacts were developed;

interstate compacts became national in scope, open to all
states. These state service compacts provided a legal framework
and they often established regulatory administrative machinery.
Seventeen new interstate compacts were proposed in the 1930s.

The other major development in the use of interstate
compacts was the blending of state and national authority in
problem-solving. The Delaware River Basin Compact of 1961 is a
multipurpose development of water resources with the national
government--by act of Congress--a full partner to the compact
and a full member of the compact body. This was the first use
of a new intergovernmental approach, the creation of a
federal-interstate compact. Since 1961, two others have been
developed--the Susquehanna River Basin Compact and the Agreement
on Detainers.

With the uses of the compact device broadened by these
pioneering compacts, the subjects now covered by interstate
compacts include: air and water pollution, bridges and tunnels,
fisheries conservation, forest fire protection, mining
practices, oil and gas conservation, corrections, juvenile
delinquency, driver licensing, education, libraries, mental
health, law enforcement, taxation, vehicle safety, navigation
development, nuclear energy, pest control, planning and
development, civil defense, disaster assistance, recreational
parks, mass transit, supervision of parolees and probationers,
flood control, and placement of children for foster care and
adoption.[12]

Although many interstate compacts created interstate
agencies or commissions, some created no new agencies. This was
usually the case when the purpose of the compact was to obtain
intergovernmental action. Examples include drivers' licensing
compacts and the placement of children compacts, among many
others.

The number of states willing to cooperate and join compact
agreements varies widely depending on the issue. Some compacts
are approved by a large number of states in a relatively short
span of time. Others find approval slow in coming. A good
example of the latter can be found in the Placement of Children

Compact, first proposed in the late 1950s. The first state approved this interstate compact in 1960, but by 1973, only 16 other states had joined.

As it turns out, the spread of the compact was not impeded by any negativism about either the principles involved or their actual implementation. Rather, an absence of knowledge concerning the compact and the absence of sufficient means to assist states in learning of it and of studying its technical aspects were the inhibiting factors.[13]

Upon receiving a federal grant to increase services for the compact, the American Public Welfare Association set out to overcome the lack of knowledge about the compact. Their efforts paid handsome dividends. Within three years seventeen more states joined with seven additional ones by 1978. By 1984, there were 44 states participating in the compact.

State participation in compacts depends very directly on the compact's subject matter:

> Participation in compacts involving relatively costly programs, such as education and social programs, tends to be higher among relatively small states, as indicated by total income or total population. Participation in environmental compacts and in corrections and crime control compacts, by contrast, tends to be higher in more densely populated states, where those problems are likely to be more severe. A state which is likely to join compacts dealing with one type of issue may not necessarily be equally likely to join compacts that deal with other issues.[14]

States seem most willing to participate in non-controversial cooperative efforts. No nationwide compact dealing with controversial concerns has yet succeeded in gaining support from two-thirds or more of the states.[15]

Enthusiasm for interstate compacts seems to have waned in recent years. As the data below indicate, the use of this device is declining.

Table 3.1

NUMBER OF NEW INTERSTATE COMPACTS, BY PERIOD

Period	Number of New Interstate Compacts
1783-1920	36
1920-1929	8
1930-1939	17
1940-1949	25
1950-1959	33
1960-1969	48
1970-1979	18
1980-1985	6

The drop-off in the number of new interstate compacts in the 1970s and 1980s may be attributed to several factors. It is possible that with the large number of compacts operating, there are fewer frontiers left for this intergovernmental device. The decline could result also from disappointment with the results;[16] or from the very unsettled intergovernmental environment of the 1970s and the 1980s.[17] There can be little doubt that the financial difficulties of the federal government and the states in the mid-1970s "did not provide a friendly climate for the conception of new programs."[18]

Even though there has been a measurable slowing in the number of new interstate compacts proposed in recent years, interstate compacts have provided a legal and administrative means of "breaking through the jurisdictional and program limitations of state boundaries and also of integrating law and programmatic action on a federal-interstate basis."[19] The device has been most helpful in getting governments to tackle intergovernmental problems in concert.

National Conference of Commissioners on Uniform State Laws: Although there are a number of organizations which promote the adoption of uniform legislation, the most notable is the National Conference of Commissioners on Uniform State Laws (NCCUSL). The Conference, organized in 1892, prepares drafts of legislation for adoption by the various states.

The Conference is made up of not more than five commissioners from each state, selected by the respective governors. Commissioners are assigned to drafting committees which prepare the drafts of the proposed legislation. These drafts are then presented at the national conference meetings. At that time, the conference composes itself into the committee of the whole to debate the drafts of proposed uniform legislation. Drafts can be brought for debate either when they are in final proposal form or in mid-preparation. The minimum preparation time for these proposals is two years and is frequently longer. Over the nearly 100 years of its existence, the NCCUSL has proposed nearly 200 legislative proposals for adoption. Half of these were prepared during the past twenty years.[20]

The Conference works closely with the American Bar Association and drafts of its legislative proposals are submitted to the Association's House of Delegates. "It is significant that the uniform laws proposed and adopted so far are largely in areas outside of the normal fields of political combat...."[21] In areas of interstate competition, uniform law is difficult to develop. "Legislation is most likely to be adopted when it is highly interstate in character, when it meets a recognized need, and when it is in the area of private law where controversy is less likely to accompany social change."[22] Only three of the uniform laws have ever been adopted by all states and fewer than a dozen uniform laws have been adopted by as many as 40 states.[23]

Once the NCCUSL has drafted and approved the uniform laws, the success rate of adoption depends on the support of organizations and interests outside the Conference itself. "There is no compulsion to enact uniform acts. They rise or fall upon their substantive merits and upon the real need for uniformity."[24] The Conference itself does not function as an organized pressure group lobbying legislatures for adoption of the proposals. State bar associations often serve in that capacity. States are free to modify parts of these "uniform law" proposals. However, in spite of such localizing and in spite of varying judicial interpretations of the laws, uniform laws have helped to simplify business relations.

Regional Economic Development Commissions: Some problems of
American society refuse to fit the geographical divisions of the
American political system.   When such problems are larger than
the political jurisdictions, it is very difficult for existing
governments to solve such problems.   This "spill over," these
problems of "scale" require the improvisation of new
governmental and extra-governmental organizations.[25]

     One response has been to create regional organizations.
One of the earliest multistate regional organizations
established by the states was the Port Authority of New York
(1921).   This bi-state organization was followed within a year
by the six-state Colorado River Compact of 1922. These regional
organizations were joined by the federally-created Tennessee
Valley Authority in 1933, the first truly multifunctional
regional organization.   In spite of federal efforts to stimulate
creation of additional regional organizations, only one--the
Bi-State Development Compact (1950)--sprang up between 1933 and
1960.   The Bi-State was an effort to stimulate regional economic
development in the St. Louis area.

     The dawning of the 1960s saw that change. The 1960s would
prove to be fertile ground for the creation of regional
organizations.   In 1961, the Delaware Valley Urban Area Compact
(economic development) was organized. So also was the Delaware
River Basin Compact (see below), a federal-multistate
organization which marked the first time the federal government
had become a party to an interstate compact.

     Another new type of regional organization would result from
a specific, more "localized" problem. In the latter part of the
decade of the 1950s, much of the southeastern part of the nation
was ravaged by severe flooding.   Natural disasters such as
floods do more than temporarily destroy a portion of the
landscape and take a human toll. Often, these disasters have
long-range effects on the economic life of an area and on the
basic quality of life.   Such disasters demonstrate how
ill-equipped the political system is to deal with certain types
of problems.

     The Appalachian region of the United States had suffered

from very severe economic problems long before the flood waters
came in the late 1950s. But these problems were worsened by the
flooding. Government officials who viewed the damage caused by
the floodwaters concluded that the many problems--social,
physical, and especially economic--would have to be attacked by
a political unit larger than any of the states affected.[26]

Because the problems were general over the area, the
governors of the affected states met to try to chart the
region's recovery. During the closing weeks of the 1960
campaign, the Conference of Appalachian Governors called on the
presidential candidates to spell out their plans for aiding the
Appalachian region. One of the candidates--Democratic nominee
Senator John F. Kennedy of Massachusetts--was particularly
receptive to the governors' pleas for help. He had been deeply
affected by the poverty he had found during his primary campaign
in West Virginia. He also realized the political debt he owed
the region because of the boost the West Virginia primary
victory had given his nomination campaign.

One of the outgrowths of the governors' pleas was the
passage of the Area Redevelopment Act of 1961. The Act set some
important precedents. It established a new government
agency--in the Department of Commerce--the Area Redevelopment
Administration (ARA). The ARA was to administer the federal
government's financial assistance programs designed to combat
the region's problems. The federal government provided funds
for low interest business loans, loans and grants for the
construction of public facilities, and technical assistance
services. The aid package to the region was tripled in size
when an additional $900 million under the Public Works
Acceleration Act of 1962 was added. Well-intentioned, the Area
Redevelopment Act of 1961 was written and approved without any
real understanding of the depth and complexity of the region's
economic difficulties. The result was a too-small band-aid
approach to a very large set of problems.

The floods came again in late 1962 and early 1963. There
were more deaths and much more devastation. President Kennedy
again met with government officials from the region.

Immediately after the meeting, he created the President's Appalachian Regional Commission (PARC), and assigned it the responsibility for preparing a comprehensive program for regional economic recovery and development.

At the same time PARC was beginning its work, a debate was going on in governmental circles about the causes and cures of the problem of chronic unemployment, especially as it was reflected in Appalachia. There were some who believed that rapid obsolescence of industries and workers' skills was the culprit. There were others who believed that the causes were larger, more complex and involved flaws in the nation's economic fabric. Those who believed in the obsolescence theory tended to favor job training programs and assistance programs for especially hard hit areas. Those adhering to the hole-in-the-economic-fabric theory wanted to use fiscal and monetary policies to ensure sufficient product demand and hence create jobs for the unemployed.[27]

President Kennedy did not live long enough to see the Commission complete the assignment he had given it. He was killed before the Commission issued its final report. However, the Commission's work did not stop with Kennedy's death. Out of the deliberations of the Commission came the blueprint for the Appalachian Regional Development Act of 1965. The Act embodied elements of both of the above approaches to solving unemployment.

> The Appalachian Regional Development Act of 1965 was greeted as a major and dramatic governmental innovation. Reporters saluted the "end of the pork-barrel," noting that the Appalachian program called for the investment of funds according to "cost benefits" criteria. The program was thought remarkable in that both Congress and the bureaucracies were willing to relinquish some of their authority over the grant process, and in the new potential for cooperation among the several states involved.[28]

The Act authorized federal financial aid to help build a solid regional base for long-term economic development. Title I of the Act created a new federal-interstate regional institution, the Appalachian Regional Commission (ARC). The

ARC's governing body was a bold experiment in federal-interstate power sharing. Each state was to be represented by the governor or the governor's chosen representative. The President appointed the national co-chairperson of the Commission. ARC decisions required the approval of both the federal members and a majority of the state representatives. Thus, the national co-chairperson had a veto, but it had never been used in the first twelve years of the ARC's existence.[29] The national member was to serve as a liaison to the President, various executive branch departments and agencies, and relevant congressional sub-committees and committees.

Since the ARC only met monthly, an Executive Committee was established to direct the day-to-day activities. The Executive Committee was made up of the national co-chairperson, the Commission's executive director and the permanent liaison officer of the states, the States' Regional Representative.[30]

The ARC covered 397 counties in thirteen states, with a population of 18 million people. The multistate area shared many common problems.

> The area has continuing high unemployment, lower personal and family income, populations with low education levels and few job skills, and generally lacks adequate public facilities. These patterns have continued for decade after decade, even during periods of high affluence and economic expansion in the rest of the country. This situation provides the _raison d'etre_ for the ARC....[31]

Funding for the programs undertaken by the ARC came from a variety of grant-in-aid programs, direct federal appropriations, and state and local matching funds. The Commission undertook no projects directly, but carried out all of its activities through the state and local governments.[32]

A large number of members of Congress were naturally intrigued by the possibilities of making use of new institutional tools--such as regional economic development commissions--to help their own home areas attack the problems of chronic unemployment and poverty. It may well be that this home district interest provided the votes for passage of the ARDA.

Lyndon Johnson knew the legislative process well and he responded with a trade-off which would allow other areas of the country to utilize similar regional institutions. "As part of the trade-off for the creation of the ARC, the Congress, under Title V of the Public Works and Economic Development Act of 1965, also authorized the Department of Commerce to establish national- multistate regional development commissions."[33] The institutions which came out of this log-rolling were nicknamed Title V commissions. By 1980, there were eight of them:

- New England Regional Commission--6 states (Maryland, New Hampshire, Vermont, Massachusetts, Connecticut, Rhode Island);

- Coastal Plains Regional Commission--3 states (Georgia, South Carolina, North Carolina);

- Upper Great Lakes Regional Commission --3 states (Michigan, Minnesota, Wisconsin);

- Ozarks Regional Commission--4 states (Missouri, Kansas, Arkansas, Oklahoma);

- Four Corners Regional Commission--4 states (Arizona, Utah, Colorado, New Mexico);

- Pacific Northwest Regional Commission --3 states (Washington, Oregon, Idaho);

- Old West Regional Commission--5 states (North Dakota, South Dakota, Montana, Wyoming, Nebraska).

Life is never easy for regional organizations. By the end of 1981, the federal government had "decommissioned" the economic development commissions. The separate ARC was being cut down by substantial reductions in its budget. Even so, the seeds of regionalism had taken root and all of these Title V economic development commissions have incorporated as Councils of Governors or merged with existing organizations of states dealing with regional growth policies.[34]

River Basin Commissions: For most of the first half of the twentieth century, policies for the management of river basins originated at the federal level. Efforts involving the management of river basins were usually unifunctional in nature, e.g., projects involving flood control or pollution/ sanitation control.

The first multifunctional river basin commission was not approved until the fourth try as previous attempts in 1925, 1927, and 1951 had all failed. "The Delaware River Basin Commission (DRBC) was created in response to basinwide problems in developing adequate water supply, pollution abatement, flood control, and hydroelectric power programs to satisfy all the water users in that region."[35] In truth, the DRBC resulted from the affected states deciding to form an interstate organization in order to get out from under the United States Supreme Court managing the river. The impetus began with New York City's efforts to develop the headwaters of the river in upstate New York. Downstream communities were fearful New York City would deplete their supplies of water from the Delaware. Peaceful overtures failing, the State of Pennsylvania sued the State of New York. That lawsuit resulted in the Supreme Court divvying up the water and appointing a river master (itself) in 1954.

The compact which created the Commission gave it broad grants of power for planning, conservation, development, management, and control of the basin's water resources.[36] Because the federal government would be--in effect--an active partner in the federal-state commission, congressional opposition was heavy, but was overcome.

The creation of the Delaware River Basin Commission was not the only effort to find regional solutions to water resources problems. Activities were underway on other fronts as well. President Kennedy tried to secure passage of his Water Resources Planning Act of 1961, but congressional opposition stymied passage. Reintroduced in 1963, changes were made to meet the objections (usually relating to state involvement in the basin commissions) to the 1961 bill. It was not until the early days of the Great Society, however, that the bill was able to gain congressional approval. That bill became the Water Resources Planning Act of 1965. There was a provision in the Act which established a Water Resources Council. The Council was to be the federal coordinating agency with the power to review federal and state plans for river basin projects.[37] Title II of the Act authorized the President to establish river basin commissions when requested to do so either by the Water Resources Council or by a state lying within a proposed river basin area. Written agreement would then have to be obtained from at least half of the states affected. These river basin commissions were created to "coordinate federal, state, interstate, local and private water development plans for the basin; to prepare and keep up-to-date a comprehensive joint development plan...."[38]

As was the case with the Title V commissions, the President was to appoint one member of each commission and the governors of the member states were to select their own representatives. In addition to the appointments by the governors and the President, all federal agencies having substantial interest in the work of a commission were allowed to appoint one member per agency. This was a substantial departure from the setup of the Title V economic development commissions.

Decisions made by the river basin commissions were to be reached by consensus, not by voting. This was made necessary by the possibility of the states being outvoted by a commission's federal members, a situation which could not occur in the Title V commissions. If a consensus couldn't be reached, alternative courses of action were to be presented and considered.[39]

By 1980, six river basin commissions had been formed, the Souris-Red- Rainey, Great Lakes, New England, Ohio, and Pacific Northwest commissions in addition to the DRBC. The success of these river basin commissions is difficult to measure. Certainly, attempts to coordinate the nation's river basin planning efforts are helpful, even if not completely successful.

These five Title II commissions were strictly planning and coordinating organizations. Their powers differed considerably from the DRBC. By the mid-1970s, these river basin commissions would have staffs averaging eleven persons and budgets averaging $300,000 to $400,000.[40] In 1981, the federal government, responding to the federalism initiatives of the new president, closed down the federal-state river basin commissions established as Title II commissions. One year later, the staff of the Water Resources Council (the regional-supporting and state-supporting federal interagency) was disbanded.[41]

Even though the Reagan Administration used the axe on these regional organizations, they too, refused to die. Four of the river basin commissions became "nonprofit corporations operating as regional associations of state water resources officials;" another merged with an existing multistate commission; and only one went completely out of business.[42]

Federal Regional Councils: In March, 1969, President Nixon created a new institution of federalism as part of his own New Federalism.[43] By executive order, the President established eight (later expanded to ten) common regions for the various federal agencies. One city in each region was designated as the regional headquarters. Five federal agencies were initially involved: the Department of Health, Education & Welfare (superseded in 1980 by the Department of Health and Human Services); the Department of Housing and Urban Development; the Department of Labor; the Office of Economic Opportunity; and the Small Business Administration. The SBA never joined, but the Department of Transportation (1970); Environmental Protection Agency (1972); the Law Enforcement Assistance Administration (1972); the Department of Agriculture (1973); the Department of the Interior (1973); the Department of Commerce (1975); the Federal Energy Administration (superseded in 1980 by the Department of Energy); and the Department of Education (1980) were later added.[44]

In the same executive order in which he established Federal Regional Offices, President Nixon also established Federal Regional Councils. Membership on the councils included the regional directors of the various departments and agencies mentioned above. In addition, the Office of Management and Budget provided a liaison to each of ten Councils.[45] These inter-departmental, inter-agency organizations were established to coordinate federal assistance programs to states and localities.

The Federal Regional Councils were not authorized by law, received no direct appropriations and had no staff other than those personnel assigned by the member organizations. Meeting twice a month in the regional headquarters city, the Councils depended on the member organizations for ordinary support services. This has led one scholar to observe that: "Calling them organizations at all is stretching a point. They are forums within which member organizations meet for purposes of coordinating federal grant-in-aid administration."[46]

As Richard Nixon began his ill-fated second term, he issued a new executive order redefining the functions of the Federal Regional Councils:

> ...[to] assist State and local government by the coordination of the Federal program grants and operations through: (1) the development of better ways to deliver the benefits of Federal programs over the short term; (2) the development of integrated program and funding plans with Governors and local chief executives; (3) the encouragement of joint and complementary Federal grant applications by local and State governments; (4) the expeditious resolution of conflicts and problems which may arise between Federal agencies; (5) the evaluation of programs in which two or more member agencies participate; (6) the development of more effective ways of allocating Federal resources to meet the long-range needs of State and local communities; (7) the supervision of regional interagency program coordination mechanisms; and (8) the development of administrative procedures to improve day-to-day cooperation on an interagency and intergovernmental basis.[47]

The President took the opportunity at the 1969 National Governors' Conference meeting to toot his Administration's horn and tout his new federalism directive when he noted: "By establishing common headquarters and common regional boundaries for the various federal agencies, we have made decentralized administration possible--and made it possible for governors and mayors to do their business with those agencies at one time and in one place."[48]

President Jimmy Carter was not as sold on the value of
these two innovations as his predecessor and he asked for a
review of these regional organizations by the Office of
Management and Budget. OMB's Deputy Associate Director, W. H.
Wellford, may have reflected the President's thinking when he
noted the development of an Administration consensus that "the
councils should be scaled down one way or another while
retaining their essential functions."[49]

Several of Carter's cabinet appointees undermined even the
limited support the President gave these organizations. Joseph
Califano, Jr., Secretary of H.E.W., stripped his ten regional
directors of their titles and most of their authority. The ten
had operated as mini-secretaries of H.E.W., supervising tens of
thousands of federal employees outside the Washington
departmental headquarters. They were relegated to positions of
lesser authority.[50]

The Department of Housing of Urban Development also
reorganized its regional offices. Frustrated with the inability
of the Department to translate program goals into direct action,
the reorganization eliminated the day-to-day operational
responsibilities of the ten regional offices. Officials from
the Department's forty area offices were ordered to report
directly to Washington rather than through the regional
offices.[51]

Additionally, there were organizational changes in the
federal bureaucracies concerned with energy problems. When the
Department of Energy was formed in late 1977, numerous changes
were made in the regional structure of its major predecessor,
the Federal Energy Administration. The responsibility of the
regional representative of the Department of Energy was changed
with the main job being to serve as a high-level spokesperson
for administration energy policies.[52]

In its evaluation of the Federal Regional Councils, the
Advisory Commission on Intergovernmental Relations was unable to
work up much enthusiasm about their accomplishments. The ACIR
offered this evaluation of the first eight years of the Federal
Regional Councils:

> To this date, the Federal Regional
> Councils have made but limited progress
> toward the objectives set in 1969, when the
> council system was first initiated. At
> present, the FRC's contribution to the
> improved management of Federal assistance
> programs is modest, and their activities have
> in most instances only marginally strengthened
> relations among the governmental levels within
> the Federal system.
>
> The disappointment and frustration with
> which the councils are widely regarded,
> however, may reflect unrealistic expectations
> as well as limited performance. The councils
> probably were oversold....[53]

Advisory Commission on Intergovernmental Relations: The ACIR, established in 1959, was hardly a spur-of-the-moment creation. During the mid-1950s, at the request of President Eisenhower, Congress established the 25-member Commission on Intergovernmental Relations, better known by the name of its chairman as the Kestnbaum Commission. Among the Kestnbaum Commission's many charges were to examine not only the theoretical side of the federal system, but also the actual functioning of the system, especially the various federal aid programs. The Commission was directed to offer in its final report specific recommendations on the re-allocation of functions and responsibilities of the federal government and the state governments.[54]

Following the issuing of the Commission's final report with recommendations, several things happened. President Eisenhower named a Deputy Assistant to the President as his full-time federal-state relations expert; the Bureau of the Budget acquired its first full-time staffer in intergovernmental relations; and committees in both houses of Congress conducted hearings to follow up on the many recommendations made by the Commission. Two years after the final report of the Kestnbaum Commission, Eisenhower proposed--at a meeting of the National Governors' Conference-- formation of a Joint Federal-State Action Committee. The Committee was to study methods of returning to the states certain federal functions, and to examine the revenue situation of both levels of government.[55]

The Committee issued several reports outlining programs which could be shifted to the states from the federal government as well as other programs the states could take over.[56] After Congress ignored the plan, a substitute was offered. It too was ignored.[57] The Committee was dissolved at its own request, in the spring of 1960, chiefly due to the fact that Congress had established the ACIR in 1959.

The Act (PL 86-380) which established the ACIR specified a 26-member bipartisan group, with members coming from the federal executive branch of government, both houses of Congress, state governors and legislators, mayors, elected county officials, and private citizens.[58] The ACIR would become the nation's leading public forum on intergovernmental relations, bringing together representatives from all levels and branches of government. The Commission was to study federal grant programs, recommend allocation of governmental functions among the levels of government, make available technical assistance to the federal government, and conduct studies of various intergovernmental problems and organizations.[59] Over the years, the ACIR has done many excellent studies on a wide variety of subjects.

> Legislative and administrative recommend-
> ations, including draft bills, were transmit-
> ted to the appropriate level and organ of
> government and made available to interested
> private groups. The Commission maintained
> special ties with the Council of State Govern-
> ments, the American Municipal Association, the
> National Association of Counties, and the
> United States Conference of Mayors.[60]

The ACIR and the Kestnbaum Commission have spent 25 years undertaking a continuous review of federalism. The most important conclusion reached in this on-going review came in an early report of the Commission's predecessor, the Kestnbaum Commission, in 1955:

> The national government and the states
> should be regarded not as competitors for
> authority but as two levels of government
> cooperating with or complementing each other
> in meeting the growing demands on both.[61]

The recent period of American federalism--1960-1985--has witnessed some startling changes. New institutions have been born. Some have survived. Some have been killed. The blossoming of these new organizations marked the beginning of a new chapter featuring regional, federal-interstate relations.

> The shift in the sixties then was in response to a new and different cluster of problems, the most significant of which was the spill-over character of certain pressing policy issues. Common to all of these recent regional efforts was the view that the traditional interstate compact approach involving only the participating States was inadequate for certain program purposes and that the Federal-single State relationship did not cover adequately the interstate ramifications of these functional concerns. Put more positively, the Federal-multistate partnership concept emerged as a popular formula for resolving some of the administrative, political and fiscal difficulties that had emerged--at least in certain regions--in the economic development and water resources planning and management fields.[62]

The range of governmental institutions of federalism is vast. Interlevel cooperation has never been easy. As former governor Terry Sanford (D-N.C., 1961-1965) explained: "Interstate cooperation, like so many other programs that involve groupings of governments or cooperative endeavors, has grown slowly because some states felt that each of these arrangements were somehow a surrender of state sovereignty."[63]

NEW EXTRA-GOVERNMENTAL INSTITUTIONS OF FEDERALISM

In addition to these governmental institutions, there are other institutions of federalism, institutions which have no official governmental connection. Many such organizations serve a particular set of public officials--e.g., the U.S. Conference of Mayors, the National Conference of State Legislatures, the National Governors' Association and the National Association of State Budget Officers. Besides the extra-governmental organizations representing elected and appointed officials, several organizations represent governmental units or levels of government. Any list of these organizations would necessarily include the National Association of Counties, the National League of Cities, and the Council of State Governments.

In order to provide a perspective on the nature and position of these new creatures of federalism, this section will focus on four of the major extra-governmental institutions of federalism.

Council of State Governments: One of the common descriptions of the Council of State Governments (CSG) labels it "the most significant association of states and state officials."[64] The CSG is one of the more interesting and diverse of the new breed of extra-governmental institutions.

The Council of State Governments is a non-profit, state-supported and directed service organization which "collects and distributes information, promotes interstate cooperation, and works to improve state administration and management."[65] Like many of these organizations, the CSG isn't new as much as it was reborn and vastly changed during the quarter-century 1960-1985.

In 1925, Colorado State Senator Henry W. Toll almost singlehandedly founded the American Legislators' Association. The Colorado legislator had been concerned about the lack of shared information available to state legislators from different states. He wheedled, wrangled and coaxed into being an organization out of nowhere and although the second annual meeting of his fledgling organization had only two legislators and three journalists in attendance, the idea and the organization somehow took root.

Once the ALA was able to stand on its own and had begun to function as an information clearinghouse, it became clear to Toll that the need for shared information transcended the states' legislative branches. Following a meeting of the ALA's Board of Managers in October of 1933, Toll presented the board with a draft of articles of organization for a "league of state governments." The Board agreed with the need and unanimously adopted the articles which were to become the charter of the CSG. Twenty years after he had left the CSG, Leonard D. White honored Toll's work by observing:

> Throughout their long history until a
> bare 20 years ago, the states possessed no
> such common ground on which they could stand
> as states, consider their common problems,
> and, so far as they cared to do so, act
> collectively with respect to the federal
> government. The organization of the Council
> of State Governments during the 1930s was thus
> an event of major portent as well as a
> triumph of organizing skills on the part of
> its founder, Henry W. Toll of Colorado.[66]

From the beginning, the CSG set out to serve all three
branches of state government. The CSG has as its primary
purposes the advancement of the position of the states in the
federal system and furthering the cause of intergovernmental
cooperation:

> The purpose of the Council shall be to
> strengthen state government and preserve its
> role in the American federal system by: force-
> ful expression of the views of the States;
> assisting the States in improving their
> legislative, administrative and judicial
> practices; promoting state-local and inter-
> state cooperation; facilitating state-federal
> relations; and serving as a broad instrument
> for bringing together all elements of state
> government.[67]

The CSG is set up much like the federal system itself,
sporting different levels of organization with overlapping
jurisdictions. The central headquarters of the Council is
located in Lexington, Kentucky. In addition to being
responsible for the business and accounting functions of all
offices, the central headquarters serves as secretariat to the
Council's Executive Committee and its Governing Board. The
central office also edits and publishes CSG's many periodicals
and research publications. The Council conducts a considerable
amount of research and produces many studies for state
governments as well as suggesting legislation for consideration
by the states. The organization serves as the authoritative
clearinghouse for state governments.

Second, the real cornerstone of the Council is its regional
office concept. There are four regional offices serving

sections of the nation: the Western Region (established in 1940, 13 states, headquartered in San Francisco); the Midwestern Region (established in 1969, when the central office moved from Chicago to Lexington, 12 states, headquartered in suburban Chicago); the Southern Region (established in 1959, 15 states, headquartered in Atlanta); and the oldest, the Eastern Region (established in 1938, 10 states, headquartered in New York City). These regional offices--"nearly autonomous in operation and issue development"[68]--are assigned several basic duties:

1. To serve the duly constituted Regional Conferences of the Council (established independently by the States in the East, the Midwest, the West and the South, with their own articles or rules).

2. To serve regional meetings of legislators, Governors, Attorneys General, Budget Officers and of other organizations affiliated with the Council.

3. By field trips, to be in regular communication with state legislators and state officials at the state capitols.

4. To serve as secretariat to the standing and special committees established on a regional basis.

5. To meet regularly with Commissions on Interstate Cooperation in the States comprising each region.

6. To serve as key sources of information for newsletters and other publications published in the headquarters office.

7. To provide subsidiary information and inquiry services on matters of regional interest.

8. When appropriate, to administer special regional or subregional projects requested by States within the region.

9. When appropriate, to administer special conferences which blanket the Country in sequence.[69]

Each regional office holds regional conference meetings of state officials from all three branches of state government. A good part of the activities of these conferences is devoted to analyzing issues and trying to develop policy.

Third, the CSG operates a Washington, D.C. office, in operation since 1938. Internal documents indicate the Washington office's functions to be:

> To provide a modest CSG presence in Washington for the benefit of affiliated and associated organizations, regional conferences, and other Council offices; to foster state-federal cooperation; to maintain liaison with federal agencies and with state-county-city organizations headquartered in Washington; and to deliver reliable, non-lobbying information for the States in the form of newsletters and special reports.[70]

The Council's Washington office has undergone some drastic changes in recent years--including a modification in mission and a drastically reduced budget from $293,496 in FY 1972-1973 (18 percent of the entire CSG budget) to $167,622 for FY 1977-1978 (only 8 percent of the CSG budget). By FY 1984-1985, $184,992 was budgeted for the Washington office, but the Washington office share had shrunk to only 5 percent of the CSG budget.

Many of these changes in the Washington office can be attributed to changes in the missions of the National Governor's Association (NGA) and the National Conference of State Legislatures (NCSL). These two public interest groups began--in the mid-1970s--to change their direction and their mission and to increase their lobbying efforts with Congress and with executive branch departments and agencies.[71]

On the other hand, the CSG has steadfastly continued to abstain from lobbying:

> Most notable in the past year have been decisions by the National Governors' Conference and National Legislative Conference to vigorously expand their activities, to heighten the impact of Governors and State Legislators on federal policy decisions, and to assure more state inputs to federal legislation. The Council of State Governments stands ready to cooperate in any way it can to support the NGC and the newly formed NCSL. However, the Council's mandate of service does not and should not include lobbying as an organizational function.... For the Council to be present in the lobbying arena would be

63

to fail its main mission.[72]

This split in the ranks was not only doctrinal and philosophical in nature, but also involved the power positions of each of the three organizations. Prior to the split, the CSG had since 1938, served as secretariat to the NGA and the NCSL. The struggle among the three was very much a power struggle. The struggle and the fallout from that struggle precipitated both the resignation of long-time (1958-1977) CSG Executive Director Brevard Crihfield in February, 1977, as well as the efforts preceding Crihfield's resignation to begin the process of redefining the mission of the Council of State Governments. The severing of relationships involved the establishing of three separate and distinct Washington staffs. The Council's Washington Office had at one time served all three organizations.

In September, 1976, the CSG Executive Committee had appointed a committee to study and make recommendations about the role and mission of the Council. That committee produced an Interim Report in December of 1976. Contained in that report were these observations on the state (as of 1976) of the organization: that the CSG was facing problems of changing constituent demands based on the changing role of the states; that it was weakened by the splitting away of two major public interest groups; that the opportunities for duplication and overlap of staff effort among the three organizations had subsequently increased; that the CSG's ties to a specific constituency of state officials were the most tenuous of the three groups; that because the NGA and the NCSL had decided to participate more directly in the federal policy-making process as lobbyists, the CSG must significantly alter its organizational structure if it were to survive.[73]

Having stated the problem, the Committee proceeded to make these recommendations:

> 1. CSG must expand its capability and concentrate on serving as a source of information and research for state governments.

2. In order to be directly responsive to
the needs of the two major state public
interest groups, the Committee believes
that the CSG governing structure should be
made up of eight state officials. Four of
these officials should be governors and
should be the officers of NGC or their
designated representatives from the NGC
Executive Committee. Four should be state
legislators and should be the officers or
their appointees from the Executive
Committee of the NCSL.

3. The Governing Board of CSG should review relationships with affiliated and associated organizations and make decisions about
the services to be provided to each on an
individual basis.

4. Within three years, the regional office structure of CSG should be phased into a
regional support structure of the National
Governors' Conference and the National Conference of State Legislatures.[74]

As might be expected, such a report was not unanimously
accepted. Indeed, there was such a fuss from a variety of
quarters that an Evaluation Committee of Sixteen was appointed
by the CSG Executive Committee to review the report of the
Select Committee. The Evaluation Committee voted to table the
Select Committee's report, but decided to continue to study the
issues and problems raised in that report.[75]

In 1985, the Council began refocusing its efforts as an
organization which conducts research on current issues of
importance to the states and on state roles in the federal
system. A part of that refocusing resulted in the creation of
four specialized research centers: agriculture and rural
development; management, administration and productivity;
environment and natural resources; and financial
management.[76] The four research centers are grouped together
under a new State Government Research Institute. A board of
directors is to set policy for the Institute and each of the
centers is guided by a policy steering committee.[77]

The CSG provides secretariat services to five of nine of
its affiliates: the National Conference of Lieutenant Governors
(date of affiliation--1962); the National Association of State

Purchasing Officials (1947); the National Association of State Auditors, Comptrollers and Treasurers (1980); the National Association of Secretaries of State (1935-1941, 1983); and the National Conference of State General Services Officers (1983). In 1966, the Council had served eight "affiliates" with secretariat services, but the withdrawal, in 1975, of the National Governors' Conference and at the governors' request the move of the Council of State Planning Agencies and the National Association of State Budget Officers to Washington lessened the number of affiliated organizations. In 1975, the National Conference of State Legislatures was established and moved its headquarters to Denver, Colorado. In addition to secretariat services, the Council provides a variety of support services to 27 "cooperating" organizations.

The Council of State Governments has always raised a sizable amount of its budget from "dues" paid by the state members. In FY 1972-1973, the states anted up $1,646,392.50 (83 percent of total CSG revenues).[78] In FY 1977-1978, $1,500,000 came from the states, the District of Columbia and the five territories amounting to 90 percent of total revenues.[79] Efforts to broaden the Council's financial base have been successful as by FY 1983-1984, state "dues" amounted to $2,616,257, accounting for only 61 percent of the organization's total revenues.[80]

The CSG is governed by a large and somewhat unwieldy Governing Board, made up of nearly 200 persons. The Board meets once a year and its chief responsibilities are to set policy guidelines and approve the Council's budget. The Governing Board is made up of all governors, one member from each house of the state legislature in each state, representatives from each of the regional conferences of the CSG, and representatives from each "affiliated" organization. There is an Executive Committee of 40 members which acts for the Board between annual meetings.[81]

Both the Governing Board and Executive Committee are heavily weighted in favor of governors and state legislators. Approximately 80 percent of the Governing Board members are

either chief executives or legislators. The same can be said of
36 of the 40 members of the Executive Committee. A governor has
always served as President of the Council of State Governments
while a state lawmaker has always served as Council Chairman.
Among the nine affiliated and associated organizations, the NGA
and the NCSL are clearly the political powerhouses. Therefore,
it is not surprising that they are proportionately
over-represented in the Council's decision-making bodies.

National Governors Association: The Association was begun in
1908 at the insistence of a former governor of the State of New
York. President Theodore Roosevelt was the moving force behind
establishing a national governors' organization. The President
invited the nation's governors to the White House to discuss one
of his favorite topics--conservation. Somewhat surprisingly, 34
governors attended this first conference of governors. The
conference of 1908 would be the first and last devoted to a
single subject.

Between its founding and the Depression, the organization
developed essentially as a "social club" made up of political
peers.[82] Glenn Brooks, who has done the major research work
on the organization has noted:

> Reflecting the weak position of the governors
> at the time, the early Governors' Conference
> was neither a vigorous nor a decisive body.
> With the exception of the first conference,
> the annual meetings were leisurely
> tete-a-tetes devoted to social courtesies,
> expansive oratory, and the reading of
> prepared--and usually arid--papers on
> traditional problems of state government.[83]

Very early in the Association's existence, the governors
made the decision that they should not strive to influence
national policy either formally or informally. The decision was
less than unanimous however. While governors such as Woodrow
Wilson (D-New Jersey) and Charles Evans Hughes (R-New York)
argued that the purpose of the organization was to improve state
government not to position itself in the national arena,[84]
other governors, especially Colorado Governor John F. Shafroth
(D) urged the governors to act collectively to influence

national policies. He believed the Governors' Conference was the institution capable of stemming the tide of the federal preemption of traditional state functions and responsibilities.[85]

The conference became a permanent organization in 1912. The original Articles of Organization reflected the views of Wilson and Hughes, rather than those of Shafroth. In the early years, the organization was largely ceremonial and social and attendance was generally low. The Governors' Conference was an accurate reflector of the political tenor of the times. Prior to the Depression, state responsibilities were considered separate from national responsibilities. State governments were not overly active, and there was a fear of the national government dictating state policies.[86] It is not surprising therefore, that from the early days, the Conference decided to be a somewhat informal organization which would not try to influence national policy, nor impose uniform internal policies on the states, and that the Conference would not go on record with public statements on policy questions.[87] These structural characteristics would remain in effect for a quarter of a century.

The Great Depression was a major factor in getting America's governors off of their collective duffs. The New Deal's plethora of new governmental programs required responses from the states and from their governors. Furthermore, the CSG had been established in 1933 and five years later offered its secretariat services to the Conference.[88] The Conference, now with staffing, began to be a participant in the political system.

The decade of the 1960s was a pivotal time for the Governors' Conference. The backdrop was the rapid and intrusive expansion of the federal government. For most of the years prior to the 1960s, the Governors' Conference had criticized federal programs. Beginning with the years of the Great Society, the governors--through their organization--began to request federal aid to help them solve problems.[89] In the middle of the decade, the governors added "National" to the name of their organization, emphasizing a new direction, a new focus.

In 1966, the NGC broke away from the Wilson/Hughes mindset of tending only to the advancement of state government. That year, the organization established a Washington presence when it opened an Office for Federal-State Relations, under the auspices of the Council of State Governments. For the first time, the governors had a lobby in Washington.[90]

It was also about this time that the NGC moved to become a full-time, year-round operation when it established the organization's first permanent standing committees. This effort to increase the active participation of more governors resulted in the addition of a second annual meeting of the Conference to be held each year in mid-winter.

In 1974, the Conference created the Center for Policy Research and Analysis. This Washington "think tank" was the first in-house effort to provide research on problem-solving. One year later, the governors leased a building the owner obligingly renamed the Hall of the States. This headquarters, opened in 1976, provided for the location of related public interest organizations and associations under one roof and was designed to lead to increased communication and effectiveness. The NGC also decided to sever its long-time ties with the CSG in 1975, partly because the Council was constitutionally prohibited from engaging in lobbying activities. The governors' conference took up the slack by increasing their own staff resources.

By 1977, with everything that was going on, the Conference decided that its name failed to communicate the enlarged range of its activities and the changed nature of its commitment. The 1977 annual meeting approved a name change to the National Governors' Association. By 1981, the NGA had a budget of $5.7 million (larger than the CSG's), and a staff of fifty professionals.[91]

The Association also revised its purposes: first, to provide a medium for studying, discussing, and redefining problems facing governments.[92] Second, to provide a common meeting ground for the important informal, face-to-face gubernatorial contacts. "Much of the time at these meetings is spent in informal conversation, and arrangements to deal with problems can be made. The opportunity they create for bringing public officials face to face is probably more valuable than the programs they present...."[93]

Third, to provide the governors a forum for participating in the setting of priorities by the federal government. It has become a common sight in recent years to see a parade of governors come to Capitol Hill to testify on federal legislation. Governors meet frequently with the President, sometimes at his request, sometimes at the request of the governors. As a former chairman of the NGA put it: "Governors are not content just to seek 'federal handouts,' but place increasing importance on a substantive gubernatorial role in decisions which affect and reorient domestic priorities."[94]

Fourth, to provide the governors a forum for reacting to program proposals being considered by the federal government. This function differs from the one above in that the governors often picture themselves as "spokesmen for state sovereignty and against the encroachments by the federal government."[95]

Fifth, to provide governors with information on policy developments and to monitor federal policy-making. The NGA assumed this function in 1967, when it first opened its Washington office and created a staff (of four) which operated separately from the Council of State Governments. The staff's ability to carry out this function has been aided by the reorganization of the Washington office in 1974 and the creation of the in-house Center for Policy Research and Analysis, formed to provide both technical and policy-oriented assistance.[96]

Sixth, to strengthen the system of federalism. By giving the states and their leaders an opportunity for concerted action, by giving the states a national forum, by giving the states a chance to react and to interact with the federal government, the NGA has served as well as reflected the evolving course of federalism. There are many who believe this has been the Association's major contribution to the American political system.[97]

In between the two annual meetings of the NGA, the

organization's business is conducted by a nine-member Executive Committee, no more than five of whose members may be from the same political party. The Executive Committee has grown from three members originally to the present nine. Until 1959, the Executive Committee elected the Conference Chairman. Then, the process was changed to provide for direct election by all members.[98] The NGA chairmanship alternates annually between members of the two major political parties.[99]

The 80-year history of the Association has seen a number of changes in the procedures surrounding the adoption of policy statements (resolutions). Banned in the beginning, the governors changed their stance during the early years of the New Deal. Then, resolutions were passed by majority vote. In the latter half of the 1930s, however, the Association began to require (by unwritten rule) unanimous consent for the adoption of resolutions.[100] Although it took time, the governors formally changed their rules in 1954 making it possible for three-fourths of the governors to pass resolutions. Five years later, that figure was reduced to two-thirds of the members present and voting.[101]

There is no doubt that the NGA of today is not the same NGA of 1908 or even of 1960. If any single action focuses attention on how much the NGA has changed and how far it has come, it would be the reaction of the governors' association to President Reagan's 1982 State of the Union address in which he proposed a sorting out of government functions. The President proposed restructuring the federal system "in one bold stroke"[102] and invited governors and other government officials to help him draft the restructuring.

For five months, the governors negotiated with White House advisors. The general outlines of the proposal were not satisfying state and local lobbies and the negotiations fell apart completely on the "fine printing" of the proposal.[103]

Just before the NGA meeting in August, 1982, the President phoned several governors and threw in the towel. Earlier in the summer, the President had been rebuffed by the National Association of Counties, the National League of Cities and the

National Conference of State Legislatures. As a result, the NGA's Executive Committee recommended to Association members that they go back to square one and submit their own plan for restructuring the federal system![104]   "The decision, reflect[ed] the governors' impatience with five months of inconclusive negotiations since Reagan introduced the federalism initiative...."[105]

In the end, under "strong White House pressure"[106] the governors backed away and agreed to try again to negotiate with the President.   In the first real instance of federalism brinkmanship, the governors were the ones to blink. But the message was clear, the governors--collectively--were a force to be reckoned with in the future. The governors had as much to gain in this battle as the President--and both knew the federalism package had absolutely no chance of success without the support of the nation's governors as well as the President of the United States.[107]

The President saw the federalism initiative as a way to short-term budgetary gains.   The governors did not. Their concerns were the longer-term fiscal and policy impacts of the President's proposals.[108]   Without the President's willingness to "sweeten the pot," his federalism initiative was dead. The President refused to sweeten and the governors refused to support his proposal in Congress. This was the issue over which the NGA truly came of political age.   Governor Michael S. Dukakis (D-Mass., 1975-1979, 1983-) noted of the rites of passage:

> "We also in the National Governors' Association have a much stronger federal presence.   Again, the NGA used to be a fairly weak organization.   Not so today. And most governors take their role in the NGA pretty seriously....   That's a new role for the NGA."[109]

National Conference of State Legislatures: The NCSL is the creature which emerged from the 1975 merger of the National Legislative Conference, the National Conference of State Legislative Leaders, and the National Society of State Legislators.   The Conference has three basic objectives: "To improve the quality and effectiveness of State Legislatures; to assure States a strong, cohesive role in federal decision-making; and to foster interstate communication and cooperation."[110]

The NCSL is headquartered in Denver along with the Citizens' Conference on State Legislatures. The NCSL has an Office of Federal-State Relations in Washington. That office operates rather similarly to the NGA's Washington office. Like the Association, the NCSL has broken away from the CSG although it is still considered an "affiliate" organization. The reasons for the break-up are similar to those of the NGA/CSG schism, the turn of the NCSL toward Washington lobbying.

In the NCSL, policies are developed internally by a series of task forces. The full conference then considers the resolutions at its annual meetings. The Conference is governed by an executive board of 32 members. Like its executive counterpart, the NCSL is a sizable operation with "dues" from member states making up the bulk of the organization's budget.

The NCSL rather quickly became an active organization. However, because it is a large organization (nearly 8,000 legislator-members), because its membership is a rather diverse group and because state legislatures still suffer--unfairly--from the remnants of a somewhat tainted reputation, it is not an easy organization to lead. In some ways, the NCSL is in competition with the NGA. Even with these problems, the organization has made its presence felt:

> As one of the Big Seven public interest
> groups, the NCSL is a Johnny-come-lately. It
> is apparent, however, that State legislatures
> are increasing their visibility and
> respectability. Whether these helpful but
> nonquantifiable factors can be translated into
> effective leverage on IGR (intergovernmental
> relations) decisions is an open question.[111]

Regional Governors' Organizations: In addition to these three national organizations, there are also regional organizations which have resulted from the quarter-century of change in the system of federalism. Chief among them are the five regional governors' conferences. All states belong to at last one of these organizations, and six belong to at least two. The Midwestern Governors' Conference will be the central focus of later chapters. The other conferences will be examined here in the order of their organizing.

New England Governors' Conference: The NEGC was the first to informally organize as a conference of governors. The group's informal beginnings date as far back as the 1920s. The New England area has several built-in advantages the other regions do not have. The region is small (only 66,000 square miles), there are common historical and cultural ties and the geography of the area is similar. The six states in this region are much more alike than member states of other regional governors' conferences.

The NEGC grew out of meetings of the New England Council, a sort of region-wide Chamber of Commerce. The Council is supported by business and dedicated to advancing the economic interests of the region.[112] There are still ties between the two groups. Besides their own meetings, the governors of New England states usually get together at the annual meeting of the New England Council. The NEGC sprang into formal existence as an organization in the late 1930s.[113] The reason for concerted action--problems with high freight rates.

The CSG has never provided staff for the New England Governors' Conference. They have a small, permanent staff of their own. The governors meet in one-day meetings about once every two months.[114] The ease of assembling and the small area size have made their gatherings quite different from the meetings of the other regions. The Conference has urged regional state officials to establish their own organizations, and once they are established, the NEGC has used these organizations of state officials as committees to review problems and suggest possible solutions.[115]

The NEGC is generally regarded as the "most closely-knit" of the regional governors' conferences.[116] "With few states, a historical concept and identity and some common problems, the New England Governors' Conference has become a major policy agency."[117]

Southern Governors' Association: The SGA was the first regional governors' conference to be organized on a formal basis. In 1934, nine states (Alabama, Florida, Georgia, Kentucky, Louisiana, Mississippi, North Carolina, South Carolina and Tennessee) formed the Southeastern Governors' Conference. President Franklin D. Roosevelt had suggested to the governors that they organize a permanent regional body to enhance federal-state relations.[118] That suggestion probably meant that FDR was seeking support from the southern governors for parts of his legislative program. The governors did unite—for the same reason which stirred New England governors to unified action—to fight discriminatory freight rates.

Four states (Arkansas, Oklahoma, Texas and Virginia) joined the SEGC ranks in 1939 and 1940 and resulted in the organization changing its name to the Southern Governors' Conference. The Interstate Commerce Commission ruled in the region's favor on freight rates, due in part, to the efforts of the SGC. In 1946, Maryland and West Virginia signed on as members. Since that time, two other members (Delaware and Missouri) have joined, bringing the membership to nineteen and making it the largest of the regional governors' conferences.

The Southern Governors' Conference pioneered in drafting and adopting a proposal establishing a southern regional education board. Additionally, the southern governors were the first to draft an interstate compact on nuclear energy. Southern chief executives helped get the ball rolling, donating $5,000 per state to fund the compact and pushing hard for legislative approval.[119]

Southern governors were also the first to make use of an Advisory Committee to do the agenda planning, basic research, and resolution preparation for their annual Conference meetings. Each governor appointed an aide as a member of the Committee. Southern governors have also made extensive use of task forces, each chaired and shepherded along by a "lead governor." These task forces are usually made up of subject-matter and staff experts who meet frequently (with the chairman of the task force) between annual Conference meetings.[120]

In 1981, the Southern Governors' Conference changed its name to the Southern Governors' Association, and, like the NGA it was a move to signify a more active role for the southern governors and their organization. In January, 1983, the SGA moved its headquarters from the CSG regional office in Atlanta to Washington. Together with the Southern Legislative Conference, the Southern States Energy Board and the Southern Growth Policies Board, the governors wanted to provide an increased Washington presence for the South. The joint venture of these organizations is known as the Southern States Organizations' Washington Office. The move to Washington provided the Southern states with a better opportunity to influence federal policy-making and a better chance at coordinating the efforts of several southern regional organizations.

Western Governors' Association: The WGA, like the New England Governors' Conference and the National Governors' Association began rather informally. The Association had its beginnings as a gathering of governors in 1930, governors who joined together to ask for help in fighting the effects of the Depression.

The efforts to forge an alliance of western state and Pacific Rim governors have never met with easy success. Some western chief executives saw the Western Governors' Conference as "too much concerned with the social agenda and not concerned enough with the policy agenda."[121]

Another organization, the Federation of Rocky Mountain States had been created in 1965 to focus on the problems of public land. The organization brought governors and businessmen together. This intrusion by the private sector displeased some governors.

So, yet another organization, the Western Governors' Regional Energy Policy Office (WGREPO) was formed in 1975 to tackle energy development matters. Ten western states joined WGREPO. However, this brought to four the number of western regional governors' organizations. Something had to be done about the proliferation of governors' organizations.

Several governors--among them Richard Lamm (D-Colorado, 1975-1987) and Calvin Rampton (D-Utah, 1965-1977) set out to create a new western governors' organization--one which would replace all of the others. The effort at consolidation led to some deep divisions among western chief executives. Political divisions, organizational divisions, personality clashes and even lobbying by the WGC staff in opposition to the consolidation[122] created some deep wounds. The resulting bitterness split western governors and as a result not all of them joined the new organization.

At their 1977 conference, the governors created a new regional coordinating organization. The ten chief executives in attendance agreed to form a Western Governors' Policy Office (WESTPO) to consolidate the activities of the several existing multistate organizations, including the Energy Resources Policy Office.[123] Eight WGA member states agreed to participate in the new venture. They were joined by the governors of North Dakota and South Dakota. The North Dakota and South Dakota chief executives have been attending WGC meetings for a number of years even though neither state held formal conference membership. The WGC continued to remain in existence.

For seven years, the two organizations both fought to represent western governors. In February of 1984, the governors of sixteen western states and the three Pacific territories met in Washington during the winter meeting of the NGA and agreed to form the Western Governors' Association. The new organization was formed through the merging of the Western Governors' Conference and the Western Governors' Policy Office. The new organization was to help strengthen regional ties and gain a stronger, more unified voice in Washington.

The Association resulted, in part, from the powerlessness felt by many westerners.[124] The passing of several senior members of Congress from Western states contributed to the feeling of powerlessness.

The new WGA should end any confusion about the two organizations and end interstaff competition as well. The new group, to be headquartered in Denver, will have a staff of twelve and a first year budget of $1,000,000.[125] The Association will continue to maintain a Washington office. The governors are expected to meet five or six times a year to discuss and reach agreement on matters of regional interest.

At the organization's first meeting, the governors displayed unexpected unity on diverse issues. Governor Scott Matheson (D-Utah), one of the leaders in forming the new organization explained that the unity resulted from necessity: "This region is so small in terms of the clout of individual states we have to stick together to get anything done. So there's a camaraderie and political support among Western politicians that really transcends all of the other political considerations."[126]

Other Regional Governors' Conferences: Other regional governors' conferences are quite numerous. Some are based on a single issue, a single concern or a single problem. An example would be the Missouri River Basin Governors' Conference which met in St. Paul in 1976. The ten Missouri River Basin governors met to see about setting priorities for the use of Missouri River water.[127] The meeting had been arranged by Governor Richard Kneip (D-S.D., 1971-1978) and the Missouri River Commission Chairman John Neuberger. Governors spent their time at the meeting discussing the role of the states in settling water rights conflicts and the role of the Commission itself in water disputes.

Some regional governors' conferences are outgrowths of other multistate organizations. The Mid-Atlantic Governors' Conference was formed in 1965 as an outgrowth of the Delaware River Basin Commission.[128] There were four charter members (New Jersey, New York, Pennsylvania and Delaware) and with the exception of Delaware, none of the other three were affiliated with any other regional governors' conferences. Since that time, two additional states—Maryland and West Virginia—have joined. Both hold membership in other regional conferences as well.

On occasion, regional conferences are created as a reaction

to something. Just such a reaction created the Coalition of North Eastern Governors. Founded in 1976, the nine-state Coalition (Vermont, Connecticut, New Jersey, New York, Pennsylvania, Massachusetts, Rhode Island, Maine and New Hampshire) was formed to help the Northeast flex its political muscles.[129] Seeing the federal dollars flowing to other regions coupled with the loss of employment opportunities stirred the governors of this area to action. The governors also organized to complement the efforts of the Northeast-Midwest Economic Advancement Coalition, a congressional caucus which was organized in late 1975.[130] Member-state governors and members of Congress are hopeful this two-level attack will help lead to solutions of the many problems of this region.

Finally, some regional governors' organizations spring up out of a commonality of interests. Such an organization would be the Council of Great Lakes Governors. The eight-state Council, formed in 1983, began more informally as a Great Lakes Governors' Caucus meeting over breakfast at the annual meetings of the Midwestern Governors' Conference. The governors met to talk over problems relevant to the Great Lakes. Shipping and pollution are among the problems discussed at these breakfast confabs.[131] Another similar organization is the Conference of Appalachian Governors and their concerns about coal and natural gas.[132]

There are still other governors' organizations including partisan organizations. Though only a few have their own staff, none attempt to compete with the larger regional organizations. These organizations are generally "discussive" organizations.

As for the more permanent regional governors' organizations, there are several conclusions to be drawn. Among their several purposes, these conferences to provide the governors with a vehicle for the "concerted expression of views on many matters of common state interests."[133] These conferences are to push for regional positions and to attempt to further the interests of those regions. Although it seems likely that cooperation between governors is enhanced, there are those who doubt that these regional organizations further a sense of regionalism: "For years, the series of regional Governors' Conferences have served, at first blush, as foci of regionalism in the states. However, this has always been more apparent than real, as they are more like gatherings than conferences."[134]

The regional conferences also provide more opportunities to talk with fellow governors than is possible at the larger NGA meetings. The opportunity to talk shop is one of the most valuable functions provided by these regional get-togethers.

These extra-governmental institutions are perhaps the most remarkable story of the last quarter-century of federalism. These organizations, without benefit of official government connection, have had to work very hard to attain position and clout in the political system. It is not an accident that most of the effective extra-governmental institutions have decided that working to affect federal policy-making is one of their more important tasks.

In Chapter Five we will look at the birth pains of a typical extra-governmental institution, born in the early 1960s. The struggle to form the Midwestern Governors' Conference is illustrative of the vast changes in the American system of federalism.

NOTES
==

[1]Deil S. Wright, Understanding Intergovernmental Relations (2nd ed. Monterey, Calif.: Brooks/Cole Publishing Co., 1982), p. 38.

[2]Ibid., p.39.

[3]Parris N. Glendening and Mavis Mann Reeves, Pragmatic Federalism: An Intergovernmental View of American Government (Pacific Palisades: Palisades Publishers, 1977), p. 185.

[4]Neil R. Peirce and Jerry Hagstrom, "The New Regionalism," National Journal, XV (May 21, 1983), p. 1044.

[5]Advisory Commission on Intergovernmental Relations, Multistate Regionalism (Washington: Government Printing Office,

1972), p. 1.

    [6]Ibid.

    [7]Roscoe C. Martin in W. Brooke Graves, American Intergovernmental Relations (New York: Charles Scribner's Sons, 1964), p. 613.

    [8]ACIR, Multistate Regionalism, p. 8.

    [9]Richard H. Leach, American Federalism (New York: W. W. Norton & Co., 1970), p. 232.

    [10]Benjamin J. Jones, "Interstate Compacts and Agreements: 1980-81," in The Book of the States, 1982-83 (Lexington, Ken.: The Council of State Governments, 1982), p. 16.

    [11]Virginia v. Tennessee, 148 U.S. 503 (1893), p. 518.

    [12]Brevard Crihfield and H. Clyde Reeves, "Intergovernmental Relations: A View from the States," The Annals, CDXVI (November, 1974), 101; The Book of the States, 1984-85 (Lexington: The Council of State Governments, 1984), pp. 12-14.

    [13]Frederick L. Zimmermann and Mitchell Wendell, "Interstate Compacts," in The Book of the States, 1974-75 (Lexington: The Council of State Governments, 1974), p. 269.

    [14]David C. Nice, "State Participation in Interstate Compacts," Publius 17 (Spring, 1987), p. 83

    [15]David C. Nice, "Cooperation and Conformity Among the States," Polity, XVI (Spring, 1984), pp. 494-505.

    [16]Ibid., p. 505.

    [17]Ibid.

    [18]Frederick L. Zimmermann and Mitchell Wendell, "Interstate Compacts," in The Book of the States, 1976-77, p. 573.

    [19]Ibid., p. 575.

    [20]The Book of the States, 1984-85, pp. 175-79.

    [21]Phillip Monypenny, "Interstate Relations--Some Emergent Trends," The Annals, CCCXLIX (May, 1965), p. 55.

    [22]Glendening and Reeves, Pragmatic Federalism, p. 193.

    [23]The Book of the States, 1976-77, pp. 190-95. For an analysis of why some states cooperate in such cooperative ventures as uniform state laws and other states refuse to, see Nice, "Cooperation and Conformity Among the States," pp. 494-505.

[24] John M. McCabe, "Uniform State Laws," in The Book of the States, 1976-77, p. 187.

[25] Martha Derthick, Between State and Nation, Regional Organizations of the United States (Washington: The Brookings Institution, 1974), p. 6.

[26] ACIR, Multistate Regionalism, p. 17.

[27] Ibid., p. 19.

[28] Advisory Commission on Intergovernmental Relations, Improving Federal Grants Management (Washington: Government Printing Office, 1977), p. 28.

[29] Glendening and Reeves, Pragmatic Federalism, p. 211.

[30] Ibid.

[31] Ibid.

[32] Neal R. Peirce, The Border South States (New York: W. W. Norton & Co., Inc., 1975), p. 25.

[33] Glendening and Reeves, Pragmatic Federalism, p. 209. For a more complete study of regional development commissions and the Appalachian Regional Commission in particular, see ACIR, Improving Federal Grants Management, pp. 25-44.

[34] Bruce McDowell, "Regional Organizations Hang On," Intergovernmental Perspective VIII (Winter, 1983), p. 15.

[35] ACIR, Multistate Regionalism, pp. 99-100.

[36] Derthick, Between State and Nation, p. 15.

[37] Congressional Quarterly Service, Congress and the Nation: 1965-1968, pp. 498-499.

[38] Ibid., p. 499.

[39] ACIR, Multistate Regionalism, pp. 109-110.

[40] Derthick, Between State and Nation, p. 16.

[41] Bruce McDowell, "Regional Organizations Hang On," p. 15.

[42] Ibid.

[43] ACIR, Improving Federal Grants Management, p. 163. Although the idea was not officially unveiled until 1969, the idea was not in fact new. The efforts at coordinating date back to the 1930s. See ACIR, Improving Federal Grants Management, pp. 181-185.

[44]ACIR, _Multistate Regionalism_, p. 172.

[45]Derthick, _Between State and Nation_, p. 158.

[46]_Ibid._, p. 16.

[47]_Ibid._, p. 157.

[48]"Statement on Establishing Common Regional Boundaries for Agencies Providing Social and Economic Services," _Public Papers of the Presidents of the United States, Richard M. Nixon, 1969_ (Washington: Government Printing Office, 1971), pp. 256-57.

[49]Mercer Cross, "Carter's Federalism: How Real in Practice," _Congressional Quarterly Weekly Report_, XXXV (April 9, 1977), p. 679.

[50]"Califano Alters HEW Regional Offices," _Kansas City Star_, July 20, 1977, p. 5C.

[51]Editorial, _Kansas City Star_, October 17, 1977, p. 26.

[52]John M. Wylie, "New Identity No Crisis for Energy Offices," _Kansas City Star_, November 27, 1977, p. 39A.

[53]ACIR, _Improving Federal Grants Management_, p. 198.

[54]Commission on Intergovernmental Relations, _Final Report_ (Washington: Government Printing Office, 1955).

[55]Congressional Quarterly Service, _Congress and the Nation: 1945-1964_, p. 1395. See also Deil S. Wright, _Understanding Intergovernmental Relations_, pp. 53-56.

[56]Congressional Quarterly Service, _Congress and the Nation: 1945-1964_, p. 1395.

[57]_Ibid._

[58]_Ibid._, p. 1396.

[59]William G. Colman, "The Role of the Federal Government in the Design and Administration of Intergovernmental Programs," _The Annals_, CCCXLIX (May, 1965), pp. 26-27.

[60]Congressional Quarterly Service, _Congress and the Nation: 1945-1964_, p. 1396.

[61]Commission on Intergovernmental Relations, _Report to the President for Transmittal to the Congress_ (Washington: Government Printing Office, 1955), p. 2.

[62]Glendening and Reeves, _Pragmatic Federalism_, p. 210.

[63]Terry Sanford, _Storm Over the States_ (New York: McGraw-

Hill Book Co., 1967), p. 121.

[64]Ibid., p. 114.

[65]The Book of the States, 1984-85 (Lexington: The Council of State Governments, 1984), p. 1.

[66]Frederick L. Zimmermann, "Fourteen Creative Years," State Government News, XXVI (December, 1983), p. 72.

[67]Council of State Governments, Articles of Organization, Article I, Section 2, (December 3, 1976).

[68]"The Council of State Governments 1974," (Lexington: The Council of State Governments, 1975), p. 4.

[69]Council of State Governments. "Budget Summary--Program Narrative, FY 1977-1978, Appendix B," CSG/Lexington (CSG/L) files.

[70]Ibid., p. 12.

[71]"The Council of State Governments 1974," p. 8.

[72]Ibid., p. 6.

[73]Select Committee, Interim Report of the Select Committee to Study the Role and Missions of The Council of State Governments (Lexington: The Council of State Governments, December 3, 1976), pp. 2-4.

[74]Ibid., pp. 4-12.

[75]Evaluation Committee, CSG Evaluation Committee Summary of Developments through April 2, 1977 (Lexington: The Council of State Governments, 1977), p. 1.

[76]"Council Close-Up," State Government News, XXIX (January, 1986), p. 15.

[77]Ibid.

[78]"Council of State Governments Budget Summary," p. 1.

[79]Ibid.

[80]"Annual Report 1984," State Government News, XXVII (November, 1984), p. 24.

[81]Ibid., p. 16.

[82]Glenn E. Brooks, When Governors Convene: The Governors' Conference and National Politics (Baltimore: The Johns Hopkins Press, 1961), p. 3.

[83]Ibid., p. 5.

[84]Carol S. Weissert, "The National Governors' Association: 1908-1983," State Government, #2 (1983), p. 45.

[85]Ibid., pp. 45-46.

[86]Brooks, When Governors Convene, pp. 14-21.

[87]Ibid.

[88]Ibid., pp. 30-44.

[89]Larry Sabato, Goodbye To Good-time Charlie: The American Governorship Transformed (2nd ed.: Washington: CQ Press, 1983), pp. 172-73.

[90]Ibid.; Deil S. Wright, "The States and Intergovernmental Relations, Publius, I (July, 1968), pp. 41-42.

[91]Sabato, Goodbye to Good-time Charlie, p. 174.

[92]See Joseph P. Harris, "The Governors' Conference: Retrospect and Prospect," State Government, XXXI (Summer, 1958), p. 196; Glendening and Reeves, Pragmatic Federalism, p. 203; Brooks, When Governors Convene, p. 164.

[93]Glendening and Reeves, Pragmatic Federalism, p. 192.

[94]Marvin Mandel, "A Progress Report on the National Governors' Conference," State Government, XLVI (Autumn, 1973), p. 228. Mandel (D) was Governor of Maryland, 1969-1977.

[95]Joseph E. Kallenbach, The American Chief Executive: The Presidency and the Governorship (New York: Harper & Row, Publishers, 1966), p. 523.

[96]The Book of the States, 1976-77, p. 566.

[97]Harris, "The Governors' Conference," p. 191; Glendening and Reeves, Pragmatic Federalism, p. 203.

[98]Brooks, When Governors Convene, pp. 44-45.

[99]The Book of the States, 1976-77, p. 566.

[100]Brooks, When Governors Convene, pp. 45-48.

[101]Ibid.

[102]"Is This the End for Reagan's New Federalism?" National Journal, XIV (August 14, 1982), p. 1407.

[103]Ibid.

[104]David S. Broder and Dan Balz, "Governors Break with President," Washington Post, August 9, 1982, p. 1.

[105]Ibid.

[106]David S. Broder, "Governors Relent, to Seek Accord on Federalism with Reagan, Washington Post, August 11, 1982, p. 1.

[107]Broder and Balz, "Governors Break with President," pp. 1, 9; Broder, "Governors Relent," pp. 1, 8; Dan Balz and David S. Broder, "Governors Question Balanced Budget Bill," Washington Post, August 10, 1982, p. 5A; Donald Haider, "Intergovernmental Redirection," The Annals, CDLXVI (March, 1983), p. 176; Dave Durenberger, "A Resolution of National Purposes, National Civic Review, LXXI (November/December, 1982), pp. 521-525; William F. Winter, "A Concept Transformed," National Civic Review, LXXI (November/December, 1982), pp. 510-11.

[108]Timothy J. Conlan, "Federalism and Competing Values in the Reagan Administration," in Laurence J. O'Toole, Jr., ed., American Intergovernmental Relations (Washington: CQ Press, 1985), p. 270.

[109]Michael S. Dukakis quoted in John H. Alfrich et al., American Government: People, Institutions, and Policies (Boston: Houghton Mifflin Co., 1986), p. 104.

[110]The Book of the States, 1976-77, p. 567.

[111]Wright, Understanding Intergovernmental Relations, p. 282.

[112]David B. Walker, "New England and the Federal System," Publius, II (Fall, 1972), p. 45.

[113]"Governors Confer on Regional Basis," National Civic Review, LV (October, 1966), pp. 512-13.

[114]Sanford, Storm Over the States, p. 112.

[115]Edwin W. Webber, "Regional Cooperation: A Modus Vivendi for New England," State Government, XXXVIII (Summer, 1965), p. 189.

[116]ACIR, Multistate Regionalism, p. 138.

[117]Thad L. Beyle, "New Directions in Interstate Relations," The Annals, CDXVI (November, 1974), p. 111.

[118]Memorandum, Charles M. Byrley to Governor Michael V. DiSalle, July 13, 1960, CSG/L files.

[119]Robert H. Solomons III, "The Southern Interstate Nuclear Compact and Board," State Government, XXXVI (Winter, 1963), pp. 40-43.

[120]Brevard Crihfield, private interview with author, Lexington, Kentucky, March 1, 1977.

[121]Scott M. Matheson, _Out of Balance_ (Salt Lake City: Peregrine Smith Books, 1986), p. 232.

[122]Ibid., p. 233.

[123]"Water Concerns Western Governors," _State Government News_, XX (October, 1977), p. 10.

[124]"Western States Form Group to Gain Greater U.S. Impact," _New York Times_, March 11, 1984, p. 56.

[125]Ibid.

[126]Iver Peterson, "Unity is Credo of Western Governors' Group," _New York Times_, May 24, 1984, p. 22A.

[127]"States' Rights, River Use Tied," Kansas City Star, August 4, 1976, p. 20A.

[128]"Governors Confer on Regional Basis," pp. 512-13.

[129]Neal Peirce, "The Northeast Campaign," _Washington Post_, December 22, 1976, p. 19A.

[130]Ibid.

[131]"$175 Million Asked for Lakes," _Lansing State Journal_, July 31, 1974, p. 12B.

[132]Council of State Governments, _State Headlines_, #77-23 (November 14, 1977), p. 4.

[133]Kallenbach, _The American Chief Executive_, p. 522.

[134]Beyle, "New Directions in Interstate Relations," p. 111.

CHAPTER FOUR

THE GOVERNORSHIP: CHANGED AND CHANGING

ROLES AND RESPONSIBILITIES

The quarter-century from 1960 to 1985 witnessed a truly
mindboggling transformation of the American governorship. Early
in that quarter-century, New York Times columnist James "Scotty"
Reston would write of the then-current crop of governors: "The
state capitols are over their heads in problems and up to their
knees in midgets."[1] At the end of that quarter-century,
political analyst Neal R. Peirce would make this observation
about the governors in office in the 1980s:

> ...there had been a distinct fading of the
> breed so aptly depicted as "good-time
> Charlies".... The glad-handing,
> intellectually vacuous, administratively inept
> breed that populated governors' conferences
> until the late '60s faded in favor of
> generally younger, more incisive, better
> educated, manager type executives.[2]

Had the American governorship really changed as much as
these two starkly different evaluations seemed to indicate? The
evidence would seem to indicate that an affirmative answer is
appropriate. Some analysts have been so bold as to declare that
the American governorship has "gone through a political
revolution."[3] Seen once as "political homebodies with few
responsibilities or interests beyond the boundaries of their
home states,"[4] the changes in the federal system which took
place during 1960-1985, have erased that image once and for
all. As noted in earlier chapters, the changes in the American
system of federalism almost guaranteed a significant change in

the office of governor. Governors were no longer able to enjoy the somewhat splendid isolation which resulted from a position as a political homebody. The most recent quarter-century gave witness to a new phenomenon in gubernatorial politics--the sight of governors cooperating with other governors, on a regional as well as a national basis.

In some ways, state governors are like presidents. As the office has become more and more the focal point of state government, governors (and presidents) are expected to be able to accomplish more and more. The increased visibility of the governorship has proven--in some cases--to be a rather mixed blessing. Increased visibility coupled with a strengthened governorship has led to an increase in controversy surrounding gubernatorial decisions and roles. In some cases, the controversy has been sufficient to cause a governor to be defeated in a re-election bid.

GUBERNATORIAL ROLES

There are a sizable number of roles governors are expected to fulfill. Some of these roles are as old as the office of governor itself, while others are of a much more recent vintage. Some of the new or expanded roles have resulted from the larger systemic changes in American federalism.

The tendencies of the last quarter-century have been toward creation of a strong governorship. Governors have assumed responsibility as the state's major policy leader, a responsibility spread over several different gubernatorial roles. Governors are also expected to wield power as a manager of state government. As fiscal belts have been repeatedly tightened in the 1960s and 1970s, this responsibility has loomed larger and larger.

Governors--in almost every state--are exercising greater power. The office and the office-holder are more important than previously, leading to an expansion in the roles of governors. Today, there are several important roles a governor must fulfill.

First, the governor must be the chief legislator in his

state.   Governors bring to office a statewide perspective much
larger   and   less   parochial   than the perspective any legislator
brings   from   a   single   legislative   district.   It is not at all
surprising,   therefore,   that   most   of   the   major   legislative
proposals   for   programs   will   be   at the governor's suggestion.
Supported by a sizable supporting cast in the executive branch,
a governor is uniquely positioned to propose solutions to the
state's problems.

The   governor   is   also   in   a   singular   position   to offer
leadership not only in policy but also in performance. Nowhere
will   those   positions   be   more   sorely tested than in the chief
executive's   efforts   to   work   with   a   co-equal,   but   clearly
separate   branch   of government.   In serving as chief legislator,
and   in   lobbying the legislature for approval of his legislative
proposals, a governor finds a branch of government which has
also   undergone   substantial   changes   during   the last 25 years.
State   legislatures   have   moved   to   strengthen   their own role,
their   own   position   in   the   governmental   system.   Increased
professionalism   and   the   many   improvements resulting therefrom
have   created   stronger,   more   independent   and   less easily led
legislators.

Always   difficult,   the   governor's   task   of   legislative
leadership is made even more difficult when the governor and a
majority of members of at least one house of the legislature are
from   opposite   political   parties.   Over this quarter-century,
never   fewer   than   21   states   were so "divided" and that figure
climbed as high as 28 states.

A   second   gubernatorial role and one closely related to the
first   is   the   governor as chief budget officer.   Budget
preparation powers are one area of gain for many governors over
the   last   25   years.   In many states, governors have now assumed
the   major   responsibility   for   preparing and submitting a budget
to   the   legislature.   Realizing   the potential, governors have
begun   to   use their budget proposals as additional statements of
their policy andspending priorities.

Although   state   legislators   are   empowered   by   the   state
constitution   to   approve   (or reject) a budget, much of the time

state legislators go along with most portions of a governor's proposed budget. That legislators must face the pressures of time, the lack of financial expertise, the shortage of qualified staff, and the difficulty in sculpting an acceptable alternative are all factors working in the governor's favor in budget battles. Even so, it is a battle fought more evenly than before.

Third, a governor is expected to be the state's chief executive. That is, the governor is expected to be the leader of the executive branch. This role is no easier than the first two roles. The existence of independently- elected executive branch officials, the multitude of executive branch agencies, commissions, departments, and bureaus present roadblocks to effective gubernatorial control. Toss in the loss of patronage jobs, the continued incursion of civil service, the overlapping and staggered terms of executive branch appointees, and the challenges to a governor's control become even more difficult to overcome. Most governors do not have the time, nor do they usually desire to commit the precious resources necessary to provide firm executive branch leadership.

A quite unrelated aspect of the governor as chief executive is one as chief lobbyist for his own state government. This expansion and extension of an old role have been dramatically affected by the events of the past quarter-century. The decision by many states to create a state office in Washington, the new look of the National Governors' Association as a lobbyist for all governors, an increased role in regional governors' associations, and the more-and-more frequent appearances of governors to lobby Congress, the president and/or relevant executive branch agencies and departments all speak to the rising importance of this newest gubernatorial responsibility.[5]

Fourth, a governor must serve as the leader of his chosen political party. This remains an important role even in an era in which political parties have continued to grow weaker and more ineffectual in many of the states. Only a handful of states can lay claim to the existence of strong state party organizations. We have witnessed more and more gubernatorial candidates winning nomination without party support and more and more gubernatorial nominees being elected with the help of personal organizations and professional campaign managers rather than depending on the help of party organizations.

Even so, a governor must seek to lead his party. Party members in the legislatures are normally likely to be legislative allies. Party leaders as well as members are often sources of names of persons to be appointed to various positions. Partisan identification remains of enormous importance to a large majority of American voters. It is the cue card which helps them to exercise their right to vote. A governor who leads his political party has a major political asset in his corner.

Fortunately for most governors, the roadblocks to party leadership are few. There are unlikely to be many competitors for the leadership of the party. Other potential rivals--especially U.S. Senators and members of the state's congressional delegation of the governor's party--are at somewhat of a disadvantage in a battle for party control as their base of operations is out of the state.

Fifth, a governor must be a leader of public opinion. Atop his state's political and governmental structure, a governor has several means available to attempt to mold and shape public opinion. A governor has an annual "state of the state" message which can be used to stake out priorities and to highlight problem areas. A governor constantly commands media attention. Governors can make use of press conferences (sometimes carried live on television and radio), "fly-arounds" (a series of airport press conferences held in different parts of the state), in addition to the usual publicity-generating devices including bill signings, public appearances and official proclamations.

If a governor is successful as the leader of public opinion, such success will give a governor "clout" to use in marshalling support for his ideas, programs and proposals. Such success will contribute to a governor's success in being a true political leader even when such leadership requires sacrifice on

the part of citizens (such as those times in which a governor
must lead a charge to increase taxes).

Sixth, an additional new responsibility has evolved in
recent years. In this new role, governors find themselves
serving as "federal-systems- officials."[6] In this role, the
governor becomes a coordinator of policy. Changes in both the
legal position of the states in the federal system and the
increased level of intergovernmental program activity have
placed governors in a very crucial and pivotal role in
intergovernmental relations.[7]

While governors are elected independently of the federal
government, no governor governs independently of the huge
federal conglomerate. A rash of new federal programs to be
administered by the states, the creation of federal project
review procedures and requirements (such as A-95), the federal
pressure to upgrade the management capacity of state government,
the creation of a grants-based intergovernmental economy which
has led to the ascendancy of program professionals in state
government, the resulting tension between these professionals
and elected state officials have all worked to place the
governor in a quasi-federal position[8] as the "grand
coordinator, controller, connector, and compromiser of the
executive branch."[9]

These changed roles have contributed to the transformation
of the American governorship. The transformation has not come
cheaply nor without difficulty. There is a very real
possibility that the new administrative and managerial demands
made on governors require "time, energy, resources, and skills
notably different from the political and policy-leadership
skills normally required for high elective office."[10] A
question which cannot yet be answered is whether governors can
administer and manage while at the same time performing all of
these other functions. An equally important, but also
unanswered question is whether governors really have any choice
about the new administrative and managerial functions thrust on
them.

GUBERNATORIAL POWERS

Just as gubernatorial roles have undergone significant changes, so have the powers of the 50 state chief executives. The last 25 years have witnessed some major gains in the formal powers of governors.

In the early 1960s, Joseph Schlesinger constructed an index of the formal powers of the governors.[11] Governors were evaluated on the basis of tenure potential, budget powers, appointment powers, and veto powers. Schlesinger classified 13 governors as "strong," 18 as "medium strong," and 17 as "weak" chief executives.[12]

In a 1977 revision of Schlesinger's analysis, John Straayer (utilizing data from the Book of the States as Schlesinger had done), classified 28 state chief executives as "strong," 17 as "medium strong," and only three as "weak."[13] Since that revision, even more efforts at strengthening the American governorship have been successful. Over the quarter-century, the number of "strong" governors increased from 25 percent to approximately 70 percent. Truly the governorship has become an office of new trappings, new powers, new roles.

The last quarter-century has been crucial to the emergence of the modern governorship. The signposts of that emergence have included: the change to four-year terms of office, the removal of re-election restrictions, the development of the executive budget, the establishing of administrative management agencies in the governor's office, the power to reorganize the executive branch, and the centralization of publicity in the governor's office.

The states have carefully built frameworks for policy, development, coordination and administration of state functions. State after state made substantial moves to strengthen the office of governor. Some states made the changes by writing entirely new constitutions between 1963 and 1976, others by constitutional amendments or changes in statutes. Whatever the medium of change, governors emerged better equipped to do battle with the problems of the remaining decade and a half of the twentieth century.[14]

Tenure Potential: Between 1960 and 1985, 12 states changed governors' terms to four years, bringing the total to 46 states.   The longer terms—which freed governors from never-ending campaigning (much as members of the U.S. House of Representatives must conduct)—did not come cheaply.   In 1960, 25 states had no restraints on re-election, by 1985 that number was still basically unchanged.   By 1985, only Kentucky prohibited consecutive re-election, but 23 states had established an absolute limit of two terms or eight years, a quadrupling of the number 25 years earlier. Much like Amendment XXII to the United States Constitution, many states placed constitutional limits on gubernatorial tenure.

Development of the Executive Budget: In government, as in the rest of society, money has come to represent power. If a governor wants to use the power of his office, he must keep on top of the state's budget.   In 1960, 37 governors had the responsibility (though it was often shared with executive branch agencies outside of the governor's office) for developing the state's budget.   By 1985; that number had increased to 47 states.

   "The budget provides the basic structure for policy making in state government....   It is not only good budgeting and planning practice, but also good politics for a Governor to know the fiscal consequences of all decisions before making them."[15]   These words of advice are contained in a handbook especially prepared for newly elected occupants of governors' chairs.   Realizing that the budget is both a spending plan and a policy tool, it is obvious that the budget had become an important tool in the governor's effort to establish priorities, design public policies, and manage and administer the business of the state.

Establishment of Administrative Planning Agencies: Beginning in the 1960s, many states—at the urging of the federal government—sought to write comprehensive plans for both private- and public-sector activities.   Many states moved to make planning an ongoing part of the policy process and in so doing created executive branch planning units.

Planning was seen as a key element in the management of state government--both in the short-run as well as over the long-term. The efforts to utilize planning were given an additional boost as economic development plans began to make their appearance.

Early on, governors realized the potential benefits--including political benefits--of planning properly done. It was no surprise when governors sought to bring the planning units directly under their control. By the early 1970s, most governors were able to claim that the major components of management and planning had been centralized under their direct control.

Appointment Powers: Governors in most states have been empowered to appoint a growing number of state officials. More importantly, however, governors have gained greater control over the appointment of key executive department administrators than was possible 25 years ago. Correspondingly, governors have increased powers of removal of these same officials. This is of considerable significance in the governors' attempts to set policy.

Although many governors seem willing to give them up and although the courts have dealt major blows to the spoils system, there still exist some patronage appointments to minor posts. These are often used as bargaining chips to influence legislators and others a governor needs to influence.

Veto Powers: Another of the areas in which governors have had their hand measurably strengthened is in the area of veto powers. In 1960, only slightly more than half (29) of the nation's governors had executive veto powers. By 1985, all but North Carolina's chief executive had been given the veto.

Not only did almost all governors possess the veto, but a large number of states added additional veto powers. In 1960, the 29 governors possessing a veto were essentially like the President of the United States, they could only veto a bill in its entirety.

By 1985, many state governors had greater veto powers than the chief executive of the nation; 43 governors had available a line item veto to be used on appropriation bills. Eight also had a reducing veto, the power to reduce legislatively appropriated amounts. A few governors (15) had a fourth veto power--the amendatory veto. This veto gave governors the opportunity to correct clerical errors in a bill and in a handful of states, such as Illinois, to actually suggest "amendments" to a legislative bill, subject of course to the concurrence of the legislature. A governor--as legislative leader--with these veto powers was in a much stronger position vis-a-vis the state legislature.

Reorganization of the Executive Branch: Although state governments have--with few exceptions--resisted the movement to reorganize, the passage of time has brought new wisdom. Beginning in the late 1950s with a trickle, executive reorganization became a torrent of reform by the late 1960s and early 1970s. In spite of entrenched centers of power and the inertia of the bureaucracy, the movement pushing for executive reorganization gained momentum.

Executive reorganization was centered around the principles of reducing the number of executive branch departments, agencies, bureaus, and the like; of matching authority with responsibility,[16] and strengthening the power of the governor in the role of chief executive. If a governor is to be an effective manager, "the key to control is the reorganization of state government...."[17] Impressively, one-third of the states provide for executive reorganization by the governor--subject only to legislative review and veto.

Other Changes in the Executive Branch: In addition to the changes in the office of governor, three other trends were evident. The first was a move to strengthen the governor's political hand by moving elections for governor to the off-years, away from presidential elections. The move to four-year terms made this change possible and by 1984, only 9 four-year governors' chairs would be up for electoral grabs. Two years earlier in a non-presidential election year, 32 four-year term states had held elections for governor.

A second trend was also designed to strengthen the

governor's political hand by moving to elect the governor and the lieutenant governor as a team. In 1960, no states held team elections, but by 1985, 22 states provided for joint election. Of those, however, only a handful provided for joint nomination in addition to joint election.

A third reform movement also surfaced during this quarter-century. This movement was an effort to remove the lieutenant governor from the duties and responsibilities as the presiding officer of the upper house of the state legislature. By 1985, one-third of the states had removed the constitutional or statutory requirement to preside. This reform was an attempt to ease the problem of the lieutenant governor having to straddle the executive/legislative fence. For the most part, lieutenant governors were assigned a variety of executive duties to make up for the loss of legislative responsibilities.

Staffing: As the roles, responsibilities and powers of the governors increased, it became apparent that most governors were still having to "make do" with inadequate staffing. Not only was it necessary to provide more clerical support staff, but as the governorship was strengthened, more professional staff assistance was needed as well. A properly staffed governor's office--it was reasoned--could further broaden a governor's power and influence and enable a governor to manage government and make those major policy decisions which needed to be made.

In 1956, the average governor's staff had 4.3 persons.[18] By 1966, the figure had only risen to 6.6 persons.[19] But, by the early 1980s, the average governor's office staff size was 34.[20]

CHANGING POLITICAL ENVIRONMENT

As the powers and responsibilities of governors have increased, so has the visibility of the office as well as of the officeholder. When the office and the officeholder become involved in controversy, the visibility increases even more. Events and the general pressures affecting state government require strong political leadership. That leadership can only be exercised by the governor of a state. The visibility, the controversy, and the necessity for a governor to assume the mantle of political leadership have all contributed to making governors the central political and governmental leader in their states. The press and the public alike watch carefully the actions of the governor.

Gubernatorial Elections: As the importance of the office has changed, so has the political environment of the governorship. Competition for the office has increased substantially. While members of the United States House of Representatives have enjoyed a post-World War II re-election rate of 91 percent[21] and while United States Senators have enjoyed a 75 percent re-election rate[22] for the same period, governors have proven more vulnerable to challenges.

Governors are re-elected at a rate of approximately 65 percent over the last 25 years. In the last decade, however, that rate has edged upward with governors winning re-election 70 percent of the time. The increased visibility/leadership/vulnerability of the new governorship has not been a great boon at re-election time, but it is less fatal than it first appeared.

Tenure: Having mentioned the problems many governors have faced in trying to be re-elected it is important to note a counter-trend. Governors are serving for longer periods of time. In the first two decades of this century, fewer than 16 percent of governors served five or more years in office. In the decade of the 1950s, the figure rose to 29 percent. Since 1970, the figure has exceeded 50 percent.[23]

The change from two-year terms to four-year terms and the increasing importance of the office have led to the office becoming "a more extended stage in a political career."[24] As a result, politicians are making a greater effort to win the office. Nowhere is this more visible than in the related areas of campaign finance and professional campaign management.

The cost of running for governor has shot upward as though propelled by a cannon. According to one observer, the cost of a gubernatorial campaign in a small state in 1956 was about $100,000 with a figure of $300,000 in heavily populated states.[25]   Thirty years later, it was not uncommon to find campaigns in which the total spending exceeded $10,000,000.[26]

The use of professional campaign consultants is a fairly new wrinkle in gubernatorial campaigns. Professionals arrived on the scene to fill the vacuum left by the continued weakened positions of the two political parties. Gubernatorial politics have become more competitive, there is more ticket-splitting, greater efforts are expended in wooing the independent voter, and it is hard to overestimate the importance of television in political campaigns. These changes in the electoral environment are important in explaining the changes in the types of politicians who would be governor.

Career Patterns: In the first 50 years of this century, the penultimate or last office held before election as governor was evenly divided between governors who held statewide elective office and those who held some sort of law enforcement position.[27]   For the most recent 25-year period, the trend has been to find governors coming from the ranks of state legislators.   By 1985, one in three sitting governors had been elected from a position in the state legislature.[28]

CHARACTERISTICS OF GOVERNORS

In order to gain a better understanding of who the governors are, a sampling of some personal and political characteristics would seem helpful.[29] This study concentrates on those persons who served as governor during the time period of 1960-1985. When helpful, comparative data from other periods will be presented.

Birthplace: During the decade of the 1960s and 1970s, 71 percent of the governors of the fifty states were "native born" in the state they governed. There was no decline in this figure in the first half of the 1980s.

Veterans: As might be expected of those who were growing up during World War II, the Korean War or the war in Vietnam, many governors had served in the military. Approximately two-thirds of all the nation's governors during this time period were veterans.

Education: The percentage of governors who have attended
college continues to move upward. In the 1940s, slightly less
than 90 percent had attended college. During the 1950s, the
figure would edge up just over the 90 percent mark. By the
1960s, the pattern was set as 95+ percent had attended college.
Almost all (99 percent) of the occupants of the statehouses
since 1970 have attended college. Governors were likely to have
attended college in their home states. Increasing numbers of
governors were likely to have completed an advanced degree (most
of those were in law).

Age: Governors continued to be younger and younger. In the
1950s, the average age of governors at inauguration was 47. In
the 1960s, the average dropped a full year. That figure has
declined by another 6 months on the average for the period
1970-1985.   At least 25 governors in their thirties were sworn
into office during those 15 years.

Vocations: The majority of persons elected governor in the last
quarter- century were lawyers.   Between 55 and 60 percent of
those who served as governor were attorneys, eclipsing the
second-place vocational choice--businessman, a career choice of
one fifth of the governors.

     These personal and political characteristics help to shed
some light on the nature of those providing the central
political leadership in the states over the last 25 years. The
so-called "typical" chief executive during this time period was
likely to be home grown, well-educated, politically experienced,
young, and thoroughly trained for the responsibilities of the
new governorship.

     As shown above, the position of governor has been one of
growing powers, growing influence and growing visibility. With
this growth in the ability of governors to more effectively deal
with problems came many new responsibilities. A sizable number
of these new responsibilities resulted from and were related to
matters of intergovernmental policies and politics. The last
quarter-century has seen a major increase in the number of
matters of an intergovernmental nature with which governors must
deal.   Thus, the roles of the governors themselves as well as

the roles governors play in organizations such as regional
governors' conferences have taken on added importance and
meaning.

FEDERALISM AND THE CHANGES IN THE ROLES OF GOVERNORS

For governors who came to office during the decade of the
1970s, it was immediately clear that major changes in American
federalism had occurred, changes which had profoundly altered
the nature of intergovernmental relations. In 1970, federal
agencies provided $24 billion to state and local governments.
This amount doubled to $49.8 billion by mid-decade and further
increased to $91.5 billion by 1980.[30]

It was not just that the amount of federal aid had
increased so dramatically, it was also the fact that the number
of federal programs and the number of entangling federal
regulations had grown so enormously. Thus, it became
crystal-clear that "no governor could afford to maintain an
insular attitude."[31] To do so was to risk losses due to
changes in distribution formulas, in federal grant conditions,
or in appropriation levels. The intrusion of the federal
government into state and local affairs, and the general
disorder and chaos of the federal grant-in-aid system led
governors to seek an expanded role for themselves. In seeking
to define such an expanded role, governors took a look at the
politics of the new federalism. As one intergovernmental
relations student has observed: "Whatever approach or posture a
governor adopts, it seems certain that a governor cannot escape
from entanglement in a web of intergovernmental political,
policy, and administrative relationships."[32]

Governors spelled out the most significant
intergovernmental management problems they regularly encountered
in a report entitled Federal Roadblocks to Efficient State
Government:

> 1. Lack of coordination among federal
> departments or agencies limits the
> effectiveness of programs in solving problems
> and increases the administrative burden on the
> states.

2. The federal executive branch exceeds its proper authority in some areas, encroaching on matters which are within the proper jurisdiction of the states.

3. Federal regulations are prescriptive in methodology rather than oriented toward results.

4. Excessive reporting and paperwork requirements must be met by states participating in federal programs.

5. Funding and program implementation are delayed by lengthy approval procedures, absence of program guidelines, and other administrative practices that cause serious dislocation and inequities at the state level.

6. Lack of federal coordination and consistency in implementing indirect cost determination procedures creates continuing administrative confusion for States.[33]

In order to deal with the substantial increase in federal-state relationships, many governors hired intergovernmental relations directors or coordinators.[34] Although the responsibilities of these units varied greatly, they all shared one common purpose--to consolidate federal-state relations in the governor's office. It was one effort designed to try to eliminate some of the "roadblocks." It is worth noting, that in the handbook provided to new governors by the National Governors' Association, only the chapter on budgeting was longer than the section on state-federal relations.[35]

Governors found that the new federalism thrust them into the middle. That middle position was titled "federal-systems-officer." A governor must not only take the lead in policy innovation, but must also lobby Washington for funds to put the policy into effect. If the funds are made available, the governor--again in the middle--tries to ensure that the federal dollars are spent in line with his goals and program ideas.[36] To ensure that, a governor must also lobby his own legislature for authority, support and/or matching funds.

More and more, governors are going outside their states to encourage action at the national level and secure for the governor a larger role in channeling federally financed

> programs and services through the states.
> This might be called the federal-systems-
> officer role at the state level. Increasing-
> ly, governors seem to be playing this role to
> a greater extent than the traditional textbook
> roles assigned to chief executives.[37]

A survey of governors who served between 1960 and 1980 found that on average, governors spent one workday a week on state-federal matters.[38] Governors who served in the 1970s were devoting much more time to state-federal relations than their counterparts who served in the 1960s. The increase occurred because of a proliferation of grant-in-aid programs, the new federal-state partnership which was developing, the reversal of the federal power flow and the increasing power of governors.[39]

The last quarter-century has seen a new governorship created. Governors who served during this time period have become "active and assertive in their state's relations with the federal government."[40] Anyone who would seek to understand state government, federalism, or the American political system in general, quickly comes to the realization that such an understanding is only possible when one gains an understanding of the contemporary American governorship.

NOTES
==

[1] James Reston, New York Times, 1962.

[2] Neal R. Peirce and Jerry Hagstrom, The Book of America: Inside 50 States Today (rev. ed., New York: Warner Books, Inc., 1984), p. 19.

[3] Glenn E. Brooks, When Governors Convene: The Governors' Conference and National Politics (Baltimore: The Johns Hopkins Press, 1961), p. vii.

[4] Ibid.

[5] For a discussion of this role see Thad L. Beyle and Lynn R. Muchmore "Governors in the American Federal System," in Being Governor: the View from the Office, ed. by Thad L. Beyle and Lynn R. Muchmore (Durham: Duke University Press, 1983), pp.

104

17-18.

[6] Parris N. Glendening and Mavis Mann Reeves, _Pragmatic Federalism: An Intergovernmental View of American Government_ (Pacific Palisades: Palisades Publishers, 1977), p. 48; Deil S. Wright, "Governors, Grants, and the Intergovernmental System," in _The American Governor in Behavior Perspective_, ed. by Thad Beyle and J. Oliver Williams (New York: Harper & Row, Publishers, 1972), p. 188.

[7] Thad Beyle, Harold A. Hovey, and Kenneth C. Olson, "Intergovernmental Relations in the Governor's Office," _State Government_, L (Spring, 1977), p. 90.

[8] Beyle and Muchmore, "Governors in the American Federal System," pp. 17-18; Deil S. Wright, _Understanding Intergovernmental Relations_ (2nd edition, Monterey, Calif.: Brooks/Cole Publishing Co., 1982), pp. 273-77; Glendening and Reeves, _Pragmatic Federalism_, pp. 48-49.

[9] Wright, _Understanding Intergovernmental Relations_, p. 277.

[10] Ibid.

[11] Joseph A. Schlesinger, "The Politics of the Executive," in _Politics in the American States: A Comparative Analysis_, ed. by Herbert Jacob and Kenneth N. Vines (Boston: Little, Brown & Co., 1965), pp. 207-237.

[12] Ibid.

[13] John A. Straayer, _American State and Local Government_ (2nd ed., Columbus: Charles E. Merrill Publishing Co., 1977), pp. 113-121.

[14] Kenneth C. Olson, "The States, Governors, and Policy Management: Changing the Equilibrium of the Federal System," _Public Administration Review_, XXXV (December, 1975), p. 764.

[15] Center for Policy Research, _Governing the American States: A Handbook for New Governors_ (Washington: National Governors' Association, 1978), pp. 152-53.

[16] Larry Sabato, _Goodbye to Good-time Charlie: The American Governorship Transformed_ (2nd ed., Washington: Congressional Quarterly Press, 1983), p. 60.

[17] Ibid., p. 62

[18] Ibid., p. 85.

[19] Ibid.

[20] Ibid.

[21]Jacqueline Calmes, "House Incumbents Achieve Record Success Rate in 1986," Congressional Quarterly Weekly Report, XLIV (November 15, 1986), p. 2891.

[22]Ibid.

[23]Sabato, Goodbye to Good-time Charlie, pp. 103-105.

[24]Ibid., p. 105.

[25]Coleman B. Ransone, Jr., The Office of Governor in the United States (University: University of Alabama Press, 1956), pp. 105-106.

[26]Sabato, Goodbye to Good-time Charlie, pp. 148-51.

[27]Ibid., p. 40.

[28]Ibid.

[29]Data on personal and political characteristics were gathered from numerous sources, but especially from Who's Who in the Midwest (Chicago: Marquis Who's Who, Inc.), 1962/1963-1984/1985; Who's Who in America (Chicago: Marquis Who's Who, Inc.), 1962/1963-1984/1985; Who's Who in American Politics (New York: R. R. Bowker Co.), 1967/1968-1975/1976. Fordata on the nation's governors see Samuel R. Solomon, "Governors: 1960-1970," National Civic Review, LX (March, 1971), pp. 126-146; Samuel R. Solomon, "Governors: 1970- 1980," National Civic Review, LXX (March, 1981), pp. 120-155; Samuel R. Solomon, The Governors of the American States, Commonwealths, and Territories 1900-1980 (Lexington: Council of State Governments, 1980).

[30]Thad L. Beyle and Lynn R. Muchmore, "Governors and Intergovernmental Relations: Middlemen in the Federal System," in Being Governor, ed. by Beyle and Muchmore, pp. 192-203.

[31]Ibid., p. 193.

[32] Wright, Understanding Intergovernmental Relations, p. 271.

[33]National Governors' Conference, Federal Roadblocks to Efficient State Government, Vol. I, "A Sampling of the Effects of Red Tape" (Washington: National Governors' Conference, 1977), p. vii.

[34]Wright, Understanding Intergovernmental Relations, p. 269; Beyle and Muchmore, "Governors and Intergovernmental Relations," pp. 195-98.

[35] Wright, Understanding Intergovernmenta` Relations, p. 267.

106

[36] Sarah McCally Morehouse, _State Politics, Parties and Policy_ (New York: Holt, Rinehart and Winston, 1981), p. 224.

[37] Dennis O. Grady, "American Governors and State-Federal Relations," _State Government_, LVII (1984), p. 108.

[38] _Ibid._, p. 109.

[39] Sabato, _Goodbye to Good-time Charlie_, pp. 179-80.

[40] Grady, "American Governors and State-Federal Relations," p. 111.

CHAPTER FIVE

THE STRUGGLE TO FORM THE MIDWESTERN GOVERNORS' CONFERENCE

In this system of constantly evolving federalism, the period of
1960-1985 is marked by what one scholar has referred to as "an
extraordinary degree of interdependence between the states and
other components of the intergovernmental system."[1] During
these years, the roles and functions of the state governmental
units as well as state governmental leaders were dramatically
reshaped. Changes in the American system over the last two and
one-half decades created many new situations and responses,
heightened old tensions, exacerbated old problems and created
new ones, and led to the establishment of new governmental and
extra-governmental institutions.

These alterations in the political environment also
affected the roles and actions of the nation's governors. As
the importance of the traditional political parties declined, as
governors became "principals in the arena of federal-state
relations,"[2] and as governors emerged as executive branch
"managers," it became clear that the American governorship had
undergone dramatic changes (see Chapter Four). One of the
consequences of these changes and trends was the establishment
of regional coalitions of governors. Originally, these
organizations were established to focus on policy issues and
regionally-shared concerns and problems. Later, several of
these organizations would expand their sphere of activities to
include efforts to more directly influence policy-making in
Washington.[3]

THEORIES OF THE ORIGINS OF GROUPS

Even in a climate favorable to the formation of groups and institutions, groups do not simply spring forth automatically. We know that at the very least there must be substantial societal cleavages. Social scientists have long sought to explain the development of such groups and institutions. One of the foremost scholars in this area of study is David B. Truman, whose major work The Governmental Process theorized that groups are created when they become necessary. As a society becomes increasingly complex, he argued, new groups and institutions are formed to provide for the needs of various groups and to provide for the stabilizing of group relationships.[4]

Truman argued that the "series of disturbances and dislocations" which result from economic changes can also contribute to the proliferation of associations.[5] As groups were adversely affected by these political and economic disturbances, they would organize to correct these shortcomings. "The association articulates the interest, and by organizing its adherents provides more effective bargaining power vis-a-vis other groups."[6]

Many scholars have pointed out flaws in Truman's disturbance explanation, but it has served as a useful beginning point toward a more solid and complete theory of group origins. One of the theories proposed as a replacement for Truman's theory was offered by political scientist Robert Salisbury.[7] Salisbury took quite a different tact than Truman. He argued that leadership is the main reason any group is formed, succeeds or dies. Salisbury labeled these leaders "entrepreneurs" and said they will succeed (as will the group) if they provide attractive benefits (or incentives) to potential members. In his study of farm groups during the nineteenth century, Salisbury found that successful group entrepreneurs provided meaningful purposive, material or solidary benefits to lure members to join their organizations.

Another attack on Truman's disturbance theory came from economist Mancur Olson[8] who argued that individuals join a group because of the benefits they receive. But, Olson parted company with Salisbury when he argued that the appeal was in "selective benefits" as opposed to the collective benefits mentioned by Salisbury. Selective benefits are those available only to group members as opposed to the collective benefits available to members and non-members alike.

What is the bottom line in terms of what we know about the origins of groups and associations? First, we know some groups do evolve out of the increasing complexity of our society. Technological changes are a part of the fabric of that complexity. Second, societal disturbances can trigger new groups and associations, but many groups originate without them. Third, group constituencies vary widely and some are hard to organize, while others are easy. Because of this, organizations must provide a mix of selective benefits.[9]

GOVERNORS' ORGANIZATIONS 1960-1985

As noted above, the states and their leaders had to adjust to new situations requiring new responses and new institutions. Among these new responses were the birth and rebirth of governors' organizations. Like other public interest groups and institutions, governors' organizations are private, completely voluntary organizations. Truman noted that interest groups themselves become elements of continuity in a changing political world.[10] Governors' organizations--as interest groups--suffer from lack of a formal political position.[11] This lack of formal position has put these organizations in the strange posture of engaging in a nearly constant search for a role. In a political system that responds to and respects political power, governors' organizations have struggled to attain clout.

The revitalization of the National Governors' Conference in the mid-1960s and the formation of the Midwestern Governors' Conference (MGC) earlier in that decade were two attempts to deal with the clout problem. The need for clout was evident everywhere: (1) the states were revitalizing themselves; (2) the problems confronting the states were often common problems, problems which extended over state boundaries; (3) the roles of the governor were changing--an added role as "federal-systems

official"[12] was one of the biggest changes; (4) the
"audiences" governors had to appeal to often required concerted
action and (5) the governors' growing awareness of the stakes
involved in federal policy-making[13] and the need for channels
through which to pool resources all pointed to new
organizational needs.

Governors across the nation found themselves buried in the
plethora of new and expanded federal programs and regulations.
The decades of the 1960s and 1970s signaled a period of "federal
intergovernmental interventionism."[14] It was a period marked
by a transformation from cooperative federalism to "cooptive
federalism";[15] an era of "concentrated cooperation."[16] The
large intergovernmental lobby of today (numbering over 200
associations and groups) was spawned by the policies of
federalism during the past quarter-century. The regional
governors' organizations were forerunners of these members of
the intergovernmental lobby. It is all the more instructive,
therefore, that we understand how these groups came into being.
The vehicle for that purpose is the Midwestern Governors'
Conference.

THE PRE-1962 ATTEMPTS AT ORGANIZATION

The efforts which ultimately led to the birth of the
Midwestern Governors' Conference in 1962 were preceded by nearly
two decades and several attempts at organizing. Midwestern
governors met sporadically during the 1940s and 1950s,[17] but
all attempts to organize during these two decades ended in
failure. Part of the failure can be traced to the fact that
midwestern states were slower to develop a "distinct regional
consciousness" than states in other regions.[18] Economic
diversity within the region was one of the main reasons for this
slowness.

As far back as 1948, midwestern chief executives had tried
to organize. Governor Robert D. Blue (R-Iowa, 1945-1949)
invited four other midwestern governors (representing Illinois,
Kansas, Michigan and South Dakota) to his office to talk about
forming a conference. "Because of the lack of homogeneity and

common interest, plans for formal organization proved to be abortive."[19]

In 1951, fifteen state governors were asked to come to Omaha in an attempt to weld the Great Lakes and Missouri River Valley states into a single powerful bloc.[20] Six of the invitees came, seven more sent representatives, but two chose not to attend nor did they send representatives. The purpose was to push for the building of the St. Lawrence Seaway, which was at that time making rather unsteady progress through the national legislative quagmire.

Governor Forrest Smith (D-Mo., 1949-1953) was not enthusiastic about the proposed "Governors' Conference of Inland America." He thought: "...a bloc of Great Lakes States was trying to use the Missouri River States as a 'catspaw to high-pressure congress into spending up to $4,000,000,000 on a project which benefits one section of the country'."[21] With divisive feelings running high, the attempt to organize never was fully launched.

A fourth indication of activity is found in a 1954 letter from Governor G. Mennen Williams (D-Mich., 1949-1961), to the Executive Director of the Council of State Governments. In the letter, Williams said he favored the formation of a Great Lakes Governors' Conference and noted that several governors had tried to establish a "North Central States Governors' Conference," but the group was too large: "...with a smaller group we will have more matters of common interest and that we should get together and be able to stick together."[22]

A year later, eight governors sat down to talk about interstate highway programs. The eight states represented were all Missouri River Basin or southwest states (Colorado, New Mexico, Wyoming, North Dakota, South Dakota, Nebraska, Kansas and Iowa). After voting along party lines on President Eisenhower's highway programs, and after passing resolutions asking Congress to expedite enactment of an interstate road program, and urging the House of Representatives to bring the Gore plan "more in harmony" with the President's proposal, the eight governors adjourned.[23] That particular set of governors did not meet again.

The next attempt at mobilizing midwestern governors was a 1958 attempt by Ohio Governor C. William O'Neill (R, 1957-1959) who hoped to bring together the governors of the eight Great Lakes states to form the Great Lakes Governors' Council.[24] He invited the other seven governors to Columbus and set out the possible agenda--industrial development, freight rates, port development, regional publicity, and economics. Six weeks later, Governor O'Neill was defeated in his bid for re-election. Five other governors from that group were up for re-election. Three were defeated. The Council never got off the ground.

In December, 1958, Governor Orville L. Freeman (D-Minn., 1955-1961) invited the governors of Iowa, South Dakota and Wisconsin to meet with him. There was no specific agenda established. One of Freeman's chief aides noted: "...the discussions will no doubt have a regional flavor. It is not unlikely that they may want to consider creating a somewhat more permanent midwest conference of governors."[25] Again, nothing more occurred by way of organizational follow-up.

However, midwestern governors never quit trying. In September, 1959, Governor Michael V. DiSalle (D-Ohio, 1959-1963), wrote seven governors asking about the feasibility of forming a Council of Great Lakes Governors. The purpose of such a Council was to: "...give our states full advantage of the benefit that may be derived from the development of the St. Lawrence Seaway.[26]

This time, the effort at organizing midwest governors attracted some attention. The attention, however, was not the kind which would further Governor DiSalle's hopes for starting a regional governors' conference. The attention--in the form of opposition--came from the Executive Director of the Great Lakes Commission, Marvin Faust. The Commission (formed in 1955 by interstate compact) was to coordinate management of the water resources of the Great Lakes and to make recommendations as to their use. The Executive Director took note of the press reports of Governor DiSalle's efforts, and in a letter to

Commission members observed: "You will recall that the Commission late in 1958 [O'Neill's efforts] and again early this year [Freeman's efforts] expressed its concern over possible duplication of functions between the Commission and the proposed council and asked each state to bring this concern to the attention of its governor."[27]

Part of the friction can be traced to the fact that Ohio had not yet joined the Great Lakes Commission and did not do so for three years. New York had not joined the Commission either (it joined in 1960). The other six invitees to DiSalle's conference were Commission members.

DiSalle highlighted in a letter to Brevard Crihfield, Executive Director of the Council of State Governments the areas of mutual interest to be discussed at the first meeting as including: industrial development, freight rates, port development, publicity for the region, regional economics and other items of general interest.[28] Answering the claims of GLC Executive Director Faust that a governors' group would duplicate the Commission's work, DiSalle replied: "A review of the purposes of this organization [the Commission] limits it to a purely technical aspect of the Great Lakes. I feel that the economic purposes hereinabove outlined are outside of this scope."[29]

Finally, the Ohio governor sounded the clarion call to organize when he concluded his letter by saying: "The forces that could very well make the St. Lawrence Seaway far less effective than originally contemplated are united and are organized. This certainly calls for the Great Lakes States with mutual objectives, to meet this organized opposition on a firm basis."[30]

Press stories from this general period pointed out some interesting problems not addressed by Governor DiSalle. First, the inclusion of New York and Pennsylvania in such a conference could create a conflict of interest for them as they had Atlantic Ocean ports which could be hurt by the St. Lawrence Seaway.[31] Second, the willingness of governors to consider organizing as mentioned in the letter to Crihfield was perhaps

not as solid as the Governor thought. An article in the
Milwaukee Journal pointed out that New York and Pennsylvania had
indicated little interest in such a gathering. Indiana and
Michigan were enthusiastic but the governors of both states were
going out of office in five months, and that both Wisconsin (a
late invitee) and Illinois had strong reservations about joining
such a conference.[32]

Because of the opposition and the lack of enthusiasm on the
part of several of the eight governors, the Great Lakes
Governors' Conference never organized, never met. DiSalle would
later offer these reasons for the failure: "There was not
enough time to convince governors of the Conference's value.
There were too many changes of governors in office as a result
of the elections of 1960 and 1962."[33]

THE EVENTS OF 1962

As the attempts by Governor DiSalle to organize the
governors were failing, there were other, unrelated events
taking place elsewhere in the Midwest. The early 1960s
foreshadowed the explosion of students soon to enter the states'
systems of higher education. So many students came so quickly
that many states could not keep up with the pace. The cost of
maintaining systems of higher education was often prohibitive
for the smaller, less populated states especially for the
advanced technical, professional programs.

As a result, states began to enter into cooperative
agreements (reciprocal compacts) with one another. Such
compacts existed on a regional basis in the West, the South and
the New England states. North Dakota legislators serving on the
Legislative Research Committee worried aloud that there would
be no place for North Dakota students in professional schools in
other states due to these existing arrangements. In November,
1961, the Committee adopted a resolution urging the governor to
take the necessary action toward the entry of North Dakota into
reciprocal compacts with neighboring states in the field of
higher education.[34] In a letter, the Legislative Research
Committee asked Governor William Guy (D-N.D., 1961-1973) to

inquire of other midwestern governors at the upcoming National Governors' Conference in Hershey, Pennsylvania, whether they were interested in sitting down to talk through such a problem.

Governor Guy talked with a number of midwestern governors at the Hershey conference. Meeting over lunch they agreed to a conference of midwestern governors if Guy would organize the meeting and serve as the chairman.[35] A press release issued at the NGC meeting outlined the plans of the governors:

> In an historic move, governors of nine Midwestern states today agreed to explore the possibility of forming a regional governors' conference to study mutual problems confronting them.
>
> Support for the conference came at a luncheon meeting ...to discuss regional problems of higher education.
>
> A motion...directed Governor Guy to confer with the Council of State Governments in setting up a Midwest Conference of Governors.
>
> The motion came after the governors in attendance had discussed ways and means of initiating an organization to consider common problems of higher education. Special attention was given to the training of more students in highly specialized fields such as veterinary medicine, dentistry, public health nursing and other fields of graduate study and research....
>
> The group of midwestern governors also decided that a regional conference would also prove beneficial to study mutual problems of agriculture, water resource development, law enforcement and mental health....
>
> The governors agreed that such a conference would provide a means of communication on regional problems such as the Southern Governors' Conference had provided.[36]

Governor Guy was not the only chief executive interested in creating a midwestern governors' conference. Governor Otto Kerner (D-Ill., 1961-1968) had also been thinking along the same lines.[37]

While at the NGC, Guy moved to capitalize on the momentum which had been created. He named a six-governor Planning

116

Committee (chaired by Governor Kerner) to set up the first
meeting of the midwestern governors. The Committee members
agreed to invite the governors of twelve midwestern states to
participate in the first meeting: Illinois, Indiana, Iowa,
Kansas, Michigan, Minnesota, Missouri, Nebraska, North Dakota,
Ohio, South Dakota and Wisconsin.[38]

THE 1962 ORGANIZATIONAL MEETING OF THE MGC

In spite of the problems caused by the electoral defeat of
four governors, the organizational meeting of the MGC was held
in Chicago, December 12-14. All midwestern governors except
those from Kansas and Ohio were in attendance.

The governors moved to establish a formal, on-going
operation. The Midwestern Governors' Conference as it was to be
known formally began its existence when the Articles of
Organization were approved December 13, 1962. The seven
articles listed conference membership, spelled out the functions
of the conference, outlined meeting plans, provided for
Conference officers and established the process for Conference
consideration of resolutions.[39] Amendments would later add an
Advisory Committee (comprised of gubernatorial staffers),
provide for annual dues, and alter--numerous times--the article
on resolutions.

Desirous of expressing their collective opinion on several
matters, the Conference participants adopted five resolutions.
One dealt with interstate cooperation in higher education and
put the governors on record favoring actions to form cooperative
compacts and establish a MGC standing committee on interstate
cooperation in higher education. The conference also
established standing committees on economic growth and highway
safety. Additionally, governors were urged to ask their
legislatures to ratify the Vehicle Equipment Safety Compact and
the Drivers' License Compact.

Finally, they approved a resolution urging states to study
gubernatorial transitions and ways to improve the transition
process in their own states.[40] In addressing the 1962
gathering in Chicago, host governor Kerner gave voice to the

reasons for organizing when he declared: "Clearly, it is high time that the states of this region cooperated in their research efforts and cooperated in their political efforts to reverse a tide that has been allowed to run too long against us."[41]

CONCLUSIONS

With the advantages of a comparative perspective gained from studying the organization of the other major regional governors' conferences, it would seem useful to conclude with a few general observations about why the Midwestern Governors' Conference was successful in organizing in 1962, whereas earlier attempts had failed. The parallels between the MGC efforts and those of the other conferences should be obvious.

First, there was a single, united area of concern--higher education. It was an issue which was "politically" neutral. That is, the problem affected all states and the solutions were not definable in Republican or Democratic terms. Second, other regions of the nation already had operating higher education compacts. Midwestern states were left isolated. If there was no action soon on a regional basis, individual states would drift away, probably to try to join the New England Higher Education Compact, the Southern Regional Education Board, or the Western Interstate Commission for Higher Education.

Third, other regions of the country had previously organized regional governors' conferences. The other regions seemed to gain by being organized. The Midwest felt outmaneuvered by not being organized.[42]

Fourth, the midwestern governors felt the region was being shorted in the receipt of federal dollars for research and development, especially the dollars NASA was spreading around. Most contracts were going to areas other than the Midwest, especially to the South, and midwestern chief executives thought at least part of the credit was due to the activities of the Southern Governors' Conference.[43]

Fifth, Governor William Guy was willing to take the time to do the necessary groundwork and he served as a catalyst to see that the Conference got off the ground. The existence of a

Midwestern Governors' Conference is a tribute to his political
skills. As Governor Guy pushed cooperation in higher education,
in the process he was successful in getting a governors'
conference organized and operating.

Finally, once assembled, the governors found they had many
problems in common. The original twelve-state region was a
somewhat identifiable political entity. The early years of
nonpartisan conference activity strengthened the fragile bond of
regional unity. It also seemed possible that the condition of
the Midwest economy might be improved by collective actions.

The birth of the Midwestern Governors' Conference does not
seem to fit any one of the theories of group origins
exclusively. Rather, the organization's beginnings seem to
reflect parts of all of the theories. There were certainly
several societal and political "disturbances" which helped
launch the new group.[44] An examination of the history of the
founding of the association also validates the theory built on
the "personal force" of an entrepreneur.[45] William Guy has
never been more accurately described. It also seems clear that
the organization was successfully founded in 1962 because the
governors of the region were convinced that they would obtain
benefits in return for their membership in the proposed
organization.[46] The opportunity to make contact with fellow
chief executives--in an informal, private setting; the chance to
exchange information and talk shop; and the possibility of
benefits flowing from their collective action, all induced the
twelve midwestern governors to join together in a new
association.

The MGC was an organization with a relatively short-term
original purpose. Convened to solve a specific education
dilemma the governors later found other reasons for remaining
organized. Governors expressed an interest in a midwestern
governors' organization because of a variety of common problems
and needs. The MGC was to help midwestern governors with the
job of being governor, with regional problems, with research and
with increasing their Washington clout. After more than two
decades of false starts, a midwestern governors' organization

had finally become a reality.

NOTES
===

[1] Deil S. Wright, "The States and Intergovernmental Relations," Publius I (Winter, 1972), p. 62.

[2] Thad L. Beyle and Lynn R. Muchmore, "Governors in the American Federal System," in Thad L. Beyle and Lynn R. Muchmore, eds., Being Governor: The View from the Office (Durham: Duke Press Policy Studies, 1983), pp. 17-18.

[3] Ibid., p. 18.

[4] David B. Truman, The Governmental Process (New York: Alfred A. Knopf, Inc., 1951), pp. 26-32.

[5] Ibid., pp. 14-44.

[6] Robert H. Salisbury, "An Exchange Theory of Interest Groups," Midwest Journal of Political Science, XIII (February, 1969), pp. 3-4.

[7] Ibid., pp. 1-32; see also his "Interest Representation: The Dominance of Institutions," American Political Science Review, LXXVIII (March, 1984), pp. 64-76.

[8] The Logic of Collective Action: Public Goods and the Theory of Groups (Cambridge: Harvard University Press, 1965).

[9] Jeffrey M. Berry, The Interest Group Society (Boston: Little, Brown & Co., 1984), pp. 73-82.

[10] Truman, The Governmental Process, pp. 519-20.

[11] Donald H. Haider, When Governments Come to Washington: Governors, Mayors and Intergovernmental Lobbying (New York: The Free Press, 1974), pp. 306-308.

[12] Parris N. Glendening and Mavis Mann Reeves, Pragmatic Federalism: An Intergovernmental View of American Government (Pacific Palisades: Palisades Publishers, 1977), p. 48.

[13] Haider, When Governments Come to Washington, p. 23.

[14] David B. Walker, "American Federalism--Then and Now," in The Book of the States, 1982-83 (Lexington: The Council of State Governments, 1982), p. 26.

[15] Ibid., p. 24.

[16] Daniel J. Elazar, American Federalism: A View from the States (3rd ed.; New York: Harper & Row, Publishers, Inc., 1984), p. 85.

[17] Jay A. Sigler, "Governors Confer on Regional Basis," National Civic Review, LV (October, 1966), pp. 512-13.

[18] Boyd R. Keenan, Illinois Office of Governor: Expanding Regional Role Within National Politics (Urbana: the Institute of Government and Public Affairs, 1982).

[19] Letter from Catherine M. Barrum to Jerry Poston, Assistant to the Governor of Ohio, February 29, 1960, Council of State Governments/Lexington (CSG/L) Files.

[20] William M. Blair, "Seaway Backers Ask MW Aid," New York Times (June 19, 1951), p. 8.

[21] Ibid.

[22] Letter from G. Mennen Williams to Frank Bane, April 1, 1954, CSG/L Files.

[23] Seth S. King, "Governors Split Over Road Bills," New York Times (June 2, 1955), p. 29.

[24] Copy of letter from C. William O'Neill to other Great Lakes governors, September 25, 1958, CSG/L Files.

[25] Letter from Arthur Naftalin to Brevard Crihfield, December 18, 1958, CSG/L Files.

[26] Copy of letter from Michael V. DiSalle to other Great Lakes governors, September 16, 1959. CSG/L Files.

[27] Copy of letter from Marvin Faust to members of the Great Lakes Commission, September 24, 1959, CSG/L Files.

[28] Letter from Michael V. DiSalle to Brevard Crihfield, July 7, 1960, CSG/L Files.

[29] Ibid.

[30] Ibid.

[31] "Eight Governors Act to Help Seaway," New York Times (June 29, 1960), p. 67.

[32] Perry C. Hill, "Seaway Use Unit Slated," Milwaukee Journal (June 29, 1960), p. 20.

[33] Michael V. DiSalle, private interview with author, Washington, D.C.; March 10, 1977.

[34]Resolution, Subcommittee on Education, Legislative Research Committee, November, 1961, William L. Guy Papers, Chester Fritz Library, University of North Dakota.

[35]William L. Guy, private interview with author, Casselton, North Dakota, June 6, 1977.

[36]Press Release, Hershey, Pennsylvania, July 2,1962, William L. Guy Papers.

[37]Kennan, Illinois Office of Governor.

[38]Meetings of the Planning Committee, Minutes, August 31, 1962, CSG/Chicago (CSG/C) Files.

[39]Ibid.

[40]Ibid.

[41]Minutes of the Annual Meetings of the Midwestern Governors' Conference, Chicago, Illinois, December 12-14, 1962, CSG/C Files.

[42]Crihfield, private interview with author.

[43]Ibid.

[44]Truman, The Governmental Process, pp. 14-44.

[45]Salisbury, "An Exchange Theory of Interest Groups," pp. 1-32.

[46]Olson, The Logic of Collective Action, p. 146.

CHAPTER SIX

THE MACHINERY OF THE MIDWESTERN GOVERNORS' CONFERENCE

Over the years, the Midwestern Governors' Conference has made use of a number of different in-house as well as adjunct "institutions." Each was intended to serve a particular and distinct purpose. Many of these institutions evolved from their predecessors.

THE CONFERENCE SECRETARIAT

The Midwest office of the Council of State Governments in Chicago (CSG/C) is the secretariat for the MGC as well as for several other regional organizations such as the CSG Midwestern Conference and the Midwestern Conference of Attorneys General. The Governors' Conference is the only one of these regional organizations having as members states which are not in the twelve-state region assigned to CSG/C by the Lexington office. The assigned region is comprised of the twelve states which were charter members of the governors' conference.

The Chicago office, established in 1969--when the organization's national office was moved to Lexington, Kentucky--is one of four regional Council offices (see Chapter Three). As the secretariat of the governors' conference, the office has several duties. Chicago office staff members work closely with the host governor's staff people in charge of the annual Conference meeting. At annual meetings, CSG/C staffers attend all meetings, make recordings of all speeches and discussions for transcription into a written meeting summary. Any post-meeting follow-up is usually done by the CSG/C staff.

Between annual meetings, the staff provides relevant information of varying types to the governors, does "spot research" for the governors, works closely with the Conference's task forces on research (see below), and provides clerical support services.[1]   The CSG/C also works with the MGC Advisory Committee (see below) and serves as liaison between the Advisory Committee and the various task forces. The six professionals in the office complemented by three support staffers spend what has been estimated at 20 to 30 percent of their time serving the Midwestern Governors' Conference.[2]

STEERING COMMITTEE

At the conclusion of the 1962 organizational meeting of the MGC, Chairman William Guy (D-N.D., 1961-1973), felt it would be helpful to have some type of interim Conference organization. Such a mechanism would help prepare the next annual meeting agenda and serve as a prod to the Conference's standing committees.   Thus, the Steering Committee came into existence. The Committee was comprised of the Conference chairman and vice chairman as well as the chairman of each of the three standing committees.

On May 3, 1963, Chairman Guy called the Committee together for what was to be its only meeting between the 1962 and 1963 annual meetings.   Discussion topics included the work (or lack thereof) of the standing committees, the Midwest Governors' Research Institute proposal (see below), and plans for the upcoming 1963 annual meeting.[3]

The Steering Committee next met not long after the 1963 annual meeting, in Chicago on January 31 and February 1, 1964. At that two-day session, the five governors in attendance made plans for holding two special conferences--one on mentally ill offenders and the other on economic development in the Midwest. The Steering Committee approved continuation of the three standing committees and appointed members to each.[4]   The Steering Committee also gave the go-ahead for the North Star Research and Development Institute to undertake a study asked for by the Conference's Committee on Economic Growth. Member states had pledged the $15,000 necessary to conduct the study.[5]

Additionally, the Steering Committee approved a resolution urging a more equitable distribution of federal research dollars and protesting NASA's location of an electronic research center in Boston rather than in the Midwest. This resolution had been prepared for consideration at the 1963 annual meeting but when the meeting abruptly adjourned because of the assassination of President Kennedy, all resolutions had been set aside.[6]

During the second day of its meeting, the Committee turned its attention to further discussion of the proposed Midwest Governors' Research Institute. The consensus was that if they could create such an in-house Conference organization, that would be preferable to the more formal research institute approach. The latter approach had been the one chosen by Southern governors in creating the Southern Growth Policies Board. This board, created to identify problems and work out solutions, had been formed in 1971 by executive orders of nine Southern governors. Sensing that the consensus on what form the research institute should take was not yet formed, the CSG/C staff suggested the creation of an Advisory Committee as "an extension of the existing Conference" and as an immediate answer to the research needs of Conference governors.[7]

ADVISORY COMMITTEE

Upon the recommendation of the Steering Committee, an advisory committee was created. The Advisory Committee would have one member from each Conference state. In order to give the Committee needed political clout, the Steering Committee recommended "that the governors appoint their executive secretaries or other key staff aides."[8]

The chairman of the MGC would be responsible for naming the director of the Advisory Committee. In practice, the director was always one of the Conference chairman's top aides. The director was to report annually to the Conference on the activities of the Advisory Committee. Member states were responsible for financing the travel expenses of aides while on committee business. The Steering Committee specified the following functions for the Committee:

> The Advisory Committee shall attend and monitor all meetings of the Midwestern Governors' Conference. It shall serve as a policy and coordinating body in dealing with all matters requiring research which may come before the Conference. It shall be authorized to establish special committees of state officials to carry out various Conference programs and activities, including research projects. It is intended that the Advisory Committee should have broad powers and responsibilities in order to increase in every possible way the total effectiveness of the Midwestern Governors' Conference.[9]

In creating a committee of top gubernatorial aides, the Steering Committee put itself out of business. The Advisory Committee was incorporated into the MGC's Articles of Organization (Article V) in 1965.

From its inception, the Advisory Committee has been a powerful, active body. The Committee schedules meetings and special workshops, establishes the agendas for the Conference's annual meetings, reviews amendments to the Articles of Organization and carries on research projects for the Conference.

One of the more important functions performed by the Advisory Committee is that of follow-up, of checking on whether decisions made at Conference meetings are carried out. For example, in 1964, the governors had decided to create a committee to look into the prospects, problems, and possibilities of an interstate compact on nuclear energy. By the time of the first Advisory Committee meeting following that decision, governors had not yet sent in the names of aides who were to be named as members of the ad hoc committee to investigate the proposed compact. The Advisory Committee undertook the follow-up to make certain that appointments were made.[10]

The Committee generally meets once or twice a year, unless circumstances dictate additional meetings. Attendance at these meetings of the Advisory Committee usually averages eight or nine aides. The attendance is higher when the Committee meets during the NGA winter meetings.

Over the years, the success of the Advisory Committee has depended on the people named by the governors and how much of the governor's ear each commanded. In looking at the lists of those gubernatorial staffers who have served on the Advisory Committee, it is clear that most governors sent their top aides. Most of the Committee members are members of their governor's inner circle and have the trust of their governors. On the other hand, individuals named to the task forces (see below) are more often subject matter experts, rather than political generalists. The aides assigned to task forces are not usually among the top level of gubernatorial assistants. This has not necessarily been true of task force chairmen, but of the general membership of the task forces.

With the introduction of task forces in 1973, the Advisory Committee began to spend more of its time planning for the annual Conference meeting and coordinating the activities of the various task forces. The CSG/C staff and relevant gubernatorial staffers apprise the Committee of the work being done by the various task forces. The Committee is empowered to review changes in the Articles of Organization, providing an opportunity for representative gubernatorial input on the changes proposed.

COUNCIL OF ECONOMIC DEVELOPMENT DIRECTORS

As might well be expected, the Conference has always paid special attention to the condition of the Midwest's economy. It is a topic discussed at every annual meeting. In July, 1964, the MGC sponsored a special conference on economic and industrial development in the Midwest.[11] One of the outgrowths of that special conference was the creation of the Council of Midwestern Economic Development Directors.[12] At that meeting, Council members agreed to have reports on a number of topics--ranging from the St. Lawrence Seaway to state development organizations--readied for the September Midwestern

Governors' Conference meeting.

The Council had the various reports ready for the governors at their 1964 meeting. The Council had also prepared recommendations on administering federal programs through state development agencies, on regional transportation systems, on regional planning, and on science advisory committees.[13]

The governors approved the reports of the Council and accepted the recommendations of the economic development directors. They went one step farther by establishing priorities for the Council including establishing a Science Advisory Committee for the Midwest; setting up the administration of federal programs through state economic development agencies; analyzing and reporting on export trade; examining university extension services; and exploring the possibilities of each governor creating a staff position to work with industries on improving their chances of federal procurement.[14]

Although existing simultaneously with the Midwest Resources Association (see below), the Council flourished. Its members were directly or indirectly involved in many different projects. The 1966 report of the Council chairman indicated the wide variety of Council undertakings:

> That we do exist as a cohesive entity with economic and political strength is tangibly evidenced by the following: establishment of the Midwest Resources Association in January, 1966; three of the six sites recommended by the National Academy of Sciences for the Atomic Energy Commission's proposed 200 bev portion accelerator are in this region; seven of the states submitted testimony earlier this month opposing toll increases on the St. Lawrence Seaway system; ten of the thirteen states organized foreign trade missions during the last two years (some more than once); tourism directors for the states are meeting and developing programs of mutual regional benefit; the directors of the land grant college agricultural experiment stations of the North Central Region have assigned one of their members to work with the Department of Agriculture to give guidance in the long range locational planning of agricultural research laboratories.[15]

The Council of Economic Development Directors continued to function until approximately 1968. The date of its demise is uncertain. The facts are that its functions were taken over by other conference bodies and that the changes in the format of Conference meetings contributed to the death of the Council. The last official notation relating to council activities was in the 1967 Annual Meeting Minutes.

MIDWEST GOVERNORS' RESEARCH INSTITUTE

In the early part of the decade of the 1960s, most state chief executives had small office staffs. In more than half of the states, extensive borrowing of aides from various departments was necessary if a governor were to do even the minimal tasks expected of him. This was especially true of the smaller, less-populated states in the Midwestern Governors' Conference. Most governors simply did not undertake long-range planning. These were still the days before state planning departments--helped along by generous federal funding--were to spring up.

Nonetheless, there were problems which required research and information sharing. Governor Guy informally proposed the creation of a Midwest governors' research institute at the 1962 organizational meeting. It would be, as he envisioned it, an information clearing house and coordinating body for regional research and promotion in such areas as higher education and economic expansion.[16] Although he had talked up such a body, the North Dakota chief executive did not offer a motion on the matter at that first meeting. Given the fact that it was far from certain before that first meeting that there would even be a Midwestern Governors' Conference, member governors may have decided to wait and see if the Conference was to endure before attempting to create auxiliary organizations. The Conference deferred the matter for action to a later date, pending further study.

Governor Guy was not easily discouraged. Early in 1963, he wrote to each MGC governor requesting that each of them include in their budget requests an appropriation for such a research

institute.   Guy recommended an appropriation rate of ten cents
per college student enrolled in each state.[17] He also asked
fellow governors to support his proposal formally organizing the
Midwest Governors' Research Institute.

At   the   first   meeting   of   the   Conference's   Steering
Committee, members had discussed creating a research institute,
and how such an institute might be financed.[18] The Steering
Committee decided to draw up a draft of a compact to establish
the MGRI and discuss it at their next meeting. The second draft
of the proposed compact was presented at the September 19, 1963
meeting of the committee.[19]   The reworked draft of a compact
which emerged from that Steering Committee meeting set up a
research institute and spelled out its purposes, which were to:

> (a) Improve cooperation among the party
> states in research and investigation, planning
> and   utilization   of educational and other
> institutions and services.
>
> (b) Promote economy and efficiency in
> government by such cooperation.
>
> (c) Facilitate the study of means of
> furthering   agricultural   and   economic
> development of the Midwest and its several
> subregions.[20]

The research institute was to be run by a board of
directors made up of one member from each state. The board
could hire an executive director who could hire a staff of up to
five persons.   The board was empowered to contract for services
and to receive grants and other monies.[21] The board was also
empowered to:

> (a)   Study   the educational and other
> institutional facilities and services of the
> party states, and develop and recommend plans
> and   arrangements   for   the   cooperative
> establishment, operation or use of such
> facilities and services with a view to
> improving their utility for the region as a
> whole, or of such subregion or subregions as
> may be appropriate.
>
> (b) Study and make recommendations with
> respect to programs for the development of
> agriculture, industry and natural resources in
> the Midwest, which study responsibilities do
> not fall within the area of responsibility of

any other interstate agency of the states.

> (c) Encourage and facilitate research and studies by governmental agencies and private organizations or institutions in any field of interest to it.

> (d) Make contracts for research or studies in any field of interest to it.

> (e) Do all things necessary and proper to the carrying out of the exercise of its powers as granted by the terms of this compact.[22]

Strangely, the compact draft did not contain explicit funding provisions. It is quite possible that agreement on such provisions was impossible at that time. This would prove to be the fatal flaw as funding proved to be one of the stickier issues.

Responses to the letter Governor Guy had written to his fellow governors in February, 1963, were not encouraging. Of seven recorded replies, only one governor pledged his state's share (based on the rate of ten cents per enrolled college student). All others expressed the opinion that it would be very difficult for them to obtain state funds for such an organization.[23]

At the September 19, 1963 meeting of the Steering Committee, it became clear that Guy remained the prime mover in trying to create such an information clearing house. Another member of the Committee, Governor Karl Rolvaag (D-Minn., 1963-1967) was not pleased with the idea of an interstate compact and proposed instead an "executive agreement" arrangement.[24]

Two months later, the governors gathered in Omaha for the second annual MGC meeting. In terms of the research institute, nothing had been settled. The agenda for the meeting contained an announcement of a panel presentation on the proposed research institute with time set aside following the panel for discussion by the full Conference membership.

At the meeting, Governor Guy began the session on the research institute by calling the proposed institute a "special research arm of the Midwest governors which would pursue specialized investigations of regional problems,..."[25] Three other speakers on Guy's panel explored the proposed institute. Brevard Crihfield of the Council of State Governments explained that his organization would not be adversely affected by the creation of such an institute. He went on to say that the CSG could not undertake, in behalf of the Midwestern Governors' Conference, the research projects contemplated for the institute.[26]

Mitchell Wendell, Counsel to the CSG, explained that the interstate compact approach had been selected as the preferred vehicle for the institute because it would establish a legal entity separate from any of the member states but which could raise and manage funds, while appearing to be accountable and permanent organizationally.[27] Wendell went on to explore alternative methods of organizing including the non-profit corporation, executive agreement, and "unilateral but parallel statutes" in each of the member states.[28]

The third panelist was one of Governor Guy's chief aides, Lonell W. Fraase, Director of Administration for North Dakota. His topic was the delicate matter of financing the institute. He suggested that the governors first try to obtain seed funds from private foundations to start up the institute:

> The conclusion that I have reached is that assistance for our purpose should be available from several of the larger foundations. In general terms, it appears that basically these foundations are interested in pioneering or experimental projects and seldom aid the operational phases of established programs. This is significant since this is the point which we are at, and at such time as the programs of this conference become operational, I think we will all agree that this would be the responsibility of the various individual states themselves.[29]

The length of the panel presentations limited the discussion following the presentations and the Conference chairman noted that the final business session on Saturday, November 23 would allow time for full-scale discussions and perhaps a final decision on the institute.[30] The Saturday

morning business session was never held. President John F.
Kennedy was murdered on Friday, November 22 and the MGC quickly
adjourned early Friday afternoon, without completing the
scheduled agenda. President Kennedy's death signaled the death
of the proposed Midwest Governors' Research Institute. The
Institute was never discussed again nor formally voted on by the
conference.

There were many obstacles which contributed to the
institute's demise. The biggest problem was that of funding.
At the Steering Committee meeting in January, 1964, the
governors in attendance agreed they "did not wish to create
expensive machinery or organization with sizeable staff to carry
out research."[31] The problem of securing legislative
appropriations for such an institute was a difficult one for
most of the governors. They met with little success when they
asked their legislatures to appropriate money for an institution
over which they would exercise only 1/12 control.

Second, there was the stumbling block of creating a formal
legal entity by means of an interstate compact, as "...they [the
governors] appeared to favor a form of organization which would
be less formal in nature than an interstate compact."[32]
Because withdrawal from an interstate compact would not be easy,
several governors favored a less formal organization giving the
governors greater maneuverability.

Finally, there was concern about the institute's role
vis-a-vis the Midwestern Governors' Conference itself. The
fledgling organization was only two years old and still trying
to carve out a role for itself. Several governors felt that the
institute would not be particularly helpful in that search for
an identity.

Therefore, the Steering Committee killed the idea of a
Midwest Governors' Research Institute and in its place
unanimously approved the creation of the Advisory Committee. If
special research projects needed to be undertaken, the Advisory
Committee was empowered to establish special committees of state
officials to carry out such research.[33]

MIDWEST RESOURCES ASSOCIATION

Long before the successful attempt to establish a midwestern governors' conference, governors were expressing their concerns about the economic vitality of the region. Almost every annual meeting of the conference has featured speakers and panels on the midwest's economic health and welfare.

One of the concerns manifested itself in the general feeling that the Midwest as a region was not getting its fair share of the federal pie. Many felt this condition was traceable to a lack of unified aggressiveness on the part of the midwestern states. Out of this concern and somewhat defensive posture came the idea for a new organization, an organization which would serve as a regional unifier; an organization which would act as a forum for policy planning on federal programs and proposals which affected the Midwest. The idea--first tossed about during the early months of 1964--was to form a regional organization which would work to better the economic conditions of the region. The proposed organization would be called the Midwest Resources Association. "Defense and space spending--or the loss of these to other regions--was a main impetus to the formation of MRA."[34]

It is here that any similarity to previously considered organizations ends. The Association would have as members all MGC governors, the twenty- four United States Senators from the twelve states of the region, and all members (numbering 125 in 1965) of the United States House of Representatives delegations from these twelve states. In other words, it would be an organization of 161 members.

Those governors who were interested in pushing such a proposal--among them Democrat Frank Morrison of Nebraska (1961-1967) and George Romney (R- Mich., 1963-1969)--got together in February and again in June, 1964, to talk over plans for forming such an organization. In July, ten of the twelve governors met in Washington with eighteen of the twenty-four senators. As a report on that meeting noted: "The tenor of the conference was that the senators were unanimous in their opinion that a complete action organization should be established."[35]

In August, eleven of the twelve governors met in Washington again, this time with approximately 100 members of the House of Representatives. Members discussed the uses of and need for such an organization and conducted a mini-survey on regional strengths and weaknesses. Midwestern members of the House agreed to explore the possibilities of such an organization. Shortly thereafter, a committee of two governors, two senators, and two House members was selected to recommend an organizational structure.[36]

The committee recommended an organization be formed and that it be governed by a rather large 24-member Steering Committee and a six-member Executive Committee.[37] Following the reading of a brief statement on the Association, the Midwestern Governors' Conference "...approved the formation of the Midwest Resources Association, but deferred action on financing the Association."[38] The governors also agreed to naming the Conference chairman and vice chairman as the Conference members on the Executive Committee.

The Conference Advisory Committee met January 24-26, 1965, and among various items of business taken up was consideration of a draft of the proposed Association by-laws. A summary of the meeting indicates lengthy discussions about the proposed association.[39]

The organizational meeting of the Association's Steering Committee was held in Washington early in February, 1965. As outlined in the organization's by-laws, the MRA's purposes were to:

> 1. Act as a forum for the planning, development, and coordination of regional programs in such areas as research and development, foreign trade, natural resources, transportation and agricultural products utilization.
>
> 2. Consolidate and disseminate information on state, regional and national programs and program proposals, both public and private, which would affect the Midwestern region's welfare.
>
> 3. Harmonize and coordinate such

programs and proposals into a dynamic,
internally consistent action program designed
to increase the Midwest's contribution to the
nation's growth.[40]

The chairman of the Midwestern Governors' Conference would
serve as the chairman of the Association, chairing both the
Steering and Executive Committees. There were to be two vice
chairmen, one from the U.S. Senate contingent and one from the
U.S. House of Representatives delegations.[41]

The twenty-four member Steering Committee was designed to
be the governing body of the Association. The committee was
empowered to adopt a biennial budget and adopt "whatever
policies it may deem appropriate for the promotion of the
Association's interests."[42]

The Executive Committee was to have two members from each
of the three groups of office-holders. The two governors were
to represent opposite parties and the same would be true of the
pairs of senators and representatives. Each grouping would
select its Executive Committee membership from among the
Steering Committee membership. The chairman and both vice
chairmen would automatically be Executive Committee
members.[43] The Executive Committee was to act for the
Steering Committee during the interim between regular meetings
and was also charged with supervision of the Association's
executive director.[44]

The matter of financing was settled by deciding to "tax"
each state according to the size of its congressional
delegation.[45] An annual assessment of $810 per House seat was
approved.[46] The "taxes" levied on the member states ranged
from a high of $19,440 for Illinois to a low of $1,620 for North
Dakota.[47] With the problems of finances seemingly behind
them, the Steering Committee approved a $100,000 budget for the
Association for the 1965-1966 biennium.[48]

The by-laws were approved by the governors in September,
1964, and were ratified by both congressional groups in January,
1965. The Midwest Resources Association became official with
the adoption of by-laws at its organizational meeting on
February 3, 1965. The new organization was finally off the

drawing board. But, as we will see, there were many hurdles yet in the organization's path.

At the MGC Advisory Committee meeting in the summer of 1965, the Association again received top billing on the agenda. Nine of the 13 member states had pledged money for the Association. Once the money had been pledged, the organization began to move. A decision was made by the Executive Committee to open a Washington office. A press release dated July 21, 1965 carried the news of the organization's new office:

> The Governors emphasized that the office will be non- partisan. Its principal objective will be that of the Midwest Resources Association--to strengthen the combined economic position of the Midwest Region. It will act as a special arm of the Congressional delegation on Washington matters of Midwestern concern and it will work closely with the home States. Planning, development and coordination of regional programs, particularly in the economic sphere, will be a major task of the Association, which was officially established in February.[49]

In deciding to establish a Washington office, the Executive Committee also decided to seek an executive director for the organization. What the Association hoped to accomplish by this move was spelled out in a magazine article:

> They [the governors] voted to set up...a non-partisan office to represent the Midwest. The office will not lobby for the region, as many private offices do, but it will act as a liaison arm for the region's congressional delegations in keeping in touch with Washington's multiplicity of offices and agencies; it will be in constant touch with proper officials in the home States; and it will be a source of invaluable information for businessmen throughout the region.[50]

One of the first challenges for the executive director-less Association was the advocacy of the Midwest sites trying to secure the A.E.C. accelerator. The MGC and the Midwest Resources Association worked hard to secure the 200-BEV accelerator for the Midwest. The lobbying for the accelerator began early and continued for a long time. The competition was intense.[51]

Locating the accelerator at one of the sites in the Midwest was endorsed by the MGC's Committee on Economic Development in July, 1965.[52] The Resource Association's attractive 23-page booklet entitled "The Midwest Resources Association Proposal for the Location of the AEC 200-BEV Accelerator," explored everything from the number of scientists and engineers in each of the Midwestern states to the federal expenditures on research and development in the Midwest. The Midwestern Governors' Conference endorsed the selection of a Midwestern site at its 1965 annual meeting.[53] These were expressions of a new-found regional solidarity, and that solidarity was maintained throughout the site selection process. Regional unity was to be a most valuable asset. Governor Rolvaag, who by this time was chairman of the MGC and hence chairman of the Resources Association, made a formal presentation to the A.E.C. in behalf of the Association and the Conference. The A.E.C. announcement on September 14, 1965, that Illinois "was still very much in the running also produced escalated lobbying action in the entire Midwest, as a further expression of solidarity."[54]

At the 1966 annual meeting, Midwestern governors again approved a resolution, this one endorsing all three of the Midwestern finalist sites at Weston, Illinois; Stoughton, Wisconsin; and Ann Arbor, Michigan. This time, however, the vote was not unanimous. Governor Warren Hearnes (D-Mo., 1965-1973) abstained from voting on the resolution.[55] Most attributed his abstention to a fit of pique over the elimination of the St. Louis site.[56]

Helped by strong, well-placed and senior congressional support in addition to business and industry efforts, the site at Weston was ultimately chosen. The Midwest coalition had been victorious. The unity forged by the twelve Midwestern governors and the Midwest Resources Association had helped immeasurably in strengthening the case for the region in this very difficult fight.

During the early stages of the A.E.C. site selection, the Executive Committee was spending precious time trying to hire an executive director. The first choice of the Committee was Karl

F. Landstrom, Assistant to the Secretary for Land Utilization, U.S. Department of Interior. After failing to reach agreement on the terms of his employment, Landstrom declined.[57] At that point, Governors Romney and Rolvaag recommended their second choice, Jack Watson, Minority Counsel to the House Appropriations Committee. The Executive Committee agreed and the Steering Committee unanimously approved his hiring.[58]

The Association's Washington office opened in January, 1966. Almost at the same instant, the first money problems appeared. Two states had paid through FY 1967, but three had not yet paid for FY 1966.[59] The one problem which had plagued the organization from the beginning--and even before--was still proving to be a difficult problem. At the conclusion of their 1966 annual meeting, Midwest governors got together in a special executive session following the adjournment of the annual meeting. They agreed to several courses of action:

> 1. To call a special meeting of the MGC in conjunction with the National Governors' Conference in July, to "discuss fully the Midwest Resources Association, its future, and alternative means of achieving the basic goals and objectives embodied in the Association's By-Laws."[60] (Emphasis mine.)
>
> 2. The research including a study done by an outside agency profiling the Midwest and analyzing the impact of federal dollars on the region presented to the Association's Steering Committee be collected and assembled and prepared for dissemination.
>
> 3. A financial statement of the Association be made available to the governors at the July special meeting.
>
> 4. That the MGC Secretary/Treasurer (a staff member in the CSG/Chicago office) meet with Jack Watson, the Executive Director of the Association to "give him the benefit of the governors' discussion concerning the Midwest Resources Association."[61]

At that special meeting in July, the governors voted to close the Washington office of the Association.[62] The Association--which had seemed so promising eight short months before--was now dead. Two years of planning had gone for naught.

An obituary would have listed a variety of reasons for the shortness of its life. First, the Association's money problems were never completely resolved. Not all of the thirteen Conference states participated financially. As the Executive Director of the Association noted:

> They [the governors] summoned me into the conference room to give me the sad news. Original enthusiasm had dwindled to the point of apathy. When it was all in the dream stage, it looked so promising. But when they had to enter a line item expenditure in their budgets, it brought on the cold light of reality. Hardly any governor wanted to go to the mat to defend even a few thousand dollars, when there was no demonstrable proof of any good it was doing.[63]

Second, the fact that a growing number of Midwestern states (Illinois, Indiana, Kentucky and Ohio among them) had offices in Washington appeared to the governors of those states to be needless duplication and overlap. In some states, partisanship helped kill the Association. That is, the legislature and the governor were of opposite parties and it was difficult to get appropriations for projects favored by the governor through a hostile legislature.

Third, the Association's one-person staff (other than clerical staff) simply wasn't enough to keep track of hundreds of federal agencies and departments and thousands of federal grant programs. Some governors felt that the MGC contained states with such diverse interests that no single organization could fairly represent the entire region. There were not enough staffers to divide up the region and not enough resources to do the job. Additionally, some governors apparently felt there may have been specific "personnel problems," but declined to elaborate.[64]

Fourth, this was also the time period in which the National Governors' Conference was establishing its Washington office.[65] Coincidentally, that office would first be staffed by the former Secretary/Treasurer of the MGC, Council of States Governments' staffer Charles Byrley.

Finally, in a situation marked by intense interstate

competition for federal dollars, it was a risk betting on the success of an organization seeking to employ a one-for-all/all-for-one approach in a region where unity was still an unfamiliar new idea.[66] If this were not enough, imagine an organization whose executive director was required to take orders from an "amalgamation of [13] governors, [26] senators, and [132] representatives."[67]

Thus, an organization "which could exert a unified effort toward achieving an expanded utilization as well as development of new research capabilities within the Midwest region" died.[68] Perhaps it was from an overdose of expectations and a shortage of resources. Whatever the reasons, it was the only effort of the Midwestern Governors' Conference to land a man in Washington.

MIDWESTERN TECHNOLOGY DEVELOPMENT INSTITUTE

In 1983, the Task Force on Technology and Trade was created. It was to be chaired by Governor Rudy Perpich (D-Minn.) and co-chaired by William C. Norris, Chairman and Chief Executive Officer of Control Data Corporation.

That task force met numerous times during late 1983 and throughout 1984. At the 1984 Midwestern Governors' Conference annual meeting in November, Governor Perpich's task force presented a detailed proposal for the establishment of a Midwestern Technology Development Institute. The report recommended the implementation of structured coordination among state governments, private enterprise and research universities to spur economic growth and job creation through technology development and foreign trade strategies.

The proposed institute was to be the first step in this structured coordination. The institute was designed to be a non-profit, umbrella, policy-setting organization which would: promote cooperative research among member states and with universities and private industry; encourage equitable bilateral technology trade between regional entities and their foreign counterparts, beginning with Japan and Great Britain; establish a Midwestern Technology Trading Corporation; help establish cooperative technology development consortia to link resources of states, universities, and corporations in the Midwest and abroad.[69]

The Institute was incorporated December 27, 1984, with headquarters in St. Paul. Eight states (Illinois, Indiana, Kansas, Minnesota, Nebraska, Ohio, South Dakota, and Wisconsin) were the founding members. Each of the eight governors pledged $50,000 from his state to support Institute activities. Each governor appointed four persons to the Institute's board of directors.[70]

The Institute's board of directors met for the first time on February 5, 1985. Norris was elected chairman. The board adopted by-laws, created committees, discussed finances and began the search for a president.[71] Steve Gage was hired as president and the MTDI felt ready to try to make a contribution to economic development and job creation in member states.

It soon became apparent to all involved that--like other efforts of various types before it--the Institute would not be without cost. At the 1986 annual MGC meeting, Midwestern governors approved a resolution which reaffirmed their support for the objectives and plans of the Institute.[72] The governors also cautiously resolved that "the development of technology requires a long-term commitment before a return on the investment can be realized."[73]

To strengthen their role in the Institute's operations, the governors directed their Advisory Committee to "review and approve a three-year plan and to annually approve the MTDI budget and state assessments to ensure a level of funding consistent with MTDI's objectives."[74]

The Advisory Committee appointed a subcommittee to study the Institute's budget. That sub-committee recommended funding for FY 1987 at the requested level ($1,008,000).[75] But, the sub-committee recommended that future funding be based on success in establishing consortia. The Institute expected to have the first of these--the Family Farm Consortium and the Ceramics Consortium--operational in late FY 1986.

The Advisory Committee directed the Institute president to

develop (by January 1, 1987) a three-year work plan for consortia development with timetables. President Gage was also encouraged to pursue non-state funding thereby reducing dependence on member-state assessments. One state-- Wisconsin--was in default of its FY 1986 assessment. The committee was assured the budget had been scaled back accordingly and that Wisconsin's problems would not raise members' assessments.[76]

At this point in time, the future of MTDI is uncertain. Those who proposed the Institute knew it would not be easy. As Governor Perpich noted: "This is a creative solution to a problem that demands new answers."[77]

The Midwestern Governors' Conference provided an initial launching pad for the Institute. The hope of the governors and their Conference is that the eventual payoff "will be millions of new jobs in the Midwest and a system which will promote open, competitive and equitable conditions for trade and technology cooperation." This was the dream and the promise of Institute-promoter William Norris.

TASK FORCES

One of the more complex problems which has baffled governmental officials at all levels has been the energy crisis and its many ramifications. The tug-of-war between those who would give America the energy she desires and those who believe the environment must be protected even if energy supplies are curtailed is far from resolution.

It was chiefly this complex, multi-faceted problem which turned the MGC toward one of its most productive creations. At the 1972 MGC meeting, governors heard fellow gubernatorial panelists look at "the states' role in the energy crisis versus environmental quality." Upon the conclusion of the panel's presentations, Governor Robert D. Ray (R-Iowa, 1969-1983), invited each of the governors to send two or three of their best experts in geology, environmental protection, and energy to Des Moines for a "working session to find some direction for solving the energy crisis."[78]

Out of this invitation came the prototype of the newest creation--the task force. The Task Force on Midwest Energy Requirements and Environmental Protection met several times during its first twelve months. State delegations--which ranged in size from two to six members--were drawn from geological survey departments, environment protection agencies, state commerce commissions, departments of health, public service commissions, public utilities commissions, and departments of community and economic development. The mingling of political appointees, career bureaucrats and subject-matter experts was helpful in considering the many facets of decision-making in the energy crisis area.

The Task Force reported back to the 1973 MGC meeting as ordered, and was rewarded by being made a permanent body. That first year, the Task Force made eleven recommendations to the governors. The second year the Task Force made 13 recommendations and produced five evaluation reports on energy-related subjects. The third year (1974-1975) saw the Task Force tackle the problem of the natural gas shortage. The Task Force received a $40,000 grant from the Federal Energy Administration to study energy facility siting. The fourth year of the Task Force was yet another year of solid performance. The Energy Policy and Conservation Act enacted in December, 1975, was the result of federal officials and Task Force members jointly developing a program which focused on federal-state cooperation.

In its 1975 report, the Task Force undertook a critical self-evaluation and identified several roles for the future:

Exchange information among the states on energy issues.

Respond jointly to issues relating to federal fuel allocation programs and to proposed changes in these programs.

Advise governors of the implications of pending federal energy legislation.

Promote multi-state energy research and development projects.

Promote multi-state energy conservation programs.

Promote multi-state energy management programs such as facility siting agreements.

Promote multi-state data gathering and information systems.

Serve as a technical forum for the discussion of energy issues.

Develop proposals for state and national energy regulatory reform.

Serve as a regional energy policy forum.[79]

The Task Force rejected the urgings of several states that it function as a regional lobby in Washington. Its members felt it "inappropriate for the task force to engage directly in public information and education programs, believing that the individual states and their governors would be more effective in dealing with their citizens.[80]

Because of the energy task force's successes, other Conference task forces soon followed. At their 1973 Conference meeting, the governors approved a motion setting up a Task Force on the Future of Agriculture in the Midwest.[81] The Task Force quickly broadened its scope to include land use and in 1974, the Task Force's name was changed to the Agricultural Land Use Task Force.[82] Less wide-ranging than the energy task force, the Agricultural Task Force had only one member from each of the Conference states. The Task Force also served as the governors' liaison with the North Central Regional Center for Rural Development and helped in the preparation of a land use study which investigated the historical patterns of land use in the Midwest, the institutions and tools influencing and controlling land use, and a projection of the results of several land use policy alternatives.[83]

The incoming conference chairman for 1975-1976 Governor Richard F. Kneip (D-S.D., 1971-1978) charged the Task Force with assessing the role of the states in commercial and industrial development in rural, agricultural areas of the Midwest, with evaluating land inventories, and analyzing import-export questions.[84] The name of the task force was changed again, this time to the Agricultural Resources Utilization Task Force.

The newly-named Task Force's charge in 1976 was to serve as the mechanism to express midwestern agricultural concerns to the various agencies of the federal government. In other words, the Task Force was to lobby executive branch agencies. The Task Force was also charged with the task of looking at the future of agricultural resources.[85]

Upon assuming the chairmanship of the Conference in 1974, Governor William Milliken (R-Mich., 1969-1983) desirous of pursuing a different interest, created a new task force, the Task Force on Transportation. This was one public expression of the Governor's concern about intrastate rail transportation.[86] In charging the Task Force, Milliken urged them to:

> ...undertake immediate consideration of a unified response to the pending reduction of rail services and operations as proposed by the Federal government under the Regional Rail Reorganization Act of 1974. In addition it should monitor and evaluate pending legislation at the Federal level to ensure that the interests of the midwest are adequately represented and transmitted to Congress.[87]

Although task force members recommended continuation of the task force, its life ended when Milliken's term as chairman ended. This was an example of a task force emphasizing a concern of the Conference chairman, one apparently not shared by many other Midwestern governors.

Governor Kneip--who followed Milliken as Chairman--was one of those not as concerned with the transportation problem as Milliken. Rather, his concern was intergovernmental relations. To that end, he established a Task Force on Intergovernmental Relations to determine "what balance should exist between state governments and the Executive branch of the Federal government."[88]

This newest task force was an unpleasant surprise to some governors since it was a duplication of a National Governors' Association task force. Governor Patrick Lucey (D-Wis., 1971-1977), chair of the NGA committee, was so angered by the duplication of his committee's efforts, he refused to name a

Wisconsin member of the MGC task force. Nonetheless, the Task Force met four times and brought in a report a year later with four policy statements for the governors to consider.

Although the 1976-1977 chairman, Governor Christopher Bond (R-Mo, 1973- 1977, 1981-1985), continued the task forces on Energy and Environment and Agricultural Resources Utilization, he did not continue the intergovernmental relations group. His concern centered on health care and he created a task force to explore that problem. Additionally, Bond directed all three task forces:

> ...not to prepare lists of recommended policy statements for the annual meetings, but rather to report to the Governors on programs which are working in the states. Further, when there are pressing regional concerns that should be presented to national policy makers, the Task Forces are to react promptly, develop the proposed response, and bring it immediately to the attention of the governors for their timely action,...[89]

Over the years, the Midwestern Governors' Conference has used the task forces to study a wide range of problems. Table 6.1 shows the task forces and the years of their existence. As Table 6.1 indicates, several of the task force lasted only a year or two. It is not as though the problems of these task forces were unimportant to the governors of the Midwest. Rather, it is that they simply were not high priority concerns to many of the chief executives.

Although some of these task forces were active, viable operations, others have had a constant struggle to maintain interest, keep up attendance, and produce workable proposals. The Midwestern Governors' Conference Advisory Committee addressed each of those problems at its 1977 meeting when the Committee discussed how task forces might be better utilized.[90] One suggestion offered was to assign a "lead governor" to each task force. The governor would be responsible for the direction and work of the task force and would report on the task force and its activities at each annual meeting.[91] This is close to the model of the Southern Governors' Conference. In that conference, every governor serves on a

148

TABLE 6.1

MGC TASK FORCES

Task Force	Years in Existence
Energy/Environment	1973, 1974, 1975, 1976, 1977, 1978, 1979, 1980, 1981, 1982 1983, 1984, 1985
Agricultural Resources	1974, 1975, 1976, 1977, 1978 1982, 1984, 1985
Transportation	1975
Intergovernmental Relations	1976
Health Care	1977, 1978, 1979
Water Management	1981, 1982, 1984
Capital Formation	1981, 1983
Trade and Technology	1984, 1985

substantive task force. In the SGC, however, there are no separate staff task forces as in the MGC. The SGC's Advisory Committee undertakes all studies for the task forces.[92] At that time, the "lead governor" suggestion never advanced beyond the talking stage.

In 1981, the Advisory Committee suggested additional changes in the format of the annual meetings. These changes would have a real impact on the functioning of the task forces. In fact, the Committee felt so strongly that it adopted a policy statement--a first. The policy statement read:

> The Staff Advisory Committee...recommends that the Midwestern Governors formulate up to four action task forces emanating from the plenary session topics of the summer Conference.

> The member states of each task force would be appointed by the Chairman of the Conference. Upon the indication of their interest, a Governor will also be designated as chair. Each member state Governor will commit to:

> *appoint one private sector representative from business, agriculture, labor or

        academe to the task force

        * commit one half-time state staff person
(or secure the services of a private sector
staff person) to staff the task force

        * participate fully in implementing an
action plan developed by the task force

        A state may serve on no more than two
task forces. Each task force will be charged
with implementing the resolutions passed by
the Conference and pursuing policies coming
from the implementation process and should
meet at least four times during 1981-1982.[93]

One of the aims was to move toward having panels at the annual meetings chaired by governors. The four panels at the annual meeting in 1981 were all chaired by at least one governor, and contained at least three subject matter experts. This format was selected to avoid the problem of governors being "talked at." The new format would spread the experts out and would also allow greater interaction between governors and experts. This format was also designed to increase gubernatorial attendance and participation at the annual meetings.[94]

At the 1981 Conference, nine governors served as panel chairs and one governor served as Conference host. Not surprisingly, 10 governors were present at that meeting. It was the best-attended conference in four years.

In 1982, the Advisory Committee again set up panel sessions chaired by governors. Eight governors participated as panel chairs or moderators as they were called.[95] The number of experts was cut back even more. Not surprisingly, all eight chairs were present at the 1982 annual Conference meeting. The governors who served as panel moderators were governors who were serving as members of the various task forces. This pattern was continued at the 1983, 1984, and 1985 Conference gatherings.

Over the 13 years of their existence, the task forces have drawn mixed reviews. Some of them—like the Task Force on Energy and the Environment—have drawn national praise and have done some truly excellent work. Others have not been so successful. Nonetheless, the governors seem to believe the task forces have been helpful and useful adjuncts to the Conference and its work and deliberations.

It is clear from this examination of the "institutions" which were created to serve the various needs of the Midwestern Governors' Conference that the conference as it was founded was never intended to be just another organization whose existence was only geared to hold an annual meeting for its members to get together. From the early days in 1962, the Conference has demonstrated that it intended to be an ongoing, constantly functioning, multi-purpose organization.

The governors created internal mechanisms to keep the Conference machinery functioning. These mechanisms include the Advisory Committee (preceded by the Steering Committee) and the various task forces. In addition, the Conference governors created various auxiliary mechanisms, ranging from the earliest--the Council of Economic Development Directors--to the latest, the Midwestern Technology Development Institute. Each of these mechanisms bespoke an effort to meet a particular need. Some of these mechanisms worked and some failed. Some were replaced when they failed and others were not. The next chapter will examine the rather fragile nature of the cooperative spirit among Midwestern states. As we will see, anything which splinters this spirit of cooperation reduces the chances for any kind of substantive joint action.

NOTES
==

[1]Virginia Thrall, Assistant Director, Council of State Governments, Chicago Office, private interview, Chicago, February 16, 1977.

[2]James Bowhay, Director, Council of State Governments, Chicago Office, private interview, Chicago, February 15, 1977; Virginia Thrall, Director, Council of State Governments, Chicago Office, phone interview, July, 1986.

[3]Midwestern Governors' Conference, Minutes of Meetings of the Steering Committee, Chicago, May 3, 1963, William L. Guy Papers.

[4]Ibid., January 31-February 1, 1964, Chicago CSG/C Files.

[5]Ibid.

[6]Ibid.

[7]Ibid.

[8]Governors have honored that recommendation. Over the years, the official titles of Advisory Committee members have included: Executive Aide; Administrative Assistant; Executive Secretary; Director of Administration, Office of the Governor; Special Assistant to the Governor; Executive Counsel; Chief of Staff, Office of the Governor; Legal Assistant; Executive Administrative Assistant; Director, Office of the Governor; Assistant to the Governor for Intergovernmental Affairs; and Director, Department of Economic Development.

[9]MGC, Minutes of Meetings of the Steering Committee, Chicago, January 31-February 1, 1964, CSG/C Files.

[10]MGC, Minutes of Meetings of the Advisory Committee, Lansing, Michigan, January 25-26, 1965, CSG/C Files.

[11]MGC, Minutes of the Annual Meetings of the Conference, Minneapolis, Minnesota, September 9-12, 1964, p. 35.

[12]MGC, "The Midwestern Governors' Conference," February, 1969, CSG/C Files. (Mimeographed.)

[13]MGC, Minutes of the Annual Meetings of the Conference, 1964, pp. 39- 41.

[14]Ibid., pp. 50-51.

[15]MGC, Minutes of the Annual Meetings of the Conference, Cincinnati, Ohio, June 19-22, 1966, p. 81.

[16]MGC, Minutes of the Annual Meetings of the Conference, Chicago, Illinois, December 12-14, 1962, p. 22.

[17]Copy of letter from Governor William L. Guy to MGC Governors, February 26, 1963, CSG/C Files.

[18]MGC, Minutes of the Meetings of the Steering Committee, Chicago, May 3, 1963, William L. Guy Papers.

[19]Ibid., Chicago, September 19, 1963, CSG/C Files.

[20]MGC, Minutes of the Annual Meetings of the Conference, Omaha, Nebraska, November 20-22, 1963, Appendix "Second Draft, Midwest Governors' Research Board Compact," Article I.

[21] Ibid., Article II.

[22] Ibid., Article III.

[23] Copies of letters in the file from Governors of Illinois, Indiana, Iowa, Michigan, Minnesota, Missouri, and Ohio, William L. Guy Papers.

[24] MGC, Minutes of the Meetings of the Steering Committee, Chicago, September 19, 1963, CSG/C Files.

[25] MGC, Minutes of the Annual Meetings of the Conference, 1963, pp. 13- 14.

[26] Ibid., pp. 14-15.

[27] Ibid., pp. 16-17.

[28] Ibid., p. 17.

[29] Leonell W. Fraase, Director of Administration, North Dakota (draft of speech presented at the MGC 1963 Annual Meeting, November 21, 1963), William L. Guy Papers.

[30] MGC, Minutes of the Annual Meetings of the Conference, 1963, p. 17.

[31] MGC, Minutes of Meetings of the Steering Committee, Chicago, January 31-February 1, 1964, CSG/C Files.

[32] Ibid.

[33] Ibid.

[34] Loyal Meek, "The Midwest's Man in Washington," Milwaukee Journal, February 16, 1966, p. 10.

[35] MGC, Minutes of the Annual Meetings of the Conference, 1964, p. 36.

[36] Ibid., p. 34.

[37] Ibid.

[38] Ibid., p. 32.

[39] MGC, Minutes of the Meetings of the Advisory Committee, Lansing, Michigan, January 25-26, 1965.

[40] Midwest Resources Association, By-Laws, Preamble, CSG/C Files.

[41] Ibid., Article Two.

[42]Ibid., Article Four.

[43]Ibid., Article Five.

[44]Ibid.

[45]Ibid., Article Seven.

[46]Loyal Meek, "The Midwest's Man in Washington," p. 10.

[47]MGC, General Papers Relating to the Midwest Resources Association, CSG/C Files.

[48]Ibid.

[49]Midwest Resources Association, Press Release, July 21, 1965, CSG/C Files.

[50]Midwest Resources Association, October, 1965, CSG/C Files.

[51]Theodore J. Lowi, Benjamin Ginsberg, et al., Poliscide (New York: Macmillan Publishing Co., Inc., 1976), p. 91.

[52]Ibid., pp. 91-92.

[53]MGC, Minutes of the Annual Meetings of the Conference, Mackinac Island, Michigan, September 20-22, 1965, p. 48.

[54]Lowi and Ginsberg, Poliscide, p. 93.

[55]MGC, Minutes of the Annual Meetings of the Conference, 1966, p. 106.

[56]Lowi and Ginsberg, Poliscide, pp. 99-100.

[57]Memorandum, Charles M. Byrley, CSG to all Midwestern Governors, October 22, 1965, CSG/C Files.

[58]Ibid.

[59]MGC, Minutes of the Special Executive Session, Lexington, Kentucky, February 18, 1966, p. 5.

[60]MGC, Minutes of the Special Executive Session, Cincinnati, Ohio, June 22, 1966, p. 1.

[61]Ibid., p. 2.

[62]MGC, Minutes of the Special Executive Session, Los Angeles, California, July 6, 1966.

[63]Letter, Jack Watson, former Executive Director of Midwest Resources Association to William K. Hall, March 10, 1978.

154

[64]Private interviews with present and former Midwestern governors, conducted between January, 1977 and December, 1983.

[65]William L. Guy, private interview, Casselton, North Dakota, June 6, 1977.

[66]Darwin Olofson, "Midwestern States Office Closes Door," Omaha World Herald, December 18, 1966, p. 9.

[67]Albert Eisele, "Jack Watson is Our Man in Washington," St. Paul Pioneer Press April 17, 1966, p. 8.

[68]MGC, Minutes of the Annual Meetings of the Conference, Bismarck, North Dakota, June 25-28, 1972, pp. 3-6.

[69]"Governors Promote Technology," State Government News, XXVIII (February, 1985), p. 28.

[70]Ibid.

[71]Leonard Inskip, "Regional Institute Pursues a Cooperative Approach to Technology," Minneapolis Star Tribune, February 10, 1985.

[72]MGC, Minutes of the Meetings of the Advisory Committee, Chicago, August 24, 1986, CSG/C Files.

[73]Ibid.

[74]Ibid.

[75]Ibid.

[76]Ibid.

[77]"Governors Promote Technology," p. 28.

[78]MGC, Minutes of the Annual Meetings of the Conference, 1972, p. 4.

[79]MGC, Task Force on Energy Requirements and Environmental Protection, Report, Cincinnati, Ohio, July 23, 1975, p. 20.

[80]Ibid.

[81]MGC, Minutes of the Annual Meetings of the Conference, Rapid City, South Dakota, July 8-11, 1973, p. 33.

[82]MGC, Minutes of the Annual Meetings of the Conference, Minneapolis, Minnesota, July 28-31, 1974, p. 24.

[83]William A. Huemoeller et al., Land Uses: Ongoing Developments in the North Central Region (Ames: Center for Agricultural and Rural Development, Iowa State University, 1976).

[84]MGC, _Minutes of the Annual Meetings of the Conference_, Cincinnati, Ohio, July 20-23, 1975, pp. 41-42.

[85]MGC, _Minutes of the Annual Meetings of the Conference_, Indianapolis, Indiana, July 25-28, 1976, pp. 1-2.

[86]Jerry Moskal, "Transit Panel Takes Shape," _Lansing State Journal_, August 1, 1974, p. 6B.

[87]MGC, _Minutes of the Annual Meetings of the Conference_, 1974, pp. 25-26.

[88]_Ibid._, 1975, p. 41.

[89]_Ibid._, 1976, pp. 1-2. Governor Bond was defeated in 1976 and was replaced by the Vice Chairman Arthur Link (D-N.D.).

[90]MGC, _Minutes of the Meetings of the Advisory Committee_, April 1, 1977, p. 3.

[91]_Ibid._

[92]_Ibid._

[93]MGC, _Meeting Summary of the Meetings of the Advisory Committee_, May 4, 1981, CSG/C Files.

[94]MGC, "Annual Meeting Format Options," Advisory Committee Meeting, May 4, 1981, CSG/C Files.

[95]MGC, _Official Program of the 21st Annual Meeting_, Des Moines, Iowa, July 18-20, 1982, CSG/C files.

CHAPTER SEVEN

A TWENTY-FIVE YEAR SEARCH FOR A ROLE:

THE MIDWESTERN GOVERNORS' CONFERENCE

For the quarter-century of its existence, the Midwestern Governors' Conference has sought to establish an identity and has made every effort to organize itself as an effective regional governors' organization. In trying to establish an identity the MGC took many paths, tried many things. Some worked and some failed. Neither the successes nor the failures came easily. As the MGC discovered, these efforts to establish an identity were complicated by the fact they were taking place in a rapidly changing intergovernmental environment.

CONFERENCE MEETINGS AND PROGRAMS

As noted above, Midwestern governors decided to hold only one meeting a year. Occasionally, a brief meeting in conjunction with the winter meeting of the National Governors' Association would be held. Typical of these mid-winter meetings was the one held in 1985, when Midwestern governors met February 26 in Washington. The meeting was convened at 1:17 p.m. and adjourned 38 minutes later! During that brief meeting (and most of these special meetings were brief), governors heard details about the upcoming Midwestern Governors' Conference meeting in August, listened to a staff update on the Midwest Technology Development Institute, and approved a policy statement urging the federal government to take immediate specific steps to deal with the economic crisis in agriculture.[1] The first two annual meetings (1962 and 1963) were winter meetings, but since that time--except for 1983 and 1984--the annual get-togethers have been summer meetings (see Appendix B for list of annual meeting dates and sights).

The format of the three-day MGC annual meetings is relatively simple. Governors are generally encouraged to arrive the day before the Conference officially opens. That way, the press conferences held by many of the arriving governors can be gotten out of the way before the Conference gets underway. As an enticement, the host governor usually has a major social event for governors and spouses scheduled for the evening before the Conference is to convene.

Over a normal three-day conference, Midwest governors generally spend only 11 or 12 hours in formal sessions. The rest of their time is spent in informal sessions and in social activities. This has led to a considerable number of complaints and some pointed references--by insiders as well as outsiders--about the wasting of time at governors' conference meetings.

One governor has noted that there were too many social activities and too few "working sessions." The same governor lamented holding off the consideration of Conference resolutions (policy statements) until the end of the annual gatherings. He suggested moving that part of the agenda from the third day up to the second day. Too many governors, he said, were leaving early in the morning of the third day.[2] The 1977 Conference is a case in point. Only nine of the thirteen governors remained for the closing business session at which the resolutions were considered.

The media often focus on these charges that the meetings are too heavy on the social schedule and too light on the work schedule. These press reports convey precisely that image:

> There may be better words, but the term bacchanalian fits as a one-shot description of this conference's environment.... With all this ultra-ultra-ultra exterior, the governors showed no disposition to forego play for work.[3]
>
> One thing you can't beat about these

> pow-wows is the working hours. Yesterday's
> business session began at 9:20 a.m. and ended at
> 12:45 p.m. Most of the time is spent in play
> and attending fancy dinners.[4]

The most interesting criticism to appear in the press came not from members of the press corps, but as a quote from one of the participating governors. Governor Harold Hughes (D-Iowa, 1963-1969) left the 1968 Conference meeting in a huff "saying he had more important things in Iowa to occupy his time." Hughes said the conference was accomplishing nothing. "It's a social event," he said. "They adopt meaningless resolutions, then play golf."[5]

As might be expected, Hughes' attitude and especially his remarks angered some of his colleagues. His remarks also spawned a debate. Had Hughes really been critical of his colleagues and the Conference or had he been the victim of misquoting? "The latter," he claimed, phoning Conference chairman Warren Knowles (R-Wisc., 1965-1971). Following up his call with a telegram, the penitent Iowa chief executive noted that he had returned to his home state not in a fit of pique as the press had erroneously reported, but rather to continue his campaign for a United States Senate seat.[6]

These various criticisms notwithstanding, the meetings of the MGC have changed only slightly over the years. Early conferences featured "outside experts" as guest speakers (1962-1966) and as panel members (1967-1968). Gradually, the Conference moved away from using experts from the outside and toward a greater showcasing of the governors themselves as speakers and panel members (1969-1973). Beginning in 1974, governors served as moderators of panels made up of outside experts. This change coincided with the Conference's use of task forces (see Chapter Six).

Beginning in 1978, the governors also featured reports from their various task forces. Sometimes these reports were part of a larger panel presentation while at other times the task force reports themselves became panels. In those cases, the panels were chaired by the gubernatorial staffers who chaired the task forces. By 1981, Midwestern governors decided to follow the lead of their colleagues in the Southern Governors' Conference and assign "lead governors" to each of the task forces. As a result, the programs were rearranged to include panels chaired by those lead governors. The lead governors shared panel responsibilities with subject matter experts.

The topics discussed at the Conference meetings came from a variety of sources including those which resulted from emerging contemporary problems (e.g., the discussion of civi' disturbances in 1967, or the energy crisis in the late 1970s), from what the Conference committees or task forces presented by way of reports, from the activities the Conference was involved in (e.g., the attempt to create an interstate compact on nuclear energy--see below), or from topics the governors themselves requested (e.g., rail transportation, health care, intergovernmental relations), and from topics which interested the Conference chairman. The CSG/C staff also suggests meeting topics.

One of the interesting items of note involving the meetings of the Conference is the continued appearance and reappearance of some topic problems year after year. Table 7.1 tells the story.

In addition to regular annual meetings, the MGC has sponsored several special conferences. The first was the Conference on Economic and Industrial Development held in 1964. One of the outputs of that conference was the organization of the Council of Midwest Economic Development Directors (see Chapter Six). A second special conference also held in 1964 was an Interstate Workshop on the Mentally Disordered Offender. As a result of that meeting and two follow-up workshops, an interstate compact on mentally disturbed offenders was drafted. The conference endorsed the compact in 1965.[7] A third special conference, held in 1966, dealt with the problems of water resources and pollution and tried to formulate plans for combining federal, state and local programs to guard water resources and help fight water pollution.[8]

TABLE 7.1

TOPICS DEALT WITH BY CONFERENCE SPEAKERS
AND/OR PANELS

Topics	Years on Agenda
Education	1962, 1963, 1966, 1967, 1969, 1974, 1976, 1983, 1984
Agriculture	1962, 1963, 1966, 1968, 1971, 1974, 1975, 1976, 1977, 1978, 1980, 1981, 1982, 1983, 1984
Midwestern Economy	1962, 1963, 1964, 1965, 1966, 1967, 1968, 1970, 1975, 1978, 1980, 1981, 1983, 1984
Urban Problems	1966, 1967, 1968, 1970, 1971, 1972, 1976
Energy and the Environment	1964, 1965, 1966, 1968, 1969, 1970, 1972, 1973, 1974, 1975, 1976, 1977, 1978, 1979, 1982, 1983, 1984, 1985
Law and Order	1963, 1967, 1969, 1971, 1972, 1976
Health	1963, 1964, 1965, 1968, 1969, 1970, 1975, 1977, 1978, 1979
On Being Governor	1963, 1965, 1966, 1969, 1970, 1972, 1973, 1975, 1976
Transportation	1963, 1964, 1966, 1967, 1975, 1978, 1980
Taxes	1979, 1982
Water	1977, 1978, 1981, 1982
International Trade	1962, 1982, 1983, 1984

The MGC was a nominal sponsor of two regional gatherings organized by Governor Richard Ogilvie (R-Ill., 1969-1973). Ogilvie invited governors from the then-fifteen-state MGC to a regional conference devoted to examining the problems and benefits of nuclear power.

A few weeks later, Ogilvie hosted a larger conference, this one co-sponsored by the National Science Foundation. The focus this time was on regional potential in cooperative scientific and technological approaches. Noting that it was imperative for the Midwestern states to assume a strong leadership role, Ogilvie stated the challenge for Midwest regionalism.

> After many years of much rhetoric and little action, the Midwestern states are now demonstrating their capacity to give joint attention to the broad spectrum of problems relating to science and technology. ...we have long prized our independence here in the Midwest, but too often this independence has resulted in a provincialism that is anachronistic in an age of supersonic transportation and instant communication. As you know, we are perhaps too typically running behind other regions.
>
> I have noted elsewhere that a long overdue regional consciousness in scientific affairs is emerging in the Midwest. My major charge for you today is to nourish this consciousness.[9]

In 1984, the Midwestern Governor's Conference was one of the sponsors of "Unite for Prosperity in Agriculture," an agricultural workshop for farm leaders. The workshop was held concurrently with the 1984 MGC annual meeting.

In addition to these special conferences, the Midwestern Governors' Conference has investigated other areas (items) of concern to state chief executives. One such problem area in the mid-1960s was nuclear energy.

Southern governors, through the SGC, had created by compact the Southern Interstate Nuclear Board. The Southern Governors' Conference had approved the compact and recommended state approval in 1959.[10] The compact gave SINB no regulatory powers, but created a structure to serve as an interstate advisory and development agency for the seventeen Southern states and was charged with exploring the "full exploitation of atomic energy for economic gain."[11] The board is funded by "donations" from each of the member states.

Midwestern governors decided to look into the problems and possibilities of nuclear energy for their states and so, in 1964, they voted to create a committee to explore and study the appropriateness of an interstate nuclear compact for the Midwest.[12] The committee met in June, 1965, and heard presentations on the SINB, the Atomic Energy Commission and on interstate compacts. The committee decided to draft a compact to be presented to the governors at their 1965 MGC meeting.[13] A compact was worked up in draft form and presented to the governors at that meeting. They decided to approve the concept of a regular nuclear energy compact and appointed a committee ofgovernors to review the proposed compact.[14]

The MGC held a special meeting in conjunction with the Conference on Water Resources and Pollution. The three-member committee of governors authorized at the 1965 annual meeting was ready with its report which urged approval of the proposed compact by the Conference and adoption by Conference states.[15] Adoption of the compact was urged as representing "another major step in strengthening the posture of the Midwest in its goal for balanced economic development and expansion."[16]

As might be expected, the question of funding reared its ugly head. Committee members suggested a budget of $100,000 per year with larger industrial states bearing a larger share of the costs.[17] Additionally, the committee argued, favorable action on a compact in the nuclear energy field would aid in the region's efforts to secure the A.E.C. accelerator.

The Midwestern Governors' Conference decided to formally endorse the proposed nuclear compact and urge its adoption by the thirteen Conference states (through the individual state legislatures).[18] Following this action by the Conference, the compact ran into serious opposition.

In the first five years after Conference approval, only two states approved the compact. At the 1970 conference meeting, Midwestern governors again adopted a resolution urging adoption of the compact.[19] By the end of 1977, the compact had not yet been ratified by six states, the number necessary to submit the proposed compact to Congress for ratification. That there was never any real "sponsor" (promoter) of the compact accounts in part for the slow pace of ratification. An additional factor was the anticipated cost of the nuclear resources authority. This had been the same period (1964-1966) in which the governors were trying to fund the Midwest Resources Association (see Chapter Six) and they were feeling the economic and political pinch.

By 1970, the A.E.C. accelerator had been awarded to a site in the Midwest. Because of this victory, some governors believed that the benefits to be gained from joining such a compact no longer seemed to outweigh the continuing costs of such a venture.[20] As a result, few governors really pushed for ratification in their states.

The failure of the proposed compact rests mainly with the Conference. Conference bodies generated the idea, drafted it into proposal form, endorsed it and watched--seemingly helplessly--while the proposed compact languished amid state (legislative) inaction. There seemed to be little the Conference, as an organization, could or would do to help push the compact through the various state legislatures. It was a revealing look at the powerlessness of the Midwestern Governors' Conference when trying to get sovereign states to approve an interstate compact.

PARTISANSHIP

Because governors' organizations--whether national, regional or special interest--are composed of political office-holders who depend upon winning elections for their positions, the possibility of partisanship is always present. Governors are the de facto political leaders of their state party organizations in all but the most unusual circumstances. More than other state political officials, a governor represents "the totality of interests within his party,"[21] and most try to juggle those interests to form a program for the party.

During the time period 1962-1985, all Midwestern governors have been either Republicans or Democrats. And, as Table 7.2

indicates, the electoral pendulum has swung back and forth
between the two parties. However, except for the periods
1967-1971 and 1979-1983, the Democrats have held a majority of
the governorships.

TABLE 7.2

PARTISAN BREAKDOWN OF GOVERNORSHIPS

Year	Republicans	Democrats
1961	4	8
1963	4	8
1965	5	8
1967	7	6
1969	12	3
1971	5	10
1973	5	10
1975	7	8
1977	6	9
1979	9	5
1981	11	2
1983	6	7
1985	5	8

In addition to the fact that these officeholders are
members of different political parties, add to the equation the
fact that these same party leaders are gathering together to
discuss divisive national and state issues, that a Republican or
Democratic administration is in power in Washington, and that
administration's efforts to solve the nation's (and the
Midwest's) problems will be controversial. The possible (if not
probable) consequences are clashes triggered by political
(partisan) differences. In an organization as tenuously bound
together as a regional governors' organization, such discord
could be a major detriment to that organization's
effectiveness. The organization could become more a
battleground of partisanship than a forum for the exchange of
information and ideas.

Some evidence of this phenomenon is evident when the
governors gather for their national confabs. If the Republicans
hold the White House, Democratic governors usually take pot
shots at the administration. Republican governors have been

known to return the favor when a Democrat occupies 1600 Pennsylvania Avenue.

The Midwestern Governors' Conference has made a conscious and continuing effort to downplay partisanship. Practices such as alternating the Conference chairmanship between members of the two parties has helped as has the appointment of members of both parties to all Conference committees. Conference activities are set up so as to make an open display of partisanship difficult.

The one exception to that standard operating procedure is found in the pre-Conference press conferences held by some of the governors shortly after their arrival at the Conference site. These press conferences are generally held the day before the formal opening of the Conference itself. In this way, governors can be good card-carrying party members, but not on the Conference's time. The intent of these efforts at downplaying partisanship is not so much a matter of making the Conference meetings non-political charades, but rather to make them non-partisan gatherings of governors seeking to discuss and find answers to shared political problems.

In spite of these precautions, there have been partisan incidents. More often than not, they have stemmed from national politics, rather than from regional political circumstances. One such incident was an appearance at the 1964 MGC meeting by former Illinois governor (1949-1953) and then-United Nations Ambassador Adlai Stevenson. Stevenson delivered the main address at the State Dinner. In his remarks, the former Democratic presidential nominee defended the Johnson Administration against attacks made by the 1964 Republican presidential nominee Senator Barry M. Goldwater (Arizona). Stevenson mentioned both Goldwater and his runningmate Congressman William E. Miller (N.Y.) by name in his attack. The Chicago Tribune carried this account of the speech and the reaction to it:

> Adlai Stevenson's use of a non-political forum for a political speech was a leading topic in unofficial discussions today.... Speeches at governors' conferences are

> traditionally non-political, with the agenda
> devoted to administrative problems. Politics
> is supposedly confined to press conferences.
> Stevenson by name attacked Goldwater and
> William E. Miller.[22]

The New York Times also carried an article on Stevenson's attack.[23] The official summary of the 1964 meeting, however, carried no mention of those parts of the Stevenson speech even though the report on the speech was two single-spaced pages in length.[24]

Five years later, the Republicans were to return the favor. The featured speaker at the 1969 Conference State Dinner was former Maryland Governor (1967-1969) and then-Vice President of the United States Spiro T. Agnew. The Vice President used the forum to plump for the Administration's Viet Nam proposals and to decry those who opposed the President's war decisions. Agnew urged the governors to support the Administration, because, he said, there could be no increase in federal aid for state problems until Viet Nam was resolved.[25] One news account summarized the governors' reaction to the intrusion of foreign policy into the Conference agenda:

> Agnew's choice of subject and his
> approach to it were perplexing.... About the
> only mention of Viet Nam in two days of
> serious discussion of state problems was one
> governor's statement that the federal
> government should not wait until the war is
> over to start sharing its revenues with the
> states. Agnew received respectful applause
> after his speech, but was not applauded during
> it.[26]

In 1971, the effects of the upcoming national elections made their presence felt. Governor Warren Hearnes (D-Mo., 1965-1973), led a successful fight "to eliminate a section of an agricultural statement that would pay tribute to President Nixon for his effort to establish trade relations with mainland China."[27]

The Conference has sought to avoid partisan displays by avoiding "extending" an invitation to presidential hopefuls in election years. During the years George Romney (R-Mich., 1963-1969) was governor, a presidential "hopeful" did attend the

Conference. As a Conference member, however, Romney was careful
to be circumspect about openly politicking for his party's
presidential nomination.

Two specific incidents should further delineate the
concerted effort to keep partisanship on the back burner. In
1972, Conference members expressed a great deal of concern over
President Nixon's decision to lift the quotas on importing meat
into this country. To express their displeasure, the governors
set about drafting a resolution. The Democratic governors in
attendance hoped to use the opportunity to sharply criticize the
Republican Administration in Washington (it was, after all, an
election year).[28]   To do so without being obvious was not an
easy task.

A bipartisan two-governor--Democrat David Hall (Okla.,
1971-1975), and Republican Richard Ogilvie--resolution committee
was formed.   This was done "to avoid a partisan political
split."[29]   The resolution drafted by Ogilvie and Hall was
unanimously adopted by the Conference.   The resolution was
generally not critical of Nixon, but asked to meet with him on
the matter.[30] On their own, six of the Democrats in attendance
also okayed a much stronger, more critical statement attacking
Nixon directly.[31]

A second partisan incident also involved the presidency of
Richard M. Nixon.   In 1974, Governor Daniel Walker (D-Ill.,
1973-1977), sought to introduce a resolution which would
establish an accelerated timetable on impeachment and
conviction.   His resolution urged the House of Representatives
to complete its action on impeachment by August 15 and the
United States Senate to complete its deliberations on conviction
by October 1.[32]

This incident is also indicative of the tangled web of
parliamentary maneuverings which mark many political bodies.
Unanimous consent was required in order for Walker's resolution
to be introduced according to the Articles of Organization (see
below).   There were objections from three Republican
governors--Christopher "Kit" Bond (R-Mo., 1973-1977, 1981-1985),
William Milliken (R-Mich., 1969-1983), and Robert Ray (R-Iowa,

1969-1983)[33] Bond noted: "I think it is essential that we stay on the issues with which we as governors can deal."[34] Walker indicated he would seek a suspension of the rules at the following day's business session in an effort to have his resolution introduced for consideration.[35] When he asked for a suspension of the rules to allow introduction of the resolution he got only the vote of Governor Milliken in addition to his own![36] This was more than a little surprising since Milliken had been one of the objectors to the introduction of the resolution in the first place.

Even with all the efforts to control or at least downplay partisanship, sometimes Conference governors introduced it themselves. In his speech as outgoing Conference chairman at the 1980 Conference meeting, Governor Joseph P. Teasdale (D-Mo., 1977-1981)--a candidate for re-election as governor--stressed his record on improving Missouri's economy over the last four years. Some of Teasdale's fellow governors called his speech "campaign fodder" and expressed surprise that he had used the Conference forum for such a predominantly political address.[37] Said Lee Dreyfus (R-Wisc.) of the speech, "He gave us a good speech on his platform." "But," continued Dreyfus, "it caught me by surprise that he was campaigning here."[38] Republican Governor William Janklow (South Dakota) was less charitable in his remarks: "When I hear a political speech, I don't listen. So while he was talking, I got some reading done."[39]

The open displays of partisanship have been so infrequent, however, that most governors felt that partisanship was not really a serious problem in the MGC. Responses included these explanations: "There are fewer media people in attendance.... Smaller groups seem to be less inclined to divide along party lines.... National issues often lend themselves to partisan divisions while regional issues are less likely to divide in that manner.... The atmosphere was cooperative, cordial, friendly, non-combative.... Less 'posturing' due to absence of national press corps always in attendance at National Governors' Conference meetings.... With fewer governors aspiring to be

170

president or vice president, there was less partisan
bickering.... There wasn't much partisanship because the
governors were there to learn, not to preen in front of the
press...."[40]

Perhaps regional governors' organizations such as the
Midwestern Governors' Conference can operate successfully in a
nonpartisan mode because there is partisanship displayed at the
National Governors' Association meetings and in those partisan
governors' conferences which have more recently sprung into
being. Although some social scientists decry the non-political
facade of governors' conferences, Midwestern governors believe
it is necessary as well as helpful to be on good terms with your
neighbors.[41] For these reasons, the differences which exist
at the Midwestern gatherings generally are not partisan in
origin.

THE MGC'S ARTICLES OF ORGANIZATION

Drafters of state constitutions have done it for years.
So, when it came time to draw up a set of rules for the
Midwestern Governors' Conference, governors turned to a set of
rules already in use. The pattern for the drafting of the MGC
Articles of Organization were the "rules" governing the Southern
Governors' Conference. There were seven articles approved at
the 1962 meeting in Chicago (the Articles, as amended, can be
found in Appendix C). As originally adopted, the Articles of
Organization contained these provisions.

Article I defined the name and listed member states.

Article II spelled out the functions of the Conference:

> The functions of the Midwestern
> Governors' Conference shall be to foster
> regional development, to attain greater
> efficiency in state administration, to
> facilitate interstate cooperation and improve
> intergovernmental relationships, and to
> provide a medium for the exchange of views and
> experiences on subjects of general importance
> to the people of the Midwestern States.[42]

Article III outlined meeting plans. Annual meetings were
prescribed, with seven members constituting a quorum. The

chairman or a majority of members could call a special meeting.

Article IV provided for Conference officers--a chairman and a vice chairman. Both were to be elected and were to have a vote in conference deliberations. The chairman was to arrange the program of the annual meeting and appoint a nominating committee and a resolutions committee to serve at the annual meeting. The chairman was authorized to appoint such other committees as deemed necessary. Standing committees were to be appointed by the chairman upon their creation by the Conference. The vice chairman was to preside in the chairman's absence and succeed to the chairmanship should the chairman be unable to perform his duties.

Article V provided for the Council of State Governments to serve as the Conference's secretariat.

Article VI on resolutions was as restrictive as the rules governing resolutions in the early days of the National Governors' Conference (see Chapter Three). The Article read:

> Any proposal for an expression of opinion by the Midwestern Governors' Conference shall be prepared in the form of a resolution and shall be submitted to the Resolutions Committee.
>
> Any resolution shall be deemed adopted only upon obtaining the unanimous favorable vote of the membership present and voting.[43]

Article VII provided that the Articles of Organization could be amended by a majority vote of members present at the meeting. Notice of the amendments with explanatory statements had to be mailed to all members at least 30 days prior to a vote. If such notice was not given, a 3/4 majority vote of those present shall be necessary to amend or suspend the Articles.

Since the original Articles were adopted, a number of changes have been made. In 1965 (at a Special Meeting of the Conference), two new articles were added. A new Article V confirmed a pre-existing arrangement of governors' aides serving on an Advisory Committee (see Chapter Six) and provided official status and duties for the committee.[44]

A new Article VI provided for dues of $100 per year per

state to help defray general Conference expenses. The article also provided for a Treasurer (an assignment filled by a CSG/C staff member) and for the collection and disbursement of funds.[45] Old Articles V, VI, and VII became Articles VII, VIII, and IX respectively.

Article V would remain as originally adopted for 14 years. In 1979, however, several changes were incorporated into the article. The title of Article V was changed to "Committees and Task Forces." The revised article stipulated--with two exceptions--that no committee or task force would continue for more than one year unless specific action were taken to extend the life of such committee or task force.

The two exceptions included the Staff Advisory Committee, previously the whole subject of old Article V and the Energy and Natural Resources Task Force which by that time had been designated the Midwestern Regional Energy Advisory Board as required under Sec. 655 of the U.S. Department of Energy Organization Act.

At the regular annual meeting in September, 1965, another amendment was adopted. Article I was changed to add Kentucky as the thirteenth member of the Conference.[46] At the Conference meeting in 1967, Conference membership was raised to fifteen when Oklahoma and West Virginia were admitted as members in the presence of the governors of both states. Both were guests of the Conference during that meeting.[47]

In 1978, West Virginia withdrew from Conference membership, citing time and staff investments and the costs of participation in the NGA, the SGC as well as the MGC.[48] In 1980, Oklahoma ended its Conference affiliation for many of the same reasons.

The 1966 meeting altered the article on the adoption of resolutions. The changes allowed resolutions to be brought directly to the floor for a vote (if unanimous consent were obtained) thus bypassing the Resolutions Committee. Second, if the Resolutions Committee disapproved a resolution it could still be brought to the floor if a 3/4 majority vote were obtained. Whereas the original set of articles had required a unanimous vote for approval of a resolution, the 1966 changes pared that to a 3/4 majority of those present and voting. Lastly, provision was made for amending a resolution by a simple majority vote of those present and voting.[49]

Three years later, the article on resolutions was again the target for change. The 1969 changes abolished the Resolutions Committee. The National Governors' Conference had abolished its resolutions committee six years before, in 1963. The national group had abolished its committee as a result of the tensions which resulted from Governor Nelson A. Rockefeller's (R-N.Y., 1959-1973) efforts to get state governments to take the lead on civil rights.[50]

When the MGC abolished its resolutions committee, it provided for resolutions to be considered only when unanimous consent was obtained. The 3/4 majority vote for passage was not altered, but the vote to approve an amendment to a resolution was raised from a simple majority to a 3/4 majority of those members present and voting.[51]

The 1969 changes in the resolutions article were a result of the efforts of Conference Chairman Governor Warren P. Knowles (R-Wisc., 1965-1971) who had written the Advisory Committee about the "purpose and necessity of the profusion" of resolutions.[52] Governor Knowles also took his case to Brevard Crihfield:

> It has been ridiculous to follow the procedure of having resolutions submitted in profusion with little time to consider the proposals, and the resolutions committee saddled with the horrendous task of considering the scope, breadth, and implication of the proposals within a minimum time.
>
> I'll never forget the Lake of the Ozarks conference [1967] when Harold Hughes and I sat up until about 3:00 in the morning considering 150 resolutions, and he finally, in a state of frustration and in a bad humor, stormed out of my room saying, "To hell with it! You act any way you want."[53]

The 1969 changes also introduced a new term into the Articles, and reference thereafter was to "Policy Statements" rather than to "Resolutions." The genesis for that change may have been the National Governors' Conference. Beginning in 1969, "resolutions" came to be known as "policy statements" in that organization.

No further tinkering occurred until the 1973 Conference get-together. As was true in 1966 and again in 1969, the resolutions article was democratized some more. Policy statements could be considered by a 3/4 majority vote (down from the 1969 requirement of unanimous consent), but only if the policy statement had been submitted to the members of the Conference in writing at least 15 days prior to the opening business session of a Conference meeting. Those not in writing and not submitted 15 days in advance still required unanimous consent. Those requiring unanimous consent also had to be presented no later than the business session of the day before final adjournment and then would be voted on during the Conference's final business session.[54]

Still more changes in Article VIII occurred in 1975. So much tinkering around with the article had occurred that part of it contradicted other articles. The Conference chairman for 1973-1974 J. James Exon (D-Nebr., 1971-1979) asked the CSG Midwest Office to review the Articles of Organization and propose solutions to clear up the problems and contradictions.

The CSG staff proposed that "policy statements" be pre-filed at least 15 days in advance so as to be in the governors' hands 10 days prior to a meeting. The problem of considering policy statements at one-day special meetings was provided for.

Article VIII was extensively rewritten in 1979. The only change of any substance, however, was to require that any policy statement not properly prefiled must be submitted in writing to each attending governor no later than the day before the policy statement was to be considered.

In 1975, Article IX was changed to take care of a contradiction involving suspension of the rules. Policy statements were to be excluded from the suspension of the rules. Thus, the unanimous consent requirement for policy statements introduced later than the 15-day deadline would always be in effect.[55]

Except for the many changes in the article relating to policy statements or resolutions, over the 24-year history of the Conference, there have been remarkably few changes in the rules of the organization. The rules have generally remained simple and uncluttered, thus allowing the Conference considerable flexibility in changing its meeting format without having to change either the formal rules or the by-laws.

CONFERENCE OFFICERS

The Conference selects only two officers--Conference chairman and vice chairman. The chairman has several duties: (1) to preside at Conference meetings, (2) to arrange the program of the annual meeting, (3) to appoint any committees deemed necessary, and (4) to appoint a nominating committee to nominate Conference officers. The chairman serves in office until the adjournment of the succeeding annual meeting and until a successor is chosen.

It should be clear that with the power to determine the annual meeting agenda as well as the power to create any special committees he so desires, that the Conference goes in the direction the chairman chooses. More than a few chairmen have used the position to further causes they personally championed.

The vice chairman presides in the absence of the chairman and assists the chairman in whatever manner is appropriate. If the chairman is unable to fulfill the duties of the office, the vice chairman succeeds to all duties. That has occurred on four separate occasions. In all four cases of the inability of the chairman to fulfill his duties, the cause was the governor leaving office. Three governors--Norbert T. Tiemann (R-Nebr., 1967-1971), Christopher S. Bond (R-Mo., 1973-1977, 1981-1985), and Charles Thone (R-Nebr., 1979-1983)--were defeated in re-election bids. The other, Illinois Governor Otto Kerner, was appointed to the federal appellate bench by President Lyndon B. Johnson.

When a vacancy has occurred (as happened in 1968, 1971, and 1977), the vice chairman who has moved up to assume the duties of chairman is held over for a full year of his own, the rationale being that he did not become chairman until approximately the first of the calendar year so he has not had time to put his own imprint on the Conference.

At the 1979 meeting, an important change was made in the Articles of Organization. A paragraph was added to Article IV ("Chairman and Vice Chairman") which read: "In the case of vacancy of both offices the most recent past Chairman who is still a member shall call a meeting as soon as practicable in order to elect one or both officers." Although it may not have seemed so at the time, this was a fortuitous addition to Article IV.

On September 1, 1981, John Carlin (D-Ks.) was elected chairman (he had been vice chairman). Governor Dreyfus was elected vice chairman. This would ordinarily have meant that Governor Dreyfus would assume the chairmanship for 1982-1983. Somewhat surprisingly, Dreyfus decided not to seek a second term as governor in 1982.

At the 1982 MGC annual meeting, since Dreyfus would not be continuing as governor, the Republicans had to choose a successor to Governor Carlin as chairman. On July 20, 1982, at the final business session of the annual meeting, governors elected Charles Thone as Conference chairman. No problem.

But there was a problem on the Democratic side of the aisle. Because 11 of the 13 member governors were Republicans, there were only two Democratic governors. One was John Carlin who had just completed a term as Conference chairman. The other was John Y. Brown (Ken., 1979-1983), who would be leaving office in late 1983.

So, there were no eligible Democrats to serve as vice chairman. Rather than violating the party rotation, the governors decided to leave the vice chairmanship vacant.[56] It was expected that the 1982 elections would produce some new Democratic governors in the Midwestern states. The governors agreed to delay filling the post until their February, 1983 meeting, held in conjunction with the winter meeting of the NGA.[57]

The saga was not yet finished. Governor Thone was defeated in his bid for re-election in 1982. That left the question of who would succeed him as MGC chairman "still up in the air."[58]

The Articles of Organization provide that in the event of a vacancy in both MGC positions, the most recent Conference chairman who is still a member shall call a meeting to elect those two officers. The most recent Conference chairman was John Carlin and in early January, 1983, he notified fellow governors that there was to be a special Conference meeting on Sunday, February 27 at the beginning of the NGA winter meeting.[59]

Neither fate nor the voters had been kind to Midwestern Republican gubernatorial candidates in the election of 1982. When the smoke cleared on the day after the election, there were only six Republican governors compared to 11 before the election. One (James Thompson from Illinois) was a past chairman, one (Robert Orr from Indiana) was then serving as chairman of the Republican Governors' Association and therefore wanted to "pass at this time on MGC,"[60] and one (Terry Branstad from Iowa) had just been elected. From the short list of remaining Republican governors, Governor Christopher "Kit" Bond of Missouri was elected chairman. It was a special bit of irony as Bond's first stint as chairman had been cut short by his own defeat at the polls in 1976. Another governor's defeat would place him back in the chairmanship almost seven years later. Governor Rudy Perpich (D-Minn.) was elected vice chairman. The leadership crisis was over.

Although it is not spelled out in any of the Articles of Organization, the MGC has honored an unwritten rule of alternating the chairmanship between the two parties. Governor Guy was conference chairman in both 1962 and 1963 and he was followed by fellow Democrat Frank Morrison. Since that time, however, the chairmanship has alternated every year.

A second unwritten rule has kept any governor since 1963 from being chairman more than once unless he assumes the office in mid-term from the vice chairmanship. Governor Guy is the only governor to be elected to serve two complete terms as chairman.

A third unwritten rule is that the vice chairman is always nominated for the chairmanship. Except in cases of the vice chairman leaving the governor's office, the vice chairman has always moved up to the top rung of the leadership ladder.

A look at the list of governors (see Appendix B) who have served as Conference chairman would lead to the conclusion that the Midwestern Governors' Conference does not usually rush a governor into the chairmanship. The average length of time in office before serving as chairman is four years, an average which includes the three vice chairmen who moved up a year early to fill the chairmanship.

RESOLUTIONS AND POLICY STATEMENTS

One of the more visible activities of the annual MGC meetings is the consideration of resolutions, or policy statements as they came to be known. The introduction and consideration of resolutions usually get press coverage, especially if there is any controversy surrounding the resolutions.

From 1962 through the 1968 meeting, resolutions were routinely reviewed by the Resolutions Committee. Until the rules were changed in 1966, that was the only way resolutions could be presented to the governors. If the Committee said "no" that was that. The 1966 rules changes permitted by-passing the Committee. The Committee was subsequently abolished in 1969.

As Table 7.3 indicates, the governors' enthusiasm for resolving has waxed and waned. Over the Conference's first four meetings, only a handful of resolutions were considered. Then, in the fifth annual meeting, 13 resolutions were approved. Drawing away from passing numerous resolutions after 1968, the governors did not regain an interest in wholesale resolving until 1974. The high point in terms of sheer numbers was at the 1975 meeting when 32 resolutions were okayed.

Midwestern governors have considered a wide range of topics as subjects for policy statements. They have approved policy statements urging the establishing of meat import quotas, opposing the reduction of the federal budget for school lunch programs, supporting the deregulation of natural gas, urging uniform funding and administration on Indian reservations, urged members states to establish a uniform minimum drinking age of 21, supported the creation of a national energy supply policy, supported the President's policy to deregulate oil prices, endorsed legislative programs on state health insurance and health cost containment programs, and the request for permitting the National Guard to use military helicopters during peacetime for non-military purposes. There were so many policy statements presented at the 1976 meeting that two of those approved contradicted each other.[61]

TABLE 7.3

MGC RESOLUTIONS AND POLICY STATEMENTS

1962	5	1974	11
1963	0	1975	28
1964	3	1976	32
1965	4	1977	5
1966	13	1978	9
1967	22	1979	22
1968	11	1980	3
1969	2	1981	11
1970	4	1982	6
1971	4	1983	10
1972	2	1984	7
1973	2	1985	5

It might be assumed that any organization passing resolutions in such volume must have faith in the value of the practice. Such an assumption would be seriously weakened when one listens to individual governors comment on the subject. Comments reported at two Conference meetings are typical examples. At the 1976 confab, Governor Christopher Bond said the governors at the MGC should stop passing resolutions "on topics over which the governors have no control."[62] At that same meeting, Governor Robert Bennett (R-Kansas, 1975- 1979), criticized his fellow governors for passing "meaningless resolutions."[63] Bennett escalated his rhetoric one year later when he noted: "I'm getting a little tired of these milksop resolutions that we pass out in an effort to develop unanimity and then finally find out all we're unanimous about is that we like each other and don't want to interfere with anyone else's having a good time."[64]

These two outspoken governors represent the thinking of many of the past and present members of the Conference. A number were critical of the large number of resolutions to be considered, while others were critical of the lack of time to properly deal with the resolutions. Still others found fault with the "generality" of the policy statements.[65] A representative sample of quotes from the governors would include the observation of one chief executive that: "Resolutions were the biggest waste of time. They send them down there (to Washington) and they're forgotten." Another said: "Resolutions are one of the problems of governors' conferences. There are too many resolutions. They are too time-consuming." One governor observed: "Resolutions were very ineffectual. No one other than very junior bureaucrats ever reads them." Finally, this viewpoint: "We have to quit adopting so many resolutions. Too many governors 'posture' on the resolutions and there is seldom a 'nay' heard."[66]

In spite of these feelings a large number of resolutions are introduced as instruments of Conference policy each year. Each year finds the governors back at the same old stand--passing more resolutions. "Gubernatorial courtesy" is one of the main culprits in continuing the practice. The resolutions are often sponsored by individual governors--sometimes purely for press consumption--and governors are loathe to step in and say "no" to a fellow office-holder/office-seeker.

Although Conference members' rhetoric contain numerous references to the ineptitude and general poor condition of the federal beast in Washington, governors spend quite a lot of time asking for action by the federal government. Including resolutions requesting either positive or negative responses, 58 percent of all resolutions (128 or 221) passed during the first 24 years of the Midwestern Governors' Conference existence were addressed to the national government. Brooks' study of the National Governors' Conference found that 60 percent of the national governors' group resolutions okayed between 1943 and 1959 asked for federal government action of one kind or another.[67] It remains politic to curse the federal establishment, but it also remains politic to ask the same cursee for help in problem-solving.

What happens to the resolutions once the governors have approved them? Once the conference membership approves the resolutions, they were placed in the Minutes of the Annual Meetings (discontinued after the 1978 Conference), featured in home state press reports, and mailed to "relevant" government officials. For those governors running for re-election, the resolutions were likely to be used as evidence of the governor's concern about problem "X" and his leadership efforts to deal with the problem.

LOBBYING

It is the presentation of these resolutions to government officials that symbolizes what has been a bone of contention for many years among the nation's and the region's governors. The decision to turn to lobbying was the activity which most contributed to the breaking up of the NGC/CSG partnership in 1977. It is one answer to the nitty-gritty question about governors' conferences--what happens to the output of the conferences? What of the follow-up to decisions reached and resolutions approved at the conferences?

In seeking to follow up on the actions taken at governors' conferences, the path often leads to Washington. One question often asked is whether governors' conferences as governors' conferences should engage in lobbying. The answer to the question "to lobby or not to lobby," caused the Council of State Governments and the National Governors' Conference to go their separate ways. It should be stated at this juncture, that there are basic differences between the governors as individual governors representing their states and lobbying and the Midwestern Governors' Conference or the National Governors'

Association as conferences of governors lobbying. Let us first look at the latter case.

The MGC does not follow up on most resolutions passed at their annual meetings. Copies of resolutions requesting some type of federal action are routinely sent to members of Congress and to relevant units and individuals in the executive branch. Sometimes they are sent by the CSG/C office. Sometimes they are sent over the signature of the Conference chairman. Once they are sent out, however, the Conference does little or nothing else. There are several reasons for this.

First, the Conference as an organization is not really organized to follow-up on actions taken at the Conference meetings. Except for the various task forces working on the assigned tasks (and staffed more with subject matter experts than political generalists), the only ongoing Conference apparatus is the Advisory Committee. In recent years, the Advisory Committee has concerned itself primarily with the planning of annual meetings.

Second, the CSG/C staff cannot lobby. They are prohibited from doing so for "political reasons," because they are already understaffed, and because the IRS code currently qualifies the CSG as a tax-exempt organization, a status which might be jeopardized by the Council taking on an advocacy role for the Midwestern Governors' Conference.

Third, except for individual governors, there is no one else left. There are some who believe the Conference chairman should be the group's chief lobbyist. This might work except in those instances when the chairman may have voted on the losing side. The chairman might also have a problem as Conference spokesman when member states are evenly split on an issue, or when the chairman's home state has views at odds with the resolution which was passed.

The MGC has fought a 24-year battle with itself about the role the Conference should play in lobbying. At nearly every Conference gathering, the question has been a non-agenda topic of discussion. In the mid-1960s, the Conference established the Midwest Resources Association (see Chapter Six). The

Association was designed to be a lobbying organization with a Washington office established for that very purpose. Due to a variety of problems, however, the Midwest Resources Association lasted only about two years.

The problem facing the governors is a simple one. It is difficult to get anyone to listen to them. That is especially true of officials in the federal bureaucracy. An editorial written during the 1977 Conference meeting expressed the governors' common lament:

> Governors of the Midwestern States are meeting...this week, but anyone expecting anything important to come out of that meeting is sure to be disappointed.
>
> While the National Governors' Conference demands a certain amount of respect because of the political power the Chief Executives of the nation's States can muster, the regional meetings haven't turned out to be very influential.[68]

One of the governors in attendance at the 1977 MGC meeting put the problem of gubernatorial input on federal policy decisions even more strongly. Governor Julian Carroll (D-Ken., 1974-1978), said he had testified before numerous congressional committees (in his capacity as a representative of the National Governors' Conference), and they largely ignored his statements. "They were polite. They listened, and they asked questions," he said. "Then they did as they pleased."[69]

There would seem to be several reasons why Midwestern governors have had trouble finding a friendly ear on Capitol Hill. For one thing, they are viewed warily as potential political rivals. Governors have been known to covet the seats of sitting members of Congress, especially those sitting in the United States Senate. The position held by a governor is a political target as well. It is no secret that some members of the United States House of Representatives have been known to covet the office of state chief executive. These tendencies to covet do not necessarily result in easy, smooth, and cooperative working relationships.

Second, there is the problem of partisanship. Governors

are not always of the same political affiliation as a state's senators or a state's congressional delegation. As a result, disputes over such political stocks- in-trade as patronage appointments may contribute to cool relations.

Third, those who inhabit the national legislative chambers or the federal bureaucracy often have different perspectives on problems and how they should be solved than do those who are elected to positions of state executive leadership. Differences in institutional style of operation and time frame reference are indicative of these dissimilarities. Governors with constitutional or statutory limits on their tenure may see problems with a greater sense of urgency than do legislators or career federal bureaucrats.

Fourth, the MGC has a difficult time speaking as a single, unified, and cohesive unit on some of the pressing issues of the day. The one-time fifteen- and now thirteen-state region is quite diverse in its interests, its politics, its resources, and it economics. The old (and seemingly simpler) divisions along the bases of industrial versus agricultural and rural versus urban are long gone. The divisions of today threaten the old ways, and cause all states to re-examine their lists of allies and enemies. Many find there may have been movement between the two lists.

An excellent example of this new type of division would be the problems attendant to America's energy crisis. At the 1973 Conference meeting, Governor Patrick J. Lucey (D-Wisc., 1971-1977), sought to introduce a resolution expressing support for a study on alternate routes for the Alaskan pipeline, especially alternate routes (terminating in the Midwest) such as the Trans-Canadian route. Conference chairman Governor Robert Ray ruled the motion to introduce the resolution out of order. By a vote of 3-8, however, Conference governors voted to override the chairman's decision and suspend the rules.[70] The resolution was introduced. Standing with Ray (in defeat) were Governors Otis Bowen (R-Ind., 1973-1981) and J. James Exon (D-Nebr., 1971-1979).

Lucey later called his resolution up for discussion. There

were lengthy discussions on the issue. When the vote came, it
went five (Illinois, Indiana, Minnesota, Nebraska, and
Wisconsin) for approval of the resolution, six (Iowa, Kansas,
Missouri, North Dakota, Oklahoma, and South Dakota)
against.[71] The vote was strictly a matter of oil user versus
oil producer states. Two governors who had already left the
Conference meeting (Milliken and John Gilligan (D-Ohio,
1971-1975) were in favor of Lucey's resolution and the
resolution would have passed had they been present. Governor
Wendell Ford (D-Ken., 1971-1974) was also absent by that time,
but was known to oppose the resolution.[72] This issue did not
divide along the old familiar divisions. Partisan politics did
not figure in this vote. Instead, the vote was a reflection of
the range of needs of the various states. This dichotomous
range of needs makes the charting of a path of unity difficult.

In 1977, the MGC decided to try something new. A
suggestion was made to appoint a committee to coordinate the
lobbying efforts on energy legislation and to marshall the
forces of the 15 Midwestern governors. There was strong
sentiment among the governors present that the Conference as a
unit ought to get directly involved in the lobbying of Congress
on the problems of the energy crisis and on the Carter energy
bill. Conference chairman Arthur Link (D- N.D., 1973-1981)
named a three-member coordinating committee composed of
Governors David Boren (D-Okla., 1975-1979), Otis Bowen, and J.
James Exon.[73]

The coordinating committee proved to be a short-term
arrangement set up to deal with the President's energy proposals
before the United States Senate. It did not turn out to be the
first step toward some kind of permanent lobbying mechanism for
the Conference.

Another possibility for governors to have input in the
decision-making process is for each of the Conference governors
to contact his own congressional delegation and try to influence
policy outcomes in this way. Following the congressional
reapportionment after the 1970 census, there were 138 U.S.
Representatives from these 15 member states and 30 members of

the United States Senate. The House delegations for these
Midwestern states ranged in size from 24 members (Illinois) to
one member (North Dakota).[74] Following the reapportionment
after the 1980 census, there were 120 Representatives from these
13 member states plus 26 members of the Senate.

When governors and former governors were asked whether they
regularly took up the Conference-approved resolutions with their
congressional delegations, three out of four said they took up
only "relevant" resolutions with their delegations.[75] Quite
often, however, this "taking up" consisted of writing a letter
to the legislators with copies of the resolutions enclosed.

When governors were asked whether the MGC should involve
itself more directly and more actively in federal level
lobbying, the answers were evenly divided between those saying
"yes" and those who opposed the idea. A large number expressed
the belief that lobbying was best left to the individual
governors. Others expressed the opinion that if the Conference
did begin unified lobbying efforts, the CSG/C should coordinate
those efforts, even though it could not do the actual
lobbying.[76]

REGIONALISM AND THE MIDWESTERN GOVERNORS' CONFERENCE

Just barely below the surface is the swift, strong and
dangerous current known as regionalism. "Regionalism has been a
persistent if not always persuasive part of the American
political tradition."[77] The common tendency has been to think
of regionalism in America primarily from a geographic
viewpoint. Nonetheless, the concept of regionalism also has
attitudinal, economic, social and political dimensions as
well.[78]

By the end of World War II, the south, the west, and the
northeast were each exhibiting a distinct "regional
consciousness."[79] These regions exhibited such regional
consciousness because the governors of these states found it
helpful to join together in attacking the economic problems
which plagued their states and regions.[80]

The health of the post-war industrial giants in the Great

Lakes states and the health of the agricultural economy spared the Midwestern states--temporarily--from the necessity of having to cooperate with each other. There was little reason, little impetus to cooperate.[81]

One of the enduring problems of the Midwestern Governors' Conference is that of trying to pinpoint a definition of the Midwest as a region. One scholar has stated his view that: "The Midwest is both a geographical location and a state of mind."[82] Another has said: "Midwest, then, is simply a generic term that can be applied with only relative accuracy to portions of the Ohio-Mississippi-Missouri basins, an area that shades off imperceptibly into East, Southwest, and West."[83] Perhaps the only really practical analysis of the Midwest as a region is one which concludes: "The Middle West is the region left over after the remaining states are assigned to the Northeast, South, or West."[84]

Which states make up the "Midwest"? Which states share a distinctive "regional consciousness"? One commonly accepted definition is that the Midwest is made up of the 12 states which were charter members of the MGC. When the three additional states--Kentucky, Oklahoma, and West Virginia--joined the Conference, the definition of Midwest may have been stretched a little out of shape.

One of the questions asked of the governors and former governors interviewed was whether the existence of the MGC helped foster any sense of regionalism. The general consensus of the chief executives interviewed seemed to be that the Conference had not been a particular help to regionalism, but almost all stressed that the "region" was not as homogeneous in interests as some had thought. Comments ranged from: "The conference is too big.... The members are not a cohesive group with a community of interests.... There is a feeling of Great Lakes regionalism, but it is not common to the non-Great Lakes states.... The three new members [Kentucky, Oklahoma, and West Virginia] diluted the regional identity.... The Midwest is too large for much commonality...."[85]

Throughout the comments of the governors and throughout the

history of the MGC, there seemed to be a common thread--the feeling that the Conference and its member states lacked a shared bond to tie the members together. In fact, there is a great deal of evidence to indicate that there are many problems which work to divide the Midwest.

One recent major analysis of regionalism in America divided the 12-state Midwest into two regions.[86] The Great Lakes states--Illinois, Indiana, Michigan, Minnesota, Ohio and Wisconsin--make up the region known as the Rustbelt, the region of industrial production of all types, the region of factories and mills, of assembly lines and foundries. The Great Plains states--Iowa, Kansas, Minnesota, Missouri, Nebraska, North Dakota and South Dakota--are known as the nation's breadbasket, the agricultural giant of the world.

This division as well as others are evident in the life and problems of the MGC. Interviews with Midwestern chief executives found several who suggested a redrawing of the Conference's boundaries--along Peirce's lines.[87] In 1978, the question of whether the Conference had outlived its usefulness (because of deep regional divisions) was discussed openly at the annual Conference meeting in Lexington, Kentucky.[88]

At the 1983 Conference meeting, the governors of the six Great Lakes states banded together "to deal with mutual interests."[89] Although the governors of the Great Lakes states had often breakfasted together at the MGC meetings this was the first time a formal organization had been created. The Council of Great Lakes Governors as it was known, was established to: "foster a relationship between the federal and state governments which recognizes the unique issues in the Great Lakes region."[90] The Council opened an office and hired an executive director in 1983.

Great Lakes states share many common problems. They also share one very important commodity, water. Indeed, the Great Lakes contain one-fifth of all the fresh water in the world. Small wonder, therefore, that the Great Lakes governors see water as a weapon and vowed not to let Sunbelt states get a drop of their water.[91] The governors also vowed not to compete with one another for industry (probably a difficult decision for some governors who went on "raiding parties" to neighboring states). These states agreed to present a united front in attracting new business to the region and to pool their political influence to obtain their fair share of federal money and attention.[92]

Great Lake governors (joined by the governors of the states of Pennsylvania and New York and the ministers of two provinces of Canada) signed a "good faith agreement" to work to protect the Great Lakes against excessive consumption of water.[93] The document, known as the Great Lakes Charter has no force of law, but throws down the gauntlet to those who had hoped to divert water to the arid southwest. In February of 1986, the eight governors inked a joint statement of principle against drilling for oil in the Great Lakes. In May of 1986, the same eight governors signed a major agreement to attack toxic-chemical pollution of the Great Lakes.[94] The agreement not only contained a statement of principles but a list of 30 specific actions to be taken by member states.[95]

With these actions going on as a sort of regional backdrop, it was not completely a surprise when a resolution to dissolve the Midwestern Governors' Conference was prefiled for the 1984 annual meeting. The resolution was authored by Minnesota Governor Perpich, Midwestern Governors' Conference chairman. The Perpich resolution noted that "member states...have widely divergent interests on issues affecting the Midwest region;..."[96] The Minnesota governor also argued for dissolution because: "many MGC activities are duplicative of the activities of other regional organizations with many states also affiliating with other regional governors' organizations."[97] The resolution would have dissolved the MGC but wanted regional governors to "convene annually on an issue of major regional significance such as agriculture."[98]

The fact that Perpich prefiled the resolution indicated the seriousness of the effort. This was the first time that such a resolution had been formally introduced. An internal CSG/C memo assembled "preliminary procedural advice" related to formal consideration of the resolution.[99] The memo considered how many votes would be necessary for passage of the resolution and noted that this organizational resolution was submitted by the governor along with several policy resolutions and therefore that would seem to indicate the necessity of a three/fourths vote.[100]

The resolution did not come up for formal discussion at the 1984 meeting. Although it was undoubtedly the talk of the Conference confab, apparently it did not have the depth of support Governor Perpich had hoped. The governor did not push for its adoption at the business meeting at which resolutions and policy statements were considered.

The MGC found itself in the difficult position of trying to keep peace in a divided house. What is more, there seemed to be an oversupply of issues which divided Conference member states. The energy crisis in the 1970s triggered the opening up of the divisions. It is likely that differences in the views of energy-producing states versus energy-dependent states ultimately drove both West Virginia and Oklahoma out of the Conference.[101] Other divisive issues such as water are the dividers of today and tomorrow.

The Midwestern Governors' Conference has steered a careful course to try to minimize or avoid internal conflict. That was becoming more and more difficult. It seems very likely that the resolution prefiled for the 1984 meeting is not finally and forever dead. The very fragile nature of this coalition of Midwestern governors had been newly exposed.

NOTES
==

[1]MGC, Minutes of Winter Meetings of the Conference, Washington, February 16, 1985, CSG/C Files.

[2]Private interviews with present and former Midwestern governors, conducted between January, 1977 and December, 1983.

[3]Dick Herman, "Governors' Meet Differs from Past," Lincoln Journal, August 30, 1967, p. 1.

[4]Jep Cadou, "Midwest Governors Discuss 'Vital' Issues," Indianapolis Star, July 22, 1970, p. 25.

[5]"Gun Control Discussed by Governors," Sioux Falls Argus-Leader, July 4, 1968, p. 3.

[6]George Armour, "Governors Here Favor Kennedy for Vice President," Milwaukee Journal, July 3, 1968, p. 8-I.

[7]MGC, Minutes of the Annual Meetings of the Conference, Mackinac Island, Michigan, September 20-22, 1965, p. 15.

[8]Conference on Water Resources and Pollution, Lexington, Kentucky, February 17-18, 1966.

[9]Boyd R. Keenan, Illinois Office of Governor: Expanding Regional Role within National Politics (Urbana: University of Illinois Occasional Papers in Illinois Politics, 1982), pp. 9-10.

[10]Robert H. Solomons, III, "The Southern Interstate Nuclear Compact and Board," State Government, XXXVI (Winter, 1963), pp. 40-43.

[11]MGC, Minutes of the Annual Meetings of the Conference, Minneapolis, Minnesota, September 9-12, 1964, pp. 30-31.

[12]Ibid., p. 32.

[13]MGC, Minutes of the Special Committee to Explore the Possibilities of an Interstate Compact on Nuclear Energy, June 17, 1965.

[14]MGC, Minutes of the Annual Meetings of the Conference, 1965, p. 51.

[15]MGC, Minutes of the Special Meetings of the Conference, Lexington, Kentucky, February 18, 1966, p. 2.

[16]Ibid.

[17]Ibid.

[18]Ibid., p. 3; "Midwest Governors Set Up Atom Unit," New York Times, February 19, 1966, p. 54.

[19]MGC, Minutes of the Annual Meetings of the Conference, Columbus, Ohio, July 19-22, 1970, p. 21.

[20]Private interviews with present and former Midwestern governors, conducted between January, 1977 and December, 1983.

[21]Sarah P. McCally, "The Governor and His Legislative Party," American Political Science Review, LX (December, 1966), p. 923.

[22]Robert Howard, "Adlai's Speech Stirs Governors," Chicago Tribune, September 12, 1964, p. 3.

[23]"Stevenson Assails Goldwater Views," New York Times, September 11, 1964, p. 21.

[24]MGC, Minutes of the Annual Meetings of the Conference, 1964, pp. 18- 19.

[25]"No Federal Aid Hikes, Agnew Says," Indianapolis Star, July 2, 1969, p. 6; Seth S. King, "Agnew Says a Rise in State Aid Depends on End of Vietnam War," New York Times, July 2, 1969, pp. 1+.

[26]Gordon L. Randolph, "Opponents of War Undermine Negotiations, Agnew Asserts," Milwaukee Journal, July 2, 1969, p. 31.

[27]Ray Morgan, "Against Mills Fund Plan," Kansas City Times, July 22, 1971, p. 1.

[28]Richard Doak, "Elect Ray 1973 Chairman of Midwestern Governors' Unit," Des Moines Register, June 29, 1972, p. 4.

[29]Henry Clay Gold, "Docking Cites Crime Turn," Kansas City Star, June 27, 1972, p. 3.

[30]MGC, Minutes of the Annual Meetings of the Conference, Bismarck, North Dakota, June 25-28, 1972, p. 11.

[31]"Governors Request Meeting with Nixon on Quota Cuts," Sioux Falls Argus-Leader, June 29, 1972, p. 1.

[32]James Flansburg, "GOP Governors Reject Impeachment Timetable," Des Moines Register, July 31, 1974, p. 10.

[33]MGC , Minutes of the Annual Meetings of the Conference, Minneapolis, Minnesota, July 28-31, 1974, p. 8; Neil Mehler, "Plan to Stockpile Grain Hit," Chicago Tribune, July 31, 1974, p. 3.

[34]James Flansburg, "GOP Governors Reject Impeachment Timetable," p. 10.

[35]MGC, Minutes of the Annual Meetings of the Conference, 1974, p. 8.

[36]Seth S. King, "Governors Back Fund Disclosure," New York Times, August 1, 1974, p 58.

[37]"Teasdale's Speech is Labeled 'Campaign Fodder,'" St. Louis Globe-Democrat, August 26, 1980.

[38]Ibid.

[39] Ibid.

[40] Private interviews with present and former Midwestern governors, conducted between January, 1977 and December, 1983.

[41] Paul T. David, Ralph M. Goldman, and Richard C. Bain, The Politics of National Party Conventions (Washington: The Brookings Institution, 1960), pp. 99, 487.

[42] MGC, Articles of Organization, Article II. Adopted December 13, 1962.

[43] Ibid., Article VI.

[44] MGC, Minutes of the Special Meetings of the Conference, Washington, D.C., February 3, 1965, p. 1.

[45] Ibid.

[46] MGC, Minutes of the Annual Meetings of the Conference, 1965, pp. 31, 50.

[47] MGC, Minutes of the Annual Meetings of the Conference, Lake-of-the-Ozarks, Missouri, August 27-30, 1967, pp. ii, 83.

[48] Letter from Governor John D. Rockefeller IV to Governor Arthur Link, Chairman, Midwestern Governors' Conference, March 21, 1978, CSG/C Files.

[49] MGC, Minutes of the Special Meetings of the Conference, Cincinnati, Ohio, June 22, 1966, p. 2.

[50] Deil S. Wright, Understanding Intergovernmental Relations (2nd edition, Monterey, California: Brooks/Cole Publishing Co., 1982), p. 277.

[51] MGC, Minutes of the Annual Meetings of the Conference, Wichita, Kansas, June 29-July 2, 1969, pp. 1-2.

[52] MGC, Minutes of the Meetings of the Advisory Committee, February 28, 1969.

[53] Letter from Governor Warren P. Knowles to Brevard Crihfield, January 29, 1969, CSG/L Files.

[54] MGC, Minutes of the Annual Meetings of the Conference, Rapid City, South Dakota, July 8-11, 1973, p. 37.

[55] MGC, Minutes of the Annual Meetings of the Conference, 1974, pp. 2-3.

[56] Letter from Virginia Thrall, Assistant Director, Council of State Governments, Chicago Office to Terry Montgomery, Office of the Governor, Minnesota, January 4, 1983, CSG/C Files.

[57] Ibid.

[58] Letter from Jim H. Bowhay, Director, Council of State Governments, Chicago Office to Governor John Carlin, December 7, 1982, CSG/C Files.

[59] Draft of letter from Governor John Carlin to fellow MGC Governors, January 10, 1983, CSG/C Files.

[60] Letter, Bowhay to Carlin, December 7, 1982.

[61] T. Wayne Mitchell, "'Useless' Resolutions Will be Cut by Bond," Kansas City Times, July 29, 1976, p. 10A.

[62] Ibid.

[63] Ibid.

[64] Randall W. Myers, "Governors Aim to Grab Senate's Ear on Energy," Kansas City Times, August 9, 1977, p. 1.

[65] Private interviews with present and former Midwestern governors, conducted between January, 1977 and December, 1983.

[66] Ibid.

[67] Glenn E. Brooks, When Governors Convene: The Governors' Conference and National Politics (Baltimore: The Johns Hopkins Press, 1961), p. 53.

[68] "Fun for the 'Guys'," Tulsa World, August 9, 1977, p. 8A.

[69] Chuck Ervin, "Governors Pound Out 'Hard-Hitting' Energy Statement," Tulsa World, August 9, 1977, pp. 1+.

[70] "Governors Tackle Oil Line Issue," Milwaukee Journal, July 10, 1973, p. 2.

[71] MGC, Minutes of the Annual Meetings of the Conference, 1973, p. 25; Neil Mehler, "Governors Defeat Trans-Canada Pipeline Proposal," Chicago Tribune, July 11, 1973, p. 3.

[72] Dick Herman, "Governors Split on Oil Pipeline Issue," Lincoln Journal, July 11, 1973, p. 9.

[73] Randall W. Myers, "Governors Attack Food Policy as Good Only for Consumers," Kansas City Times, August 11, 1977, p. 2B.

[74] Congressional Quarterly Service, Guide to U.S. Elections (Washington: Congressional Quarterly, Inc., 1975), p. 531.

[75] Private interviews with present and former Midwestern governors, conducted between January, 1977 and December, 1983.

[76]Ibid.

[77]Advisory Commission on Intergovernmental Relations, Multistate Regionalism (Washington: Government Printing Office, 1972), p. 1.

[78]Ibid.

[79]Keenan, Illinois Office of Governor, p. 4.

[80]Ibid.

[81]Ibid.

[82]John H. Fenton, Midwest Politics (New York: Holt, Rinehart and Winston, Inc., 1966), p. 219.

[83]Russel B. Nye, Midwestern Progressive Politics (New York: Harper Torchbooks, 1965), p. 5.

[84]Ira Sharkansky, The Maligned States: Policy Accomplishments, Problems, and Opportunities (New York: McGraw-Hill Book Co., 1972), p. 27.

[85]Private interviews with present and former Midwestern governors, conducted between January, 1977 and December, 1983.

[86]The first of the eight-part series by Neal R. Peirce and Jerry Hagstrom, "The New Regionalism," National Journal, XXI (May 21, 1983), pp. 1044-52.

[87]Ibid.

[88]Reginald Stuart, "Midwestern Governors Express Doubts on Tax Drive," New York Times, July 16, 1978.

[89]State Government News, XXVI (July, 1983), p. 11.

[90]State Government News, XXVII (January, 1984), p. 9.

[91]Chicago Tribune, June 1, 1983.

[92]Ibid.

[93]"Governors Ink Pact on Water Diversion," Peoria Journal Star, February 12, 1985.

[94]"Governors Declare Great Lakes Oil Deposits Off-Limits," Peoria Journal Star, February 24, 1986.

[95]"Governors Sign Pollution Pact," Peoria Journal Star, May 22, 1986.

[96]"Resolution to Dissolve Midwestern Governors' Conference," Prefiled Policy Statements, November 5, 1984, 1984

MGC Files, CSG/C Files.

[97]Ibid.

[98]Ibid.

[99]Memo "Preliminary Procedural Advice on Governor Perpich's Resolution to Abolish MGC and M.O.," 1984 MGC Files, CSG/C Files.

[100]Ibid.

[101]Keenan, Illinois Office of Governor, p. 14.

CHAPTER EIGHT

EPILOGUE

As noted in earlier chapters, the period 1960-1985 witnessed
nearly unbelievable changes in the American system of
federalism. The period began with the federal government bent
on multiplying its involvement in and its influence on all
segments of American society, but especially on the sub-national
governmental and political segments. The decade of the 1960s
marked a new expansion in the role of the federal government
with the passage of numerous new programs as well as the
institution of many new requirements and regulations. The
presence of the federal government was felt everywhere.

By the mid-1980s, the federal government was in retreat.
Not the full-scale retreat promised by President Reagan in his
many speeches and public utterances on the subject, but in
retreat nonetheless. Many federal programs had been abandoned.
Others had been funded on a sharply-reduced scale. Still others
were left hanging in political limbo, victims of a shrinking
federal role and presence.

THE POST-FEDERAL ERA

By the time this quarter-century period was ending, America
had passed into what some referred to as the "post federal
era."[1] It was an era marked by the removal of many crucial
decisions from the nation's capitol. Beginning with the
presidency of Richard Nixon in the early 1970s, there had been a
conscious, concentrated attempt to reverse the flow of power to
Washington. Appearing before the nation's governors assembled

in their winter meeting, President Nixon--in office for only
eight months at the time--spoke of his plans for this reversal
of power, of his dreams for a new intergovernmental
partnership with the states.

> Washington will no longer try to go it
> alone; Washington will no longer dictate
> without consulting. A new day has come, in
> which we recognize that partnership is a
> two-way street, and if a partnership is to
> thrive, that street has to be traveled--both
> ways.[2]

That period of cooperative/cooptive federalism was one in
which some federal programs were lumped together under block
grants, one in which general revenue sharing received
congressional approval and appropriations, one in which the
federal government often by-passed the states and dealt directly
with local governmental units. This was not an effort to humble
or demean the states, but an effort to get greater grass roots
participation in decision-making.

This "post-federal era" was also the certain result of the
Nixon-Ford- Carter-Reagan efforts to return some decision-making
powers to the states. It was the aim of these administrations
to restore what they considered a "proper balance" to the system
of federalism. Translated, this meant they sought a reduction
in the role of the federal government.

This federal government withdrawal is based on the
continuous efforts of the last four presidents to return some
responsibilities and programs to the states. Trouble in
controlling the federal budget triggered the interest in
returning these responsibilities and programs to the states.
This federal withdrawal has been accompanied by a decline in
real federal aid to state and local governments. By 1985, the
end was near at hand for general revenue sharing. This federal
withdrawal was also made necessary by the awesome economic and
political effects of one staggering federal budget deficit after
another, especially under President Reagan. These changes in
the role of the federal government resulted, in part, from the
Gramm-Rudman-Hollings anti-deficit act.

The emergence of the post-federal era also resulted from a new activism on the part of many state and local governments. By 1985, a great number of state and local governments were stronger and better equipped in terms of powers and determination, and more able and willing to meet the challenges which confronted them in the mid-1980s than had been the case in the early 1960s. Earlier chapters examined the strengthening of state government as seen in the stronger governorships, but it is also true that local governments were strengthened due to the expansion and extension of home rule powers and a relaxing of the rather restrictive financial limitations on local governmental units.

A number of factors had contributed to this new activism, among them: the efforts of the United States Supreme Court and the federal judiciary to ensure political equality through the one-man, one vote and anti- gerrymandering decisions; the revision of countless state constitutions and the revision of numerous municipal charter laws; and the state-by-state nationwide efforts to strengthen the office of governor as well as upgrade the state legislatures. The rise of professional bureaucracies at the state and local levels has also been a contributing factor.

Of importance as well is the impact of new trends which are moving America in the direction of decentralization. The federal government has contributed to this decentralization with cutbacks in real federal aid to state and local governments. These cutbacks began in 1978. The federal government further contributed (albeit unknowingly) to this decentralization when it passed Great Society legislation such as the war on poverty program which required grass roots input before decisions were made and implemented. The result was a newly-reawakened and reactivated neighborhood and grass roots activism.

There has also been a recognition on the part of all levels of government of the centrality of education. Deemed necessary for the revival of the nation's long-term economic and technological health, governments and citizens alike have become aware of the fact that the real leadership in providing for education more properly rests with state and local governments, not with a financially-strapped federal government.

The economic reverses of the final decade of this period have led many leaders to doubt the ability of the federal government to control the state of the nation's economy. Wracked by the long periods of economic stagnation, state and local governments have cast aside their reliance on federal economic policy. State governments--usually in some sort of regional configuration--in conjunction with business leaders have begun to develop their own wide-ranging economic strategies.[3]

One of the major decentralizing influences has been the rise of "stronger indigenous regional organizations."[4] Any listing of these organizations would not only include the numerous regional organizations examined earlier, but would also include, for example, other regional entities such as the Center for the Great Lakes, the Southern Growth Policies Board, and the Northeast-Midwest Congressional Coalition and Institute.

The Midwestern Governors' Conference is another perfect example of this type of indigenous regional organization, born of this period, resulting from the political and issue concerns of the time. The Conference was born out of a shared concern about a specific problem. More accurately, it was a shared concern about several specific problems. Even though the original problems were shunted off to the back burner, the organization continued to exist.

The typicalness of the MGC as representational of the new breed of extra-governmental institutions of federalism is also reflected in the forces which shaped the Conference. Externally, the Conference was shaped by the direction taken by the federal government, by changes in the system of federalism, by the activities of the other regional governors' conferences, by the activities of the National Governors' Association, by the nature and type of the problems to be solved, by national events and trends (e.g., the Viet Nam war, inflation, soaring national deficits), and by public expectations of state government and their governors. It is an organization which reflects the successes and failures, the strengths and shortcomings of similar regional entities.

The decentralization which had contributed to the evolution of the post-federal era has also been affected by the changes in the relative standing of the regional configurations of states.[5] New England took perhaps the biggest dive in this quarter-century and also enjoyed one of the most impressive revivals. The Midwest region has had a tougher time of it and has recovered much more slowly from the severe blows dealt both the industrial backbone of the region and the agricultural backbone as well. The South and West regions saw growth spurts, spurts which were later tempered by reversals in the 1980s. These reversals were due to energy-related policies generated half a world away.

THE NEW REGIONALISM

In a very real sense, the story of this quarter-century is the story of emergent regionalism. Though never totally absent, the period 1960-1985 has seen a new regionalism emerge, a regionalism based not only on common geographical, historical and governmental ties, not only upon the common flow of business and political power, but also on what John Naisbitt characterized as a "tough new brand of economic regionalism, a geographic chauvinism that grows out of the unique problems and resources common to a group of states."[6]

Although some regional organizations existed before 1960, many regional organizations can be considered as among the "new institutions" of federalism. These new organizations--which include regional economic development commissions, river basin commissions, federal regional councils as well as extra-governmental regional organizations are indicative of this new development in modern American federalism.

One of the places this new regionalism has been most in evidence is in the Congress of the United States. The genesis of this congressional regionalism is in all likelihood traceable to the feud in the mid-1970s between Frostbelt and Sunbelt states over federal dollars and defense installations. Frostbelt states complained that they were not getting their "fair and just" share of the federal pie.

A study released late in 1977 concluded that Frostbelt states had lost "a disproportionate share" of the Pentagon dollar. "More fundamentally," it added, "the Defense Department rationale 'seeks to ignore the profound and lasting impact that one quarter of the federal budget (for Defense) has on regional economies, and becomes itself an implicit national policy.'"[7]

The study found that although Frostbelt states had approximately 45 percent of the nation's population and half the nation's total tax burden, the region had only 20 percent of the major defense installations, 17 percent of defense wage and salary distribution, and 16 percent of the personnel.[8]

There was more bad news later in the waning weeks of 1977. The Academy for Contemporary Problems (a public policy research center operated by the Council of State Governments, the International City Management Association, the National Association of Counties, the National Conference of State Legislatures, the National Governors' Association, the National League of Cities and the U.S. Conference of Mayors) published the results of its research into the regional distribution of federal grants-in-aid (1970-1975).

The statistics indicated that the Midwest was one of the regions receiving less federal aid than other regions and generally getting fewer federal dollars back than were sent in to Washington.[9] The Midwest sent $20 billion more to Washington (for FY 1975) than the states got back.[10] The 12 Midwestern states (Kentucky, Oklahoma and West Virginia are not included here as Midwestern states) got back only 76 cents for every dollar sent to Washington.[11] Only three of the 12 states got more back from the federal government than they had forwarded in taxes. Missouri got back $657 million more, North Dakota got back $280 million more, and South Dakota got back $220 million more.[12] Two states--Illinois and Michigan--had a give/return deficit of $10.26 billion![13]

In August, 1977, an article in an issue of Congressional

<u>Quarterly</u> began with these words: "The growing rivalry between the states over the flow of federal money is making this Congress the most regionally-minded one in recent memory."[14] Congress was a natural battleground as Congress has a major role in deciding how and where federal dollars are to be spent.

Political leaders and officeholders from Frostbelt states were anxious to increase their share of the federal dollars being handed out. One such officeholder was Representative Michael J. Harrington (D-Massachusetts, 1969-1979). From the time of his first election to the House in 1968, Harrington had been interested in forming a regional caucus to help redress the imbalance in the flow of federal dollars to Frostbelt states. He had been one of the leaders in the effort to organize the New England Congressional Caucus in 1973. In time, Harrington became disenchanted with the caucus and longed for an organization with more political muscle. An attempt to create an organization with more political clout resulted in the formation of the Northeast-Midwest Economic Advancement Coalition. The new organization held its first meeting September 1, 1976.

The Coalition--originally with members of the House from 16 states (Connecticut, Illinois, Indiana, Iowa, Maine, Massachusetts, Michigan, Minnesota, New Hampshire, New Jersey, New York, Ohio, Pennsylvania, Rhode Island, Vermont, and Wisconsin)--would grow to 18 states (with the addition of members from Delaware and Maryland) and would ultimately shorten its name--while broadening its scope of interests--to the Northeast-Midwest Congressional Coalition. Members from these states all shared similar economic characteristics and problems, among them: a slower (than the national rate) growth in manufacturing employment, many problem-ridden older cities, slower (than the national rate) economic recovery, and problems in obtaining adequate supplies of energy. Essentially, these states were losing population, business, jobs, economic power and political clout. Their numbers in the House dropped from 219 seats (an absolute majority) in the 1960s to 212 in the 1970s to 199 in the 1980s.

The Coalition was dedicated to the reformulation of federal policies that often created major obstacles to regional economic growth. It was not long before Coalition members came to realize they had a real need for information and timely analysis of public policy proposals. To provide the needed information and analysis, they created the Northeast-Midwest Institute, also a brainchild of Representative Harrington.

The Institute serves congressional members, governors, mayors, state and local officials, business and labor leaders in the region in several different ways, by devising public policy strategies that encourage economic development; by hosting conferences, hearings and seminars on critical regional policy concerns; and by producing publications that analyze federal and regional policies.

The Coalition first displayed its new found regional muscle in a vote on the Housing and Community Development Act of 1977. The Coalition was successful in writing into the bill a change in the funding schedule--a change which definitely favored the older cities of the Northeast and Midwest. The key vote on an amendment, was "along regional not philosophical lines."[15] The Northeast-Midwest Congressional Coalition members in the House had carried the day when they stuck together and voted 188-5 not to scrap the new and more beneficial allocation formula.[16]

The Coalition was also victorious in passing an amendment to the omnibus farm bill of 1977 relating to food stamps. The Coalition's goal was to permit households to deduct essential living costs from their income in calculating the amount of food stamps which could be received.[17] "The regional implications were clear; inclusion of living costs would mean more people getting food stamps in the Northeast, where rent, utility and mortgage costs are the highest in the nation."[18]

The Coalition also successfully fought for adjustments in the appropriations formulas in a jobs bill, in the awarding of Department of Defense contracts, in securing more funds for the regions under the labor surplus areas program, in passing an amendment to the Clean Water Act relating to the Great Lakes, and in obtaining increased funding for clean coal technology.

Over on the other end of the Capitol, there exists a Northeast-Midwest Senate Coalition which works closely with its House counterpart. The Senate group does not exercise nearly the influence its House counterpart does because of the Senate's ban on formal caucuses and because of greater influence wielded by small states in the upper chamber.[19] The Senate group organized about a year after the House bloc had formally organized.

The Northeast-Midwest Congressional Coalition and the Institute both operated for the first several years out of shared quarters in a House annex. But, in 1981, the House Administration Committee changed the rules and forced the Northeast-Midwest Institute as well as all other privately financed groups out of House facilities. The Institute is funded by states, foundations and federal grants. The Congressional Coalition itself was allowed to remain in the House annex because it is funded from the House allowances of its members.

In 1977, the early days of the Coalition's existence, the time in which it shared quarters with the Institute, the two organizations had a full-time staff of four.[20] By 1983, the Coalition had nine employees and 18 interns and the Institute had a staff of 18 employees.[21]

The legislative successes of the in-House Northeast-Midwest lobbying group have caused other regional blocs to develop and organize. The New England Congressional Caucus which was the model for the larger Northeast- Midwest coalition is still in business, but has changed its focus to "international problems rather than interregional issues."[22]

In 1977, Representative Charlie Rose (D-N.C., 1973-), mirrored the sentiments of many of his Southern colleagues when he casually observed: "We don't need a Sunbelt coalition."[23] It was not long, however, before the successes of the Northeast-Midwest group convinced the Southerners the need was greater than first perceived. The Congressional Sunbelt Council, formed in the House in 1981, flopped after only a year, a victim of the booming Sunbelt economy. When that economic

boom went bust, triggered by troubles in the oil and gas
industry, the House Sunbelt Caucus was formed. As a
counterbalance to the Northeast-Midwest Institute, Sunbelt
legislators also established the Sunbelt Institute in 1984. The
purpose--to "focus on the regional implications of federal
policy."[24] That purpose has a familiar ring.

On the Senate side of the Capitol, there has been less
movement to form regional caucuses. The only truly organized
bloc is the thirteen-state Senate Western Coalition formed in
1977. Most other regional groupings of senators are organized
on a more ad hoc basis.

The overhaul of the tax code, undertaken in the mid-1980s,
was the cause and legislative site of many regional skirmishes.
Though the general debate about tax reform was not cast in
regional terms, some key items such as the deductibility of
state and local taxes, tax exemptions for bonds, and taxes on
energy were all regionally-divisive issues.[25]

One of the issues pushing its way to the front burner and
sure to create inter-regional battles is the search for a remedy
to the problem of acid rain. By 1985, regional tensions were
already running high on this issue. New England wanted the
problem cleaned up, but did not want to pay the cost of cleaning
up the mess caused by other regions, especially the Midwest
which appears to be the major contributor to the acid rain. The
rain mostly results from the use of high-sulfur coal, mined in
the region and burned by utilities in the region. To shift to
low-sulfur coal (mined mostly in the West) and install expensive
scrubbers would be a serious and costly economic blow to the
Midwest. The Midwest wants all regions to share in the cost of
solving the problem but the South and the West fail to see the
equity in that sort of decision. Acid rain is not only an
inter-regional problem, but the kind of problem which could
strain the functioning of inter-regional organizations such as
the Northeast-Midwest Coalition.[26]

Though it is still early in the policy wars, regional
tensions have already been evident on other issues including
energy politics and water policies. It seems likely that as

long as there is a federal pie to be carved up, there will be
regional interests expressed as to how the carving should be
done. It also seems likely that as long as the policy interests
of regions vary and are at odds, there will be regional
interests expressed and defended.

The quarter century 1960-1985 has "seen it all" in terms of
regional institutions of federalism. This period saw the birth,
multiplication and near-total disappearance of regional economic
development commissions. The period witnessed the creation of
federal administrative units known as federal regional councils.

The new regionalism which affected these and many other
organizations also provided a vivid picture of the many problems
confronting regional organizations. Part of the difficulty has
been in trying to forge unity out of diversity. Nowhere is that
more clear than in interstate organizations. It is also quite
clear that states are the most essential and important building
blocks in the American federal system. The most immediate
problem for any regional configuration is to decide which states
should be included. In spite of the successes of the
Northeast-Midwest groups in Congress, there is something that
boggles the mind at trying to find common ground on a range of
issues for a coalition stretching from Maine to Iowa.

The problem of forging unity out of diversity has been a
particularly difficult problem for the Midwestern Governors'
Conference to solve. The divisiveness of certain issues such as
energy and water has split Conference states. The formation of
a sub-group of Great Lakes governors further strains the fragile
regional bond. The fact that only seven MGC states belong to
the Northeast-Midwest congressional coalitions is divisive. So,
too, is the fact that another MGC state--North Dakota--is a
member of the Senate Western Coalition. In fact, North Dakota
has seemed to point itself more and more to the West. In 1981,
there were indications that North Dakota might go so far as to
withdraw from the Midwestern Governors' Conference.[27]
Ultimately, nothing came of those indications, but North Dakota
now holds memberships in both the MGC and the Western Governors'
Association.

In an effort to crystalize its identity, the MGC made application for a National Science Foundation grant to allow the Conference "to experiment with various methods and mechanisms for identifying and addressing issues which will have a significant impact on the Midwest."[28] The grant was funded and in the spring of 1978, the Midwestern Governors' Conference set out to identify and address issues of significance to member states. One of the outcomes of this NSF grant was the Regional Issue Identification Project. This was an effort to sit down with member governors and their chief aides and assistants to identify issues and areas of concern. The purpose was to: (1) collect--on a state-by-state basis--a list of regional issue concerns; (2) analyze possible Conference activities with regard to these issue concerns; and (3) identify key resource persons in each state. The face-to-face interviews were conducted by staff members of the CSG/Chicago office.

The bulk of the regional issues identified fell into five categories: water resources, energy, agriculture, health care, and transportation.[29] In examining all of the regional issues advanced by governmental and political leaders, it is interesting to note that very few requested, endorsed, or opposed federal action of one sort or another. Almost all issues were expressed and analyzed in terms of how Midwestern states--acting singly or collectively--could tackle the problems.

What was also striking about the Regional Issue Identification Project were the responses as to the role of the Conference in terms of the issues identified. Suggestions for "possible Conference activity" fell into five basic categories: (1) review existing research and/or commission an in-depth study of an issue/problem; (2) refer the issue to an ad hoc committee or to a task force or create a task force to explore the issue; (3) hold a conference or seminar/workshop for appropriate officials; (4) develop a uniform policy to deal with the problem or formulate a model bill or an interstate compact; (5) take an official position on the issue/problem or send a resolution to Congress (or to some unit in the executive branch of the federal government) requesting a particular course of action.[30]

It seems clear that the views as to the role and purpose of an organization such as the Midwestern Governors' Conference held by member governors and high-ranking staffers were far from being in agreement. Some obviously envisioned an organization primarily organized to do research and analyze problems, while others viewed the organization as an interstate organization which could hammer out compromises of proposed legislative proposals or interstate compacts. Still others saw the Conference as an opportunity to pool the clout of a dozen state chief executives and to use that clout to lobby the federal government.

The history of the Midwestern Governors' Conference as reconstructed above is testimony to the search for a role, a niche. The experimentation, use, and discarding of various "in-house" Conference mechanisms; the rather continuous alteration of the meeting format; the search for ways for the MGC (as a regional governors' conference) to be heard in higher policy councils; the wondering (sometimes aloud) about whether the Conference should engage in federal level lobbying; and the desire for some type of effective liaison with the federal government, including not only the White House and the executive branch but the Midwestern congressional delegations as well are all indications of that unending search for a Conference identity. "What (who) are we?" Conference members ask themselves and each other.

This raises one of the more troublesome questions of the new regionalism. How firm is a consensus agreed upon by a group of governors? How solidly will governors stay united? We have seen a good deal of evidence which suggests that such a consensus is, at best, fragile. Deil S. Wright, an astute commentator on the federalism scene, believes that governors "cannot <u>bargain</u> as a collective entity,... Any bargaining capacity rests with the individual American governor and his or her base of support within each particular state; governors cannot pool their bargaining powers."[31]

Wright continued his analysis with the use of an analogy:

The political power generated by each American governor operates most effectively and almost exclusively within an intrastate grid. With proper construction and care of the vertical transmission lines to Washington, a governor can maintain at least a modest D.C.-directed power surge, but one which is subject to substantial variations in voltage levels and outages due to storms, earthquakes, and other uncontrollable conditions. When a governor attempts to transport power horizontally--that is, to other states, and to pool it with other governors' power grids-- there seems to be no political technology for building the transformers which make governors' different power voltages flow very effectively. Within-state power grids have their own unique voltage levels, switching mechanisms, repair techniques and the like. No governor has a central control panel where he or she manipulates power flows.[32]

SUMMARY

It is fitting that we bring down the curtain on this analysis of the new institutions of federalism with a summary of the purposes of such institutions in general and one--the Midwestern Governors' Conference--in particular. One fact seems to clearly stand out, the state is the basic unit of regional government. Regional units will likely be built upon states as the foundation. If states are the basic regional units, it must be true that "governors [who] are the central figures in state governments"[33] will be the key figures in any regional effort.

Governor Otto Kerner (D-Illinois 1961-1968) put his rhetorical finger on both the centrality of the governorship and the need for regional institutions such as governors' conferences in an interview he granted near the end of his first term of office. Kerner asserted:

Although solidly loyal to his citizenry, the governor today must display an irreverence for state boundary lines. Air pollution doesn't recognize the state line. Neither does water pollution. Nor does tax collecting. State boundaries are arbitrary lines drawn by history's happenstance. To solve common problems within a region--or to better conditions in general--state lines must be crossed, recrossed, and sometimes eclipsed. Since our original document of government provided no mechanics for fraternization between states, regional governors' conferences would fill a gap unforeseen by the founding fathers.[34]

Twenty years later, an editorial writer wondered aloud whether "governors of Midwestern states...[could] work together...toward the individual and collective good of their states."[35] That same editorial concluded by offering a set of goals such regional organizations might reasonably expect to achieve. If such institutions could be: "...joining forces where possible, sharing information, setting a common agenda and exerting regional political influence...[to] make a dent in these problems, [then] the time spent...at past and future conferences will have been well invested."[36]

In a sense, one of the biggest challenges facing every regional institution (and perhaps all other institutions of federalism as well) is that of role definition. What are the institution's roles and is this the appropriate institution to fulfill these roles? Role definition has certainly been a problem for the Midwestern Governors' Conference. Many questions remain essentially unanswered for the member states of the Conference including not only those mentioned above, but others as well. Questions such as: should the region be broken down into smaller subregions (such as Plains states and Great Lakes states)? If the Conference is the appropriate vehicle, are there structural changes which should be made?

For example, do regional governors' conference meetings achieve the stated goal of providing a "medium for the exchange of views and experiences on subjects of general importance"? There seems to be little argument that these gatherings do provide an opportunity for governors to meet with fellow governors. These meetings provide opportunities for informal dealings with political peers. The regional governors' organization is a more intimate, smaller, lower profile, less partisan, less media-event oriented gathering than the national gubernatorial conclaves. As Midwestern governors themselves noted: "The meetings were an opportunity to get to know your colleagues."   "A good chance for personal contacts."   "An opportunity to exchange ideas, talk of common problems, and compare notes on problem solving." "A chance to take a look at new problems (those problems not yet existent in your state, but likely to be there soon)."   "I found it an excellent time to discuss regional problems."[37]   One governor went on to say: "We might just sit down over a cocktail and discuss some common problem--that's the real value of the Conference. Even with the protection of anonymity, the governor hastened to add: "I know that's a bit hard to explain to people!"[38]   Do regional governors' conferences achieve the stated goal of improving intergovernmental relationships, especially relationships with the federal government?   If one of the important roles of regional governors' conferences is to analyze the impact of federal policies on the region and to respond to the federal initiatives in a unified voice,[39] how might the Washington offices of the various Midwestern states be utilized? How might the Conference relate to and work with the various congressional regional coalitions?

The quarter-century 1960-1985 ended with the states and various new institutions of federalism trying to increase their roles in the system and at the same time increase their political power. Deciding they neither could nor would wait any longer for federal leadership, the states began initiating solutions to many of their own problems. They are--to some degree--trying to reassert state sovereignty. But, the refrain is not altogether familiar as it includes a great deal of interstate cooperation through regional mechanisms. The states have been crucial actors in this new wave of cooperation. Indeed, it may well be that the last quarter-century will most be remembered in the annals of American federalism as the period which witnessed a dramatic increase in the interdependence of national, state, and local governments.[40]

Led by their governors, the states have maintained a strong federal presence. Because of new institutions which have sprung up in the last 25 years, the states also have a stronger regional presence, a stronger sense of regionalism. There is a new regional consciousness, a new regional sensitivity which was not present at the start of this quarter-century. Perhaps the future of regional governors' organizations can be glimpsed in the remark of a governor when he was asked about the value of such organizations. "The Midwestern Governors' Conference," he said simply, "is a window to the world outside my home state."[41]

NOTES
==

[1]Neal R. Peirce and Jerry Hagstrom, "The New Regionalism," National Journal, XV (May 21, 1983), p. 1044.

[2]"Address at the National Governors' Conference, September 1, 1969," Public Papers of the Presidents of the United States, Richard M. Nixon, 1969 (Washington: Government Printing Office, 1971), p. 700.

[3]Peirce and Hagstrom, "The New Regionalism," pp. 1045-46.

[4]Ibid., p. 1045.

[5]Ibid., pp. 1044-52.

[6]John Naisbitt, Megatrends (New York: Warner Books, 1982), pp.108-109.

[7]Robert Gruenberg, "Pentagon Buck Power," Peoria Journal Star, September 25, 1977, p. 1.

[8]Ibid.

[9]Charles L. Vehorn, The Regional Distribution of Federal Grants-in-Aid (Columbus: Academy for Contemporary Problems, 1977), pp. 6, 7, 14.

[10]"Federal Spending: The North's Loss is the Sunbelt's Gain," National Journal, VIII (June 26, 1976), p. 881.

[11]Ibid.

[12]Ibid.

[13]Ibid.

[14]Alan Ehrenhalt, "Regionalism in Congress: Formulas Debated," Congressional Quarterly Weekly Report, XXXV (August 20, 1977), p. 1747.

[15]Kathryn Waters Gest, "House Boosts Aid Share for Older Cities," _Congressional Quarterly Weekly Report_, XXXV (May 14, 1977), p. 891.

[16]Ibid., pp. 940-41.

[17] Ehrenhalt, "Regionalism in Congress," p. 1751.

[18]Ibid.

[19]Richard E. Cohen, "Regionalism Playing an Increasing Role in Shaping Congress's Policy Debates," _National Journal_, XV (May 21, 1983), p. 1054.

[20]Northeast-Midwest Research Institute, "Prospectus," June, 1977, p. 1 (mimeographed).

[21]Cohen, "Regionalism Playing an Increasing Role in Shaping Congress's Policy Debates," p. 1055.

[22]Ibid., p. 1054.

[23]Ehrenhalt, "Regionalism in Congress," p. 1749.

[24]W. John Moore, "Stalking Federal Dollars For a Struggling Region," _National Journal_, XIX (November 28, 1987), p. 3050.

[25]Timothy B. Clark, "Taking a Regional Stand," _National Journal_, XVIII (March 22, 1986), pp. 696-702.

[26]For a more in-depth examination of the complexity (political and otherwise) of the problem, see: Rochelle L. Stanfield, "Regionalism Tensions Complicate Search for an Acid Rain Remedy," _National Journal_, XVI (May 5, 1984), pp. 860-63; Rochelle L. Stanfield, "Environmentalists Try the Backdoor Approach to Tackling Acid Rain," _National Journal_, XVII (October 19, 1985), pp. 2365-68; Amy Stern, "Acid Rain: Both Sides Ready to Resume Battle," _Congressional Quarterly Weekly Report_, XLIV (December 27, 1986), pp. 3144-46; Leslie Cole, "Acid Rain Debate Divides Regions," _State Government News_, XXVII (February, 1984), pp. 14-16+.

[27]Letter to Paul Simmons, Executive Assistant to the Governor of Illinois from Virginia Thrall, Assistant Director, Midwestern Office, Council of State Governments, January 21, 1981, CSG/C Files.

[28]Letter to Governor James R. Thompson from Arthur A. Link, Governor of North Dakota and Chairman of the Midwestern Governors' Conference, April 13, 1978, CSG/C Files.

[29]Midwestern Governors' Conference, Regional Issue Identification Project, NSF Grant, 1978, CSG/C Files.

[30] Ibid.

[31] Deil S. Wright, <u>Understanding</u> <u>Intergovernmental</u> <u>Relations</u> (2nd ed., Monterey: Brooks/Cole Publishing Co., 1982), pp. 280-81.

[32] Ibid., p. 281.

[33] Advisory Commission on Intergovernmental Relations, <u>State</u> <u>and</u> <u>Local</u> <u>Roles</u> <u>in</u> <u>the</u> <u>Federal</u> <u>System</u> (Washington: Government Printing Office, 1982), p. 105.

[34] <u>Indianapolis</u> <u>Star</u>, April 10, 1964, as quoted in Boyd R. Keenan, <u>Illinois</u> <u>Office</u> <u>of</u> <u>Governor</u>: <u>Expanding</u> <u>Regional</u> <u>Role</u> <u>within</u> <u>National</u> <u>Politics</u> (Urbana: University of Illinois Occasional Papers in Illinois Politics, 1982), p. 7.

[35] <u>Columbus</u> (Ohio) <u>Dispatch</u>, August 27, 1985.

[36] Ibid.

[37] Private interviews with present and former Midwestern governors, conducted between January, 1977 and December, 1983.

[38] Ibid.

[39] Midwestern Governors' Conference, Regional Issue Identification Project.

[40] John E. Chubb, "The Political Economy of Federalism," <u>American</u> <u>Political</u> <u>Science</u> <u>Review</u>, LXXIX (December, 1985), p. 994.

[41] Private interviews with present and former Midwestern governors, conducted between January, 1977 and December, 1983.

APPENDIX A

GOVERNORS OF MIDWESTERN

GOVERNORS' CONFERENCE STATES

1962 - 1985

Governors	Dates of Service
Illinois	
Otto Kerner (D)	1961 - 1968a
Samuel H. Shapiro (D)	1968 - 1969b
Richard B. Ogilvie (R)	1969 - 1973
Daniel Walker (D)	1973 - 1977
James R. Thompson, Jr. (R)	1977 -
Indiana	
Matthew E. Welsh (D)	1961 - 1965
Roger D. Branigin (D)	1965 - 1969
Edgar D. Whitcomb (R)	1969 - 1973
Otis R. Bowen, M.D. (R)	1973 - 1981
Robert Orr (R)	1981 -
Iowa	
Norman A. Erbe (R)	1961 - 1963
Harold E. Hughes (D)	1963 - 1969c
Robert D. Fulton (D)	1969 - 1969d
Robert D. Ray (R)	1969 - 1983
Terry Branstad (R)	1983 -
Kansas	
John Anderson, Jr. (R)	1961 - 1965
William H. Avery (R)	1965 - 1967
Robert B. Docking (D)	1967 - 1975
Robert F. Bennett (R)	1975 - 1979
John W. Carlin (D)	1979 -

Kentucky*

Edward T. Breathitt (D)	1963 - 1967
Louie B. Nunn (R)	1967 - 1971
Wendell H. Ford (D)	1971 - 1974e
Julian Carroll (D)	1974 - 1979f
John Y. Brown, Jr. (D)	1979 - 1983
Martha Layne Collins (D)	1983 -

Michigan

John B. Swainson (D)	1961 - 1963
George W. Romney (R)	1963 - 1969g
William G. Milliken (R)	1969 - 1983h
James J. Blanchard (D)	1983 -

Minnesota

Elmer L. Andersen (R)	1961 - 1963i
Karl F. Rolvaag (DFL)	1963 - 1967j
Harold LeVander (R)	1967 - 1971
Wendell R. Anderson (DFL)	1971 - 1976k
Rudolph G. Perpich (DFL)	1976 - 1979l
Albert H. Quie (R)	1979 - 1983
Rudolph G. Perpich (DFL)	1983 -

Missouri

John M. Dalton (D)	1961 - 1965
Warren E. Hearnes (D)	1965 - 1973
Christopher "Kit" Bond (R)	1973 - 1977
Joseph P. Teasdale (D)	1977 - 1981
Christopher "Kit" Bond (R)	1981 - 1985

Nebraska

Frank B. Morrison (D)	1961 - 1967
Norbert T. Tiemann (R)	1967 - 1971
J. James Exon, Jr. (D)	1971 - 1979
Charles Thone (R)	1979 - 1983
Robert Kerrey (D)	1983 -

North Dakota

William L. Guy (D)	1961 - 1973
Arthur A. Link (D)	1973 - 1981
Allen I. Olson (R)	1981 - 1985

Ohio

Michael V. DiSalle (D)	1959 - 1963
James A. Rhodes (R)	1963 - 1971
John J. Gilligan (D)	1971 - 1975
James A. Rhodes (R)	1975 - 1983
Richard F. Celeste (D)	1983 -

Oklahoma**

Dewey F. Bartlett (R)	1967 - 1971
David Hall (D)	1971 - 1975
David L. Boren (D)	1975 - 1979
George P. Nigh (D)	1979 -

South Dakota

Archie M. Gubbrud (R)	1961 - 1965
Nils A. Boe (R)	1965 - 1969
Frank L. Farrar (R)	1969 - 1971
Richard F. Kneip (D)	1971 - 1978m
Harvey L. Wollman (D)	1978 - 1979n
William J. Janklow (R)	1979 -

West Virginia***

Hulett C. Smith (D)	1965 - 1969
Arch A. Moore, Jr. (R)	1969 - 1977
John D. Rockefeller, IV (D)	1977 - 1985

Wisconsin

Gaylord A. Nelson (D)	1959 - 1963
John W. Reynolds (D)	1963 - 1965
Warren P. Knowles (R)	1965 - 1971
Patrick J. Lucey (D)	1971 - 1977o
Martin J. Schreiber (D)	1977 - 1979p
Lee Sherman Dreyfus (R)	1979 - 1983
Anthony S. Earl (D)	1983 -

*   Kentucky joined the Midwestern Governors' Conference in 1965.

**   Oklahoma joined the MGC in 1967 and withdrew from Conference membership in 1980.

***   West Virginia joined the MGC in 1967 and withdrew from Conference membership in 1978.

a   Resigned May 22, 1968.

b   Succeeded to office, May 22, 1968.

c   Resigned January 1, 1969 to take seat in United States Senate.

d   Succeeded to office, January 1, 1969 and served until January 16, 1969.

e   Resigned December 28, 1974 to take seat in United States Senate.

f   Succeeded to office, December 28, 1974.

g   Resigned January 22, 1969 to become Secretary of the Department of Housing and Urban Development.

h   Succeeded to office, January 22, 1969.

i   His term expired March 25,1963 after the Minnesota Supreme Court had ruled that his opponent had won the 1962 election by 91 votes.

j   Assumed office March 25, 1963.

k   Resigned December 29, 1976 to take seat in United States Senate.

l   Succeeded to office, December 29, 1976.

m   Resigned July 24, 1978 to become United States Ambassador to Singapore.

n   Succeeded to office, July 24, 1978.

o   Resigned July 7, 1977 to become United States Ambassador to Mexico.

p   Succeeded to office, July 7, 1977.

Sources: Congressional Quarterly Service, Guide to U.S. Elections (2nd ed., Washington: Congressional Quarterly, Inc., 1985); subsequent election reports from Congressional Quarterly Weekly Report, 1975 - 1985; Council of State Governments, The Governors of the American States, Commonwealths, and Territories 1900-1980 (Lexington: Council of State Governments, 1980).

APPENDIX B

MIDWESTERN GOVERNORS' CONFERENCE

ANNUAL MEETING DATES, SITES, AND CHAIRMEN

(1962-1985)

DATE	SITE	CHAIRMAN
December 12-14, 1962	Chicago, Illinois	William L. Guy
November 20-22, 1963	Omaha, Nebraska	William L. Guy
September 9-12, 1964	Minneapolis, Minnesota	Frank Morrison
September 20-22, 1965	Mackinac Island, Michigan	George Romney
June 19-22, 1966	Cincinnati, Ohio	Karl Rolvaag
August 27-30, 1967	Lake-of-the-Ozarks, Missouri	James Rhodes
June 30-July 3, 1968	Milwaukee, Wisconsin	Nils Boe(1)
June 29-July 2, 1969	Wichita, Kansas	Warren Knowles
July 19-22, 1970	Columbus, Ohio	Warren Hearnes
July 18-21, 1971	South Sioux City, Nebraska	Robert Docking(2)
June 25-28, 1972	Bismarck, North Dakota	Robert Docking
July 8-11, 1973	Rapid City, South Dakota	Robert Ray
July 28-31, 1974	Minneapolis, Minnesota	J. James Exon
July 20-23, 1975	Cincinnati, Ohio	William Milliken
July 25-28, 1976	Indianapolis, Indiana	Richard Kneip
August 7-10, 1977	Afton, Oklahoma	Arthur A. Link
July 12-15, 1978	Lexington, Kentucky	Arthur A. Link(3)
August 26-28, 1979	Osage Beach, Missouri	Otis R. Bowen
August 24-26, 1980	Chicago, Illinois	Joseph P. Teasdale
August 30-Sept. 1, 1981	Milwaukee, Wisconsin	James R. Thompson
July 18-20, 1982	Des Moines, Iowa	John W. Carlin
October 9-11, 1983	Lawrence, Kansas	Christopher Bond(4)
November 14-17, 1984	Lincoln, Nebraska	Rudy Perpich
August 18-20, 1985	Mackinac Island, Michigan	Robert D. Orr

(1)Became Chairman upon the resignation of Otto Kerner.
(2)Became Chairman upon the expiration of Norbert Tiemann's term of office.
(3)Became Chairman upon the expiration of Christopher "Kit" Bond's term of office.
(4)Became Chairman upon the expiration of Charles Thone's term of office.

APPENDIX C

ARTICLES OF ORGANIZATION

of the

MIDWESTERN GOVERNORS' CONFERENCE

ARTICLE I

NAME AND MEMBERSHIP

The name of this organization shall be the "Midwestern Governors' Conference."

Membership in the Midwestern Governors' Conference shall include the Governors of the States of Illinois, Indiana, Iowa, Kansas, Kentucky, Michigan, Minnesota, Missouri, Nebraska, North Dakota, Ohio, South Dakota and Wisconsin.

ARTICLE II

FUNCTIONS

The functions of the Midwestern Governors' Conference shall be to foster regional development, to attain greater efficiency in state administration, to facilitate interstate cooperation and improve intergovernmental relationships, and to provide a medium for the exchange of views and experiences on subjects of general importance to the people of the Midwestern States.

ARTICLE III

MEETINGS

The Midwestern Governors' Conference shall meet annually at a time and place selected by the Conference, if in session, or by the Chairman.

Special meetings of the Midwestern Governors' Conference shall be held at the call of the Chairman or at the call of a majority of the membership.

Seven members present at the Annual Meeting or a special meeting shall constitute a quorum.

ARTICLE IV

CHAIRMAN AND VICE CHAIRMAN

The Chairman and Vice Chairman of the Midwestern Governors' Conference shall be elected by the Conference at the Annual Meeting or at a special meeting if both offices become vacant.

The Chairman shall hold office until the adjournment of the succeeding Annual Meeting and until his successor is chosen. He shall preside and vote at meetings of the Conference and shall arrange the program of the Annual Meeting.

He shall appoint a Nominating Committee composed of member Governors to serve at the Annual Meeting and may appoint other committees as he deems necessary.

The Vice Chairman shall preside in the absence of the Chairman and shall assist the Chairman in an appropriate manner. He shall succeed to all duties of the Chairman in case of the inability of the Chairman to perform such duties.

In case of vacancy of both offices the most recent past Chairman who is still a member shall call a meeting as soon as practicable in order to elect one or both officers.

ARTICLE V

COMMITTEES AND TASK FORCES

There shall be a Staff Advisory Committee and such other committees or task forces as the Conference Chairman may direct or the Conference may create. These committees shall report in such a manner and on such schedule as the Conference Chairman may direct. Except as provided for in this Article, no committee or task force will continue beyond the end of the next succeeding Annual Meeting unless there is specific action taken to extend such committee or task force.

The Staff Advisory Committee is a permanent committee and shall consist of one person appointed by each member Governor. The Chairman of the Staff Advisory Committee shall be appointed from among such membership by the Conference Chairman. He or she will serve until a successor is named. The Staff Advisory Committee shall assist the Conference Chairman in his responsibilities for planning annual and special meetings of the Conference, supervision of committees and task forces, implementation of adopted Conference policies and such other matters of interest to the Conference.

The Energy and Natural Resources Task Force or any direct successor task force or committee is designated the Midwestern Regional Energy Advisory Board under Section 655 of the U.S. Department of Energy Organization Act, PL 95- 91, and will continue from year to year until changed or abolished by Conference action so long as it also serves as the Midwestern Regional Energy Advisory Board. Organizational matters, procedures, reports and recommendations of the Midwestern Regional Energy Advisory Board shall be filed with the Conference Secretariat in addition to necessary and desirable reporting to member Governors and the federal government.

ARTICLE VI

FINANCE

Each member shall contribute the sum of $100 per year for the purpose of enhancing the activities of the Conference.

The Council of State Governments shall serve as the Treasurer of the Midwestern Governors' Conference. Subject to the authority of the Chairman, the Treasurer shall have custody of the funds of the Conference; shall deposit funds of the Conference in its name; shall annually report all receipts, disbursements, and balance-on-hand; and shall be bonded with sufficient sureties conditioned for the faithful performance of these duties.

ARTICLE VII

STAFF SERVICES

The Midwestern Office of the Council of State Governments shall serve as the Secretariat of the Midwestern Governors' Conference and shall render such staff assistance as may be requested by the Conference and its officers.

ARTICLE VIII

POLICY STATEMENTS

The Conference may approve policy statements. These shall be in the form of a brief statement of the issue and the conference policy position. Proposals for conference action may be submitted at the Annual Meeting or at special meetings in two ways, both of which involve the purpose of reasonable advance notice:

(1) Prefiled proposals which may be considered at any appropriate time during the formal meeting by a simple motion and a second to adopt. The procedure for prefiling such proposals shall be submission in writing to the Secretariat office at least 15 days in advance of any annual or special meeting; the Secretary will transmit such proposals at least 10 days in advance of any such meeting.

(2) Proposals which are not prefiled under the procedure in paragraph (1) above will require submission in writing to each member Governor in attendance at least on the day preceding the motion and unanimous consent to consider.

Any policy statement shall be deemed adopted upon obtaining a three- fourths vote of the membership present and voting.

Amendments to a policy statement shall be deemed adopted upon obtaining a three-fourths majority vote of the membership present and voting.

ARTICLE IX

AMENDMENTS

The Midwestern Governors' Conference at any meeting may amend these Articles of Organization by a majority vote of the members present and voting provided notice in writing of the specific amendment has been submitted to the Secretariat at least 15 days prior to the Annual Meeting or any special meeting. The Secretariat will transmit such proposed amendment at least 10 days prior to such meeting. In the absence of such prior notice, a three- fourths majority vote of the members present and voting shall be required for adoption of a proposed amendment.

Suspension of the Articles of Organization requires a three-fourths majority of members present and voting except suspension regarding Article VIII provisions for policy statements shall require a unanimous vote of the members present and voting.

* Adopted at the Organization Meeting of the Midwestern Governors' Conference, Chicago, Illinois, December 13, 1962; as amended at a special meeting in Washington, D.C., February 3, 1965; as amended at the Fourth Annual Meeting, Mackinac Island, Michigan, September 22, 1965; as amended at a special meeting held in conjunction with the Fifth Annual Meeting, Cincinnati, Ohio, June 22, 1966; as amended at the Sixth Annual Meeting, Lake-of-the-Ozarks, Missouri, August 30, 1967; as amended at the

Eighth Annual Meeting, Wichita, Kansas, June 30, 1969; as amended at the Twelfth Annual Meeting, Rapid City, South Dakota, July 11, 1973; as amended at the Fourteenth Annual Meeting, Cincinnati, Ohio, July 21, 1975; as amended at the Seventeenth Annual Meeting, Lexington, Kentucky, July 15, 1978; as amended at the Eighteenth Annual Meeting, Osage Beach, Missouri, August 28, 1979; and as amended at the Nineteenth Annual Meeting, Chicago, Illinois, August 24-26, 1980.

SELECTED BIBLIOGRAPHY

BOOKS, MONOGRAPHS, AND MAJOR ARTICLES

Advisory Commission on Intergovernmental Relations. The Federal
    Role in the Federal System: The Dynamics of Growth, An
    Agenda for American Federalism: Restoring Confidence and
    Competence (Washington: Government Printing Office, 1981).

    . The Federal Role in the Federal System: Hearings
    on the Federal Role (Washington: Government Printing
    Office, 1980).

    . The Future of Federalism in the 1980s
    (Washington: Government Printing Office, 1981.

    . Improving Federal Grants Management (Washington:
    Government Printing Office, 1981).

    . Is Constitutional Reform Necessary to Reinvigorate
    Federalism? (Washington: Government Printing Office, 1987).

    . Multistate Regionalism (Washington: Government
    Printing Office, 1972).

    . Reflections on Garcia and Its Implications for
    Federalism (Washington: Government Printing Office, 1986).

    . Regional Growth: Flows of Federal Funds 1952-1976
    (Washington: Government Printing Office, 1980).

    . Regional Growth, Historic Perspective
    (Washington: Government Printing Office, 1980).

    . Regulatory Federalism: Policy, Process, Impact
    and Reform (Washington: Government Printing Office, 1984).

    . State and Local Roles in the Federal System
    (Washington: Government Printing Office, 1982).

American Regionalism: Our Economic, Cultural and Political
    Makeup (Washington: Congressional Quarterly, Inc., 1980).

Barton, Weldon V. Interstate Compacts in the Political Process
    (Chapel Hill: University of North Carolina Press, 1965).

Beer, Samuel H. "Federalism, Nationalism, and Democracy in
    America," American Political Science Review, LXXII (March,
    1978), pp. 9-21.

228

Bender, Lewis G. and Stever, James A. (eds.). Administering the New Federalism (Boulder: Westview Press, 1986).

Berger, Raoul. Federalism: The Founders' Design (Norman: University of Oklahoma Press, 1987).

Berry, Jeffrey M. The Interest Group Society (Boston: Little, Brown & Co., 1984).

Beyle, Thad L., ed. Re-Electing the Governor: The 1982 Elections (Lanham, Md.: University Press of America, Inc., 1986).

_____, and Williams, J. Oliver, eds. The American Governor in Behavioral Perspective (New York: Harper & Row, 1972).

_____, and Muchmore, Lynn, eds. Being Governor: Views From the Office (Durham: Duke University Press, 1983).

Bingham, Richard D. State and Local Government in an Urban Society (New York: Random House, Inc., 1986).

Brooks, Glenn E. When Governors Convene: The Governors' Conference and National Politics (Baltimore: Johns Hopkins Press, 1961).

Chubb, John E. "The Political Economy of Federalism," American Political Science Review LXXIX (December, 1985), pp. 994-1015.

Cingranelli, David L. "State Government Lobbies in the National Political Process," State Government, LVI (1983), pp. 122-127.

Derthick, Martha. Between State and Nation, Regional Organizations of the United States (Washington: The Brookings Institution, 1974).

Dometrius, Nelson C. "Measuring Gubernatorial Power," Journal of Politics XLI (1979), pp. 589-610.

Elazar, Daniel J. American Federalism: A View from the States, 3rd ed. (New York: Harper & Row, Publishers, 1984).

_____, ed. Politics of American Federalism (Lexington: D. C. Heath & Co., 1969).

Fenton, John H. Midwest Politics (New York: Holt, Rinehart and Winston, Inc., 1966).

Fiorina, Morris P. Congress: Keystone of the Washington Establishment (New Haven: Yale University Press, 1977).

Foster, Charles H. W. Experiments in Bioregionalism: The New England River Basins Story (University Press of New England, 1984).

Glendening, Parris N., and Reeves, Mavis Mann. Pragmatic Federalism: An Intergovernmental View of American Government (Pacific Palisades: Palisades Publishers, 1977).

Grady, Dennis O. "American Governors and State-Federal Relations," State Government, LVII (1984), pp. 106-112.

_____. "Gubernatorial Behavior in State-Federal Relations," Western Political Quarterly, XL (June, 1987), pp. 305-318.

Graves, W. Brooke. American Intergovernmental Relations: Their Origins, Historical Development and Current Status (New York: Charles Scribner's Sons, 1964).

Gray, Virginia. "Innovation in the States: A Diffusion Study," American Political Science Review, LXVII (December, 1973), pp. 1174-1185.

Haider, Donald H. "Intergovernmental Redirection," Annals, CDLXVI (March, 1983), pp. 165-178.

_____. When Governments Come to Washington: Governors, Mayors, and Intergovernmental Lobbying (New York: Free Press, 1974).

Hanus, Jerome J., ed. The Nationalization of State Government (Lexington, Mass.: Lexington Books, 1981).

_____, and Marfin, Gary C. "State Dependency and Cooperative Federalism," State Government, LIII (Autumn, 1980), pp. 174-177.

Harbert, Anita S. Federal Grants-in-Aid, Maximizing Benefits to the States (New York: Praeger Publishers, 1976).

Henig, Jeffrey R. Public Policy and Federalism: Issues in State and Local Politics (New York: St. Martin's Press, 1985).

Herbers, John. "The New Federalism: Unplanned, Innovative and Here to Stay," Governing, I (October, 1987), pp. 28-37.

Kallenbach, Joseph E. The American Chief Executive: The Presidency and the Governorship (New York: Harper & Row, 1966).

Keenan, Boyd R. "Illinois Office of Governor: Expanding Regional Role with National Politics" (Urbana: Occasional Papers in Illinois Politics, University of Illinois, 1982).

Leach, Richard H. _American Federalism_ (New York: W. W. Norton & Co., 1970).

Lipson, Leslie. _The American Governor: From Figurehead to Leader_ (Chicago: University of Chicago Press, 1949).

Lorch, Robert S. _State and Local Politics: The Great Entanglement_, 2nd ed. (Englewood Cliffs: Prentice-Hall, Inc., 1986).

Lowi, Theodore J., Ginsberg, Benjamin, et al. _Poliscide_ (New York: Macmillan Publishing Co., Inc., 1976).

McCally, Sarah P. "The Governor and His Legislative Party." _American Political Science Review_ LX (1966), pp. 923-942.

Martin, Roscoe C. _The Cities and the Federal System_ (New York: Atherton Press, 1965).

Matheson, Scott M. [with Kee, James Edwin]. _Out of Balance_ (Salt Lake City: Peregrine Smith Books, 1986).

National Governors' Association. _Governing the American States: A Handbook for New Governors_ (Washington: National Governors' Association, 1978).

_____. _The Governor's Office_. 10 volumes. (Washington: National Governors' Association, 1976).

_____. _Governors' Policy Initiatives: Meeting the Challenges of the 1980s_ (Washington: National Governors' Association, 1980).

_____. _Reflections on Being Governor_ (Washington: National Governors' Association, 1981).

Nice, David C. "Cooperation and Conformity Among the States," _Polity_, XVI (Spring, 1984), pp. 494-505.

_____. _Federalism: The Politics of Intergovernmental Relations_ (New York: St. Martin's Press, 1987).

_____. "State Participation in Interstate Compacts," _Publius_, XVII (Spring, 1987), pp. 69-83.

Nye, Russel B. _Midwestern Progressive Politics_ (New York: Harper Torchbooks, 1965).

Olson, Mancur. _The Logic of Collective Action: Public Goods and the Theory of Groups_ (Cambridge: Harvard University Press, 1965).

O'Toole, Laurence J., Jr., ed. _American Intergovernmental Relations_ (Washington: Congressional Quarterly, Inc., 1985).

Peirce, Neal R., Hagstrom, Jerry. The Book of America: Inside 50 States Today, Rev. ed. (New York: Warner Books, Inc., 1984).

Ransone, Coleman B., Jr. The American Governorship (Westport, Conn.: Greenwood Pres, 1982).

_____. The Office of the Governor in the United States (University: University of Alabama Press, 1956).

Reagan, Michael D. The New Federalism (New York: Oxford University Press, 1972).

_____. and Sanzone, John G. The New Federalism, 2nd ed. (New York: Oxford University Press, 1981).

Reeves, Mavis Mann. "Galloping Intergovernmentalization as a Factor in State Management," State Government, LIV (1981), pp. 102-108.

Riker, William H. Federalism: Origin, Operation, Significance (Boston: Little, Brown & Co., 1964).

Sabato, Larry. Goodbye to Good-Time Charlie: The American Governor Transformed, 2nd ed. (Washington: Congressional Quarterly, Inc., 1983).

Salisbury, Robert H. "Interest Representation: The Dominance of Institutions," American Political Science Review, LXXVIII (March, 1984), pp. 64-76.

Schlozman, Kay Lehman, and Tierney, John T. Organized Interests and American Democracy (New York: Harper & Row, Publishers, 1986).

Seidman, Harold. Politics, Positions and Power (New York: Oxford University Press, 1970).

Sharkansky, Ira. The Maligned States: Policy Accomplishments, Problems, and Opportunities, 2nd ed. (New York: McGraw-Hill Book Co., 1978).

Snelling, Richard A. "American Federalism in the Eighties," State Government, LIII (Autumn, 1980), pp. 168-170.

Sundquist, James L. Making Federalism Work (Washington: The Brookings Institution, 1969).

Truman, David B. The Governmental Process (New York: Alfred A. Knopf, Inc., 1951).

Walker, David B. "Dysfunctional Federalism--The Congress and Intergovernmental Relations," State Government, LIV (1981), pp. 53-57.

          .   "The Federal Role in the Federal System? A
     Troublesome Topic," National Civic Review, LXXII (January,
     1983), pp. 6-23.

Williamson, Richard S. "Block Grants--A Federalist Tool," State
     Government, LIV (1981), pp. 114-117.

Wright, Deil S.   Understanding Intergovernmental Relations, 2nd
     ed. (Monterey, Calif.: Brooks/Cole Publishing Co., 1982).

INDEX

236

Regionalism, 38-40, 186-190, 201
Reston, James, 87
River basin commissions, 25, 51-53
Rolvaag, Karl, 131, 139
Romney, George, 134, 139, 167-168
Roosevelt, Franklin D., 14, 15, 74
Roosevelt, Theodore, 66
Rose, Charlie, 205

Salisbury, Robert, 108, 109
Safe Streets Act, 20
St. Lawrence Seaway, 111, 113, 127, 128
Sanford, Terry, 59
Schlesinger, Joseph, 93
Senate Western Coalition, 207
Shafroth, John F., 66-67
Small Business Administration, 53
Smith, Forrest, 111
Snelling, Richard A., 6, 18
Southeastern Governors' Conference, 74
Southern Governors' Association, 74-75, 117, 162, 170
Southern Growth Policies Board, 125, 200
Southern Interstate Nuclear Board, 162-163
Southern Regional Education Board, 117
Stevenson, Adlai, 166-167
Straayer, John, 93
Sunbelt Council, 205
Susquehanna River Basin Compact, 42

Teasdale, Joseph P., 169
Tennessee Valley Authority, 46
Thompson, James, 177
Thone, Charles, 175, 177
Tiemann, Norbert T., 175
Title II commissions, 52
Title V commissions, 50, 52
Toll, Henry W., 59-60
Topocrats, 31
Truman, David B., 108, 109

Unitary form of government, 9-10
U.S. Conference of Mayors, 32, 58
U.S. Supreme Court, 6, 15, 199

Vehicle Equipment Safety Compact, 116
Vietnam war, 19, 200

Virginia v. Tennesse, 41

Walker, Daniel, 168-169
Water Resources Council, 51-52, 53
Water Resources Planning Act of 1961, 51
Water Resources Planning Act of 1965, 51
Watson, Jack, 139
Wendell, Mitchell, 132
Western Governors' Association, 75-77, 207
Western Governors' Policy Office, 76
Western Governors' Regional Energy Policy Office, 75
Western Interstate Commission for Higher Education, 117
White, Leonard D., 59-60
Williams, G. Mennen, 111
Wilson, Woodrow, 29, 66
Wright, Deil S., 31, 38, 208-209

RECENT U.S. HISTORY

The General Series Editor is Professor Kenneth E. Hendrickson, Jr., Hardin Distinguished Professor of American History at Midwestern State University, Wichita Falls, Texas.

This Series includes topics from the late Nineteenth and Twentieth Centuries under the general heading of Recent American History. The specific focus will be on biographical and monographic studies at the local, state and regional levels which have implications for issues of national importance. These would include such topics as Populism, Progressivism, Politics, the New Deal, the race question, and numerous others.

Albert J. Fyfe

UNDERSTANDING THE FIRST WORLD WAR
Illusions and Realities

American University Studies: Series IX (History). Vol. 37

ISBN 0-8204-0642-2   408 pages   hardback US $ 48.95*

*Recommended price – alterations reserved

This book offers a fresh perspective on the First World War. The unmitigated calamity of that war has always encouraged numerous historians to lay the blame for the long conflict at the doors of the politicians and generals of the time. The numerous misapprehensions and distortions which followed took insufficient account of the circumstances on the Allied side which dictated that the war must be a long and costly one. Thus the British were to suffer endless adversity until they were able to play their leading role in achieving the victory.

PETER LANG PUBLISHING, INC.
62 West 45th Street
USA – New York, NY 10036